SOUNDING REAL

SOUNDING REAL

Musicality and American Fiction at the Turn of the Twentieth Century

Cristina L. Ruotolo

THE UNIVERSITY OF ALABAMA PRESS
Tuscaloosa

Tuscaloosa, Alabama 35487-0380

Manufactured in the United States of America

Typeface: ACaslon

Cover art: "The Pathetic Song" by Thomas Eakins, 1881. Corcoran Gallery of Art.
Cover design: Mary-Frances Burt / Burt&Burt

∞

The paper on which this book is printed meets the minimum requirements of American National Standard for Information Sciences—Permanence of Paper for Printed Library Materials, ANSI Z39.48-1984.

Library of Congress Cataloging-in-Publication Data

Ruotolo, Cristina L., 1963-
Sounding real : musicality and American fiction at the turn of the twentieth century / Cristina L. Ruotolo.
p. cm. — (Studies in American literary realism and naturalism)
Includes bibliographical references and index.
ISBN 978-0-8173-1798-0 (hardcover : alk. paper) — ISBN 978-0-8173-8676-4 (ebook)
1. American fiction—20th century—History and criticism. 2. Music and literature—United States—History—20th century. 3. Music in literature. 4. Musicians in literature. I. Title.
PS374.M87R86 2013
813'.5093578—dc23

2012050438

I dedicate this book to my parents.

Contents

Acknowledgments

I began to think about literary constructions of musicality during my very first semester of graduate school, in Richard Brodhead's seminar on nineteenth-century American literature and culture. As a serious violinist who had recently left the concert hall for the halls of academe, I had for some time been interested in theories of music's relationship to society (Theodor Adorno loomed large in my library). But I had never before thought seriously about social constructions of musical taste, nor about fiction's capacity to reflect and shape ideas about what music is and does. As we moved from Lawrence Levine's *Highbrow/Lowbrow* to Theodore Dreiser's *Sister Carrie*—which struck me as remarkably alert to urban music and musicality in ways that scholars had not seemed to notice—a project began to take shape that, years later, culminates in this book.

I remain deeply indebted to Richard Brodhead for this introduction to a new set of questions, and for his subsequent mentorship and support. Also crucial to the germination of this project were Carla Kaplan, Hazel Carby, Jean-Christophe Agnew, Michael Denning, Wayne Koestenbaum, Herbie Lindenberger, and Robert Stepto, all of whom contributed in significant ways to my thinking about the nexus of music, culture, identity, and politics. I also owe gratitude to Trysh Travis, Julia Erhardt, and Juliette Guilbert, a powerhouse trio of critical readers, and to Martin Berger, Karl Britto, Rebecca Laroche, Jesse Gale, Michele Janette, Cathy Shuman, Scott Saul, and David Southward, who read and commented on my work at various stages, and comprised a rich intellectual community.

In the intervening years, more people than I can name contributed to the thinking that eventually took form in this book. Wai Chee Dimock, Ron Radano, Jeffrey Melnick, Regenia Gagnier, and Bill Handley offered valuable feedback to individual chapters, as did the peer reviewers and editors who helped me hone earlier versions of three of this book's chapters for publication in *American Literature*, *American Literary Realism*, and *Literature/Compass*. I'm grateful to Chris Connery for inviting me to present my work at UC Santa Cruz's Center for Cultural Studies, and to those faculty and students who attended and offered rich feedback. I remain indebted to Gary Scharnhorst, editor of *ALR*, who encouraged me to submit this manuscript to the Studies in American Literary Realism and Naturalism series at the University of Alabama Press, and also to UAP's Dan Waterman, Joanna Jacobs, and Susan Harris for their editorial acumen. I also want to thank Donald Pizer for including my Dreiser article (first published in *ALR*) in the most recent Norton Critical Edition of *Sister Carrie*.

I have been surrounded by a remarkable group of colleagues at San Francisco State University who have supported my work in music and literature in countless ways. Loretta Stec, Laura Garcia-Moreno, Saul Steier, Mary Scott, Sandra Luft, Mike Lunine, Prithvi Shobhi and George Leonard deserve particular mention, whether for reading and commenting on drafts, for helping me think through my ideas in conversation, or for being such fabulous comrades-in-arms. My thinking has also been honed, challenged, and enriched by the many students with whom I've had the privilege of working on music-related topics in classes and thesis advising. Several of these deserve special mention: Kevin Fellezs, Steve Savage, Cookie Woolner, Lorraine Affourtit, and Jen Otter all continue to humble and inspire me with their own intellectual work. I am tremendously grateful for the support and friendship of staff and administrators at SF State, particularly Helen Goldsmith, Annette Speed, Andrea Olson, and Eva Chuck, and of two extraordinary deans, Nancy McDermid and Paul Sherwin. I'm indebted to San Francisco State University for the Presidential Scholarship that gave me time off from my heavy teaching load.

My family has been at the center of my intellectual and musical life from the start. I dedicate this book to my mother, Marcia, who set me on my own musical path and who remains in more ways than she knows my role model; and to my late father, Lucio, whose passionate engagement with literature, politics, and ideas continues to inspire me every day. Vanessa and Peter remain my musical touchstones, keeping it, and me, real with their own, rich musical lives. Finally, I owe tremendous gratitude to my daughter Lucy, whose creative spark and love of life infect me daily, and my husband Chris, without whose critical eye, keen sense of humor, and unending support I might never have finished this book. I am so lucky to have you in my life.

SOUNDING REAL

Introduction

The unnamed narrator of James Weldon Johnson's *Autobiography of an Ex-Colored Man*, recalling his first encounter with ragtime in a Manhattan club, points to a certain incommensurability between words and music: "I stopped talking to listen. It was music of a kind I had never heard before."[1] In the break opened up by these new sounds and by his silent attention to them, the narrator discovers a musical language that offers him new means of navigating his problematic relationship to the American "color line," which this novel defines, in part, as a line between (white) textuality and (black) orality. By appropriating ragtime's syncopated rhythms and improvisatory style to revise the European musical texts that had until then shaped his musical self, the narrator produces a new musical form that promises to give expression to his biracial identity and to give him agency within the emerging spaces of American urban culture. It also, however, occasions his entrapment within these spaces, as a cultural commodity destined to be bought, sold, lent, and consumed by white Americans eager for novelty.

Sounding Real proceeds from the observation that literary moments like these—moments in which musical encounters generate new imaginative possibilities and limits for modern American subjectivity—occupy a significant and underexamined place in American fiction of the late nineteenth and early twentieth century. The novels in this study have important things to say about music and about how Americans made, heard, responded to, and understood music at a profoundly transitional moment in American music and society. They also suggest that music played a significant role in *shaping* this moment in American literature, typically identified by the genres of realism and naturalism, by exerting a kind of pressure on ideas of the real and of its accessibility to language. The novels gathered here—by Theodore Dreiser, Kate Chopin, Harold Frederic, Willa Cather, Gertrude Atherton, James Weldon Johnson, and others—all give us some version of Johnson's "ex-colored man's" problematic relationship to music. They all present music as elaborating a space of authenticity, freedom, and possibility that both temporarily suspends and throws into relief the social realities—the hierarchies and ideologies of race, class and gender—that ultimately limit and contain musical spaces. Music, I will argue, represents for these diverse novels and for their central characters both a way of accessing a primitive and hidden "real" and a reminder of the limits of the realities of everyday life, of what is possible in the here and now.

Interest in music's social meanings and values has risen significantly in recent decades, as scholars have begun to recognize and scrutinize the gamut of music's participation in the production and reproduction of social identities, ideologies, and spaces.[2] A growing corpus of recent scholarship has focused specifically on American musical practices at the turn of the twentieth century. Particularly significant for the current study has been an explosion of work on black musical practices, on women's changing role in classical music in the United States, on the idea of musical nationalism, and on Americans' reception of European art music.[3] But, while scholarship on turn-of-the-century musical culture is on the rise, scholarship on realism and naturalism has been relatively slow to consider music's relationship to and place in literature. The recently published *Oxford Handbook of American Literary Naturalism*, a case in point, excludes any serious focus on music, even in a section entitled "Naturalism and the Other Arts" (which examines naturalism's relationship to drama, poetry, visual arts, and film).[4] One noteworthy exception is Philipp Schweighauser's *The Noises of American Literature*, which sees in the attention to sound given by certain naturalist writers (he focuses on Crane, Norris, and Dreiser) a "gesture towards a modernist aesthetics of noise." Their fiction, he argues, "stages a breakdown of realist-naturalist literary form in the face of the conflicts and noises of a modernity it seeks to contain."[5] Focusing on "literary acoustics" from naturalism to postmodernism, Schweighauser importantly identifies a shift in literary soundscapes at the turn of the twentieth century, and thus suggests we have something to learn from this fiction about not only how things sounded at the time but also how the very project of writing about sound involves what he calls the "orchestration of acoustic details" and the containment of chaotic and volatile noise through its representation as linear, silent text.[6]

Music, however, which receives scant mention in Schweighauser's text, is not simply a subset of noise but is already an "orchestration of acoustic details," or, in the words of Jacques Attali, an "organization of noise" in historically and culturally specific ways.[7] If fiction is already musical as it "orchestrates" the noises it represents, when it orchestrates specifically *musical* events, fiction does more than represent and manage sounds. Literary representations of music and musical events inevitably construct and reflect particular historically resonant ways of hearing, seeing, describing, and locating music, what I would like to call *musicscapes.*[8] To think about a text's musicscape is to ask questions such as: What kinds of music exist (and don't exist) in the world of the text? How are the boundaries drawn between different types of music and musicians, between who is musical and who is not, between places where music does and does not happen? What is the text's vocabulary for evoking the phenomenology of listening and performing? And, finally, what does music *do* to people who listen to and play it, and to the social spaces in which it is made?

The novels in this study accord music a special status that, if continuous with and to some degree constitutive of the more general soundscape, also stands apart from it. They approach music as participating in what Edward Said calls "extreme occasions," a term he uses to describe scenes of classical musical performance emerging in the mid-nineteenth century. With the professionalization of musicians and rise of virtuoso celebrities, he argues, the scene of performance is increasingly defined by expert performers commanding the silent attention of audiences in rarified atmospheres, bringing the private, ineffable, and often inarticulable experience of playing and hearing music into sometimes jarring contact with the conditions of public, social, hierarchical, and commercialized ritual.[9] These novels' literary musicscapes encourage us to imagine, and allow us to think critically about, that zone of contact between private and public meanings.

This study, then, presents two main arguments that I hope will initiate new avenues of discussion about music's relationship to American literature. First, I argue that the novels brought together here help us to think in new ways about music's role in turn-of-the-century identity politics, particularly around questions of gender, race, and national identity. Whether ragtime in a New York black and tan, Frédéric Chopin in a New Orleans apartment, or Mexican folk music on a small-town Colorado porch, certain musical occasions in these novels constitute temporal and spatial breaks from everyday life, "extreme occasions" in which normative social boundaries and differences dissolve at least momentarily into abstracted and seemingly collective musical experience. These moments do cultural and narrative work within their respective texts, underscoring, unsettling, or even transforming the relationships and problems otherwise at play. My argument extends from literary interpretation—from asking what music is doing within these texts—to also consider how the texts themselves constitute musical experience and understanding. By putting the musicscapes of these novels alongside contemporary discourses about music from music journals and general periodicals, I propose that fictional narrative played (and continues to play) a part in shaping musical understanding—in telling us what music is and does, and how it can be used—and that fiction thus should be considered more toward the center, than the margins, of music-cultural historiography.

While focusing on the turn of the century, I did not select the novels brought together here for their generic or canonical status as "realist" or "naturalist" novels. The vaudeville scene in Frank Norris's *McTeague*, for example, would clearly have warranted inclusion had my main intention been primarily to intervene in literary critical debates about genre. Instead, I chose novels that demonstrate a kind of attention to music and to musicality that cuts across both literary and musical genres. While Schweighauser finds the "realist-naturalist literary form" failing to "contain," through its representational strategies, the cacophony of modern American life—the noises of increasingly multicultural urban spaces, of war, and of class conflict—I read this fiction's "realist-naturalist" approach to music as betraying a more equivocal relationship to a changing musical modernity (or modern musicality) that, if not cacophonic, nonetheless challenges inherited ways of hearing, knowing, and representing. These challenges, moreover, inhere less in the "noises" or sounds of music themselves, as they push against or are contained by literary "form" than in the particular elements brought together in the performance ritual. The following chapters note that nineteenth-century European music—such as Chopin's romantic piano repertoire and Wagner's operas—produces an experience of rupture for Kate Chopin, Willa Cather, and Gertrude Atherton's characters that is remarkably similar to what ragtime produces for James Weldon Johnson's narrator. The "modernity" of these ruptures exists as much in new relationships between performers and listeners, new venues, and new kinds of musical events, as in the form and style of the music itself. Within these occasions, music's *realism* is experienced only in the moment of audition, as it gives its audience access to previously unknown or unrealized zones of reality that the written word can only describe or approximate from a representational distance. While the written word may not be able to compete with music's capacity to awaken its audience to an awareness of primitive and authentic reality, it can draw attention, much better than can music itself, to the social production, reception, marketing, and uses of what we might call musical realism.

The question of where musical agency lies, whether in musical form, in the performer's skill and expressivity, in the capacity to listen, or somewhere else, remains profoundly unsettled in this fiction. At times, music in these novels seems allied with those powerful and invisible forces that "naturalist" writers at the turn of the century increasingly evoke as inescapable determinants of and limits on individual will and agency. Johnson's ragtime, for example, takes over the bodies that listen to it, as "music that demanded physical response, patting of the feet, drumming of the fingers, or nodding of the head in time with the beat."[10] Similarly, the piano music in Kate Chopin's *The Awakening* overtakes Edna Pontellier's body such that "the very passions themselves were aroused within her soul, swaying it, lashing it, as the waves daily beat upon her splendid body. She trembled, she was choking, and the tears blinded her."[11] These two very different scenarios and musical styles similarly align music with forces that seem to transcend the performance, performers, and social conditions of performance as they pull listeners invisibly and overwhelmingly into their field of influence. That the performers in these occasions are, respectively, an uneducated black man and an unmarried white woman—neither of whom could, outside of the realm of musical performance, expect to have much social influence, and both of whom, as powerful musicians, thus threaten the status quo—underscores the complex intersection of discourses generated by narratives of musical occasions. Music here depends on the body and agency of the performer, at the same time that its disembodied, ephemeral, and invisible vibrations can be figured as forces of nature.

Joseph Horowitz's claim, almost twenty years ago, that "present-day scholars and intellectuals . . . tend to ignore classical music" is still largely true, even though, as Horowitz continues, turn-of-the-twentieth-century "classical music was as vital and contemporary as today's [classical] music business is insular and anachronistic."[12] European "classical music," a part of almost all the literary musicscapes examined in this book (Dreiser's being the one exception), is typically marginalized by American literary and cultural studies as a "highbrow" zone of white, leisure-class culture.[13] The relative dearth of literary scholarship addressing the music of this period doubtlessly also reflects a general discomfort with the racism expressed in so much of its musical discourse and practice. Compared to the blues and jazz, on which an immense amount of scholarship in literary and cultural studies continues to be produced, ragtime and the popular "coon songs" of Tin Pan Alley register Jim Crow racism as much as they also herald new, African American–inspired musical styles and forms.[14] Literary critics, and cultural critics in general, have been drawn to music that they can celebrate as authentic, or, more recently, as resistant in some strategic way to hegemonic practices. The valorization of "authenticity" in music—and particularly an authenticity associated with the musical expression of oppressed peoples—has long exerted power over our musical tastes and over the music to which scholars, living over a century later, choose to give their attention.[15] But to collapse the significance of ragtime or Frédéric Chopin entirely into their participation in hierarchies of race and class is to ignore how such music, for certain people in certain circumstances, crossed, challenged, and blurred these hierarchical boundaries between high and low, or white and black, culture. Attending to only certain forms of music and musical experience risks imposing current musical biases and categorical distinctions on a historical moment when the idea of "black music," as Karl Hagstrom Miller has recently argued, was not yet discursively available.[16]

What does tie the different musical practices and genres together at the turn of the century, and makes them worthy of our attention in their own right, is the degree to which they were bound up with the question of what constitutes American music. Because this question of American musical difference informs, directly and indirectly, all of the novels in this study, I offer in the remaining pages of this introduction an overview of the phenomenon of American musical nationalism at the turn of the century.

American Musical Nationalism

This book situates its readings of literary musicscapes in relationship to several central areas of concern in American musical life at the turn of the century: the question of the status, identity, and future of American music, a question integrally tied to notions of racial difference; the rise of Tin Pan Alley, which constitutes the first centralized national production and distribution of popular song; the consolidation of a professional and elite arena of American classical music; and the growing public presence and influence of musical women. These overlapping concerns, voiced in the pages of newspaper reviews, music journals, general periodicals, books about music, and elsewhere, arose in direct response to a number of developments in the production and reception of music, most of which have received significant attention by music historians, to whom my own work here is indebted. Most of these three areas I will address in the following chapters; the debate about musical nationalism, however, directly informs all of the chapters that follow and so is worth discussing in some detail here.

Toward the end of the nineteenth century, Americans of various stripes began to entertain the idea that they might be musical in a distinct way that said something about what it meant to be American. American popular music, of course, had by then come into its own largely through the immensely popular forms of blackface minstrelsy along with its associated songwriters. Stephen Foster was hailed, at home and abroad, as the producer of distinctly American songs, imagined (by white audiences, at least) to capture the spirit of hearth and home, as well as of the plantation. The imagined Americanness of these songs, however, was located as much if not more in its lyrics, characters, and performance styles than in the music itself, which remained largely indebted to Irish, Scottish, and English song traditions.[17] However indebted the music of blackface minstrelsy and Stephen Foster songs was to actual African American music remained shrouded in the confusion of "love and theft" that situated blackface minstrelsy in the white imagination.[18] Part of this confusion rested in whites' disavowal of a "national" identity, musical or otherwise, that included black voices and bodies. American-born composers and performers of art music, on the other hand, had been almost entirely in the shadow of Europe prior to this moment and their success depended on the degree to which they assimilated European musical traditions. The idea that the music of blackface minstrelsy, of slaves, or of popular music more generally could inform an American *classical* music had no real traction until the end of the century.[19]

Several factors conjoined in the 1890s to pave the way for Americans to begin thinking about the idea of American musicality as something to be cultivated, with conscious deliberation, as an expression of a unique national spirit. The postbellum formation of American institutions of musical training and performance—of permanent symphonies, opera houses, and conservatories—importantly established a basis for developing and showcasing native talent. As a result, a new generation of performers emerged, taking their place as soloists and symphony players alongside their European counterparts on the major stages of Europe and at home. But slower to emerge was the American composer, who was expected, increasingly, not only to develop skills commensurate with European composers but also to develop a uniquely American school of composition.

Arthur Farwell, a composer who founded the Wa-Wan Press to promote American music, described in 1907 what was considered to be at stake for these new national composers:

> To one tracing in detail the progress of American music, the present is probably the most interesting and exciting epoch through which our nation will pass. For with this generation and only with this, our composers have bent themselves to the task of genuinely mastering the technic [*sic*] of musical composition, and are thus for the first time gaining a medium through which American spirit and individuality may freely speak. From now on, we are not merely to observe how cleverly the American can imitate European modes of expression; we are to see what the American has to say for himself, for this nation, for *us,* through the medium of his art. Does he still reflect the pessimism, the melancholy, the artistic desperation of modern Europe; or does he voice the youthful, optimistic, heroic spirit of a new land?[20]

Farwell's words follow over a decade of such pronouncements, and of compositional efforts to "freely speak" an "American spirit and individuality," which most famously began with Antonin Dvořák's tenure in New York in the mid-1890s. Hired from his native Bohemia to direct the new National Conservatory of Music in New York, Dvořák urged American composers to develop a national style (as he had done for Czech music) by making use of what he saw as the richest American "folk" music: "Negro melodies" and "Indian chants." The romantic idea of a deep connection between music and national identity lay at the heart of Dvořák's sense of mission for American music. "All races," he wrote in an article for *Harper's New Monthly Magazine* that became the focus of much debate, "have their distinctively national songs, which they at once recognize as their own, even if they have never heard them before." As an outsider, Dvořák observed that white Americans, who might otherwise share very different ethnic backgrounds, seemed to embrace, in particular, the "Negro melodies" that had become, authentically or not, the basis of American popular music: "I was led to take this view partly by the fact that the so-called plantation songs are indeed the most striking and appealing melodies that have yet been found on this side of the water, but largely by the observation that this seems to be recognized, though often unconsciously, by most Americans."[21] Dvořák's idea of an "unconscious" national or racial identification with and ownership of particular folk music struck right at the heart of white American racial confusion. He was, in effect, asking Americans to acknowledge that their "racial" identity as Americans was, itself, multiracial, constituted by African American music. In this respect, he was anticipating (and perhaps influencing, as Ronald Radano speculates) W. E. B. Du Bois's argument, at the end of *Souls of Black Folk*, that the "sorrow songs" of black slaves constitute the "sole American music" and "the most beautiful expression of human experience born this side the seas."[22]

Numerous composers, including Farwell and those published by his press, experimented with versions of Dvořák's proposal and produced song cycles, sonatas, symphonies, and chamber music based on Native American and African American themes. What ensued, in response to both Dvořák's words and his own "New World" Symphony, which wove both "slave songs" and "Indian chants" into its musical fabric, was a large-scale debate over the terms of American musical identity. Critics spilt much ink over the question of what, if anything, should count as *American* folk music. Could slave songs and American Indian music really speak for the nation and for white Americans? Does essentially "barbaric" music, as both American Indian and black music was imagined to be, belong in the realm of "art" music? The problem for many in the musical establishment was that, as white, urban, northern, educated Americans, they did not hear (or *want* to hear) the music of American Indians and blacks as their own, however much they recognized the "native" character of its styles and forms.[23] But the idea of the primitive difference of black and American Indian music was, at heart, what intrigued those who sought to establish "American music" as not only distinct from but also more *authentic* than European musical art, more directly expressive of human nature and free from the artificial conventions of so-called civilization. Europeans could invoke either their own cultures' primitive folk music, in nationalist expressions, or American Indian and African American music, in modernist experiment without challenging their own sense of racial identity. White Americans, however, found themselves in the paradoxical position of having to choose between remaining in Europe's musical shadow (without a sense of distinct national identity) or crossing the color line to identify with the music of nonwhite Americans.

A number of critics circumvented this dilemma by rejecting the idea that music should be in the business of representing national identity. Some opined that the best music speaks universal truths (even if that music was composed almost entirely by Germans), while others had it both ways by arguing that America's distinctness was precisely its lack of tradition, which would allow for a freer expression of universal truths. Henry Krehbiel, for example, one of the era's most prominent music critics, predicted that American composers would achieve distinction on the basis of both their freedom from tradition, and the multicultural palette of American society:

> The characteristic mode of expression which will be stamped upon the music of the future American composer will be the joint creation of the American's freedom from conventional methods and his inherited predilections and capacities. The reflective German, the mercurial Frenchman, the stolid Englishman, the warm-hearted Irishman, the impulsive Italian, the daring Russian, each will contribute his factor to the sum of national taste. The folk melodies of all nations will yield up their individual charms, and disclose to the composer a hundred avenues of emotional expression which have not yet been explored. The American composer will be the truest representative of a universal art, because he will be the truest type of a citizen of the world.[24]

Krehbiel, who curiously leaves out "slave songs and Indian chants" from his list of folk material contributing to a potential multicultural American music, was in fact a fierce defender specifically of the artistic value of African American "folksong," which he distinguishes from its "debased offspring," ragtime.

For Krehbiel, ragtime's broad, international appeal indicated the richness of its musical roots, but also the "deplorable" commercial tastes of "the pleasure-seekers" in urban Europe and New York, who preferred "that which tickles the ears and stimulates the feet" to what Krehbiel considered the more artistic qualities of African American folk song (to which he devoted an entire book). Indeed, at the same time as composers and critics debated the question of, in Krehbiel's words, "whether or not the songs were original creations of these native blacks, whether or not they were entitled to be called American and whether or not they were worthy of consideration as foundation elements for a school of American composition,"[25] ragtime was quickly becoming Tin Pan Alley's most popular song form, identified at home and abroad as America's most distinct musical contribution. A term loosely applied to music that featured syncopated rhythms, ragtime was generally acknowledged to have originated from African American sources, although its most popular and best paid performers and composers were, by 1900, white (or, in the case of James Weldon Johnson and his brother, who wrote "rag-time" songs for musical theater and Tin Pan Alley, were presumed to be white by many of those buying or perusing the sheet music).[26] The critical debate over ragtime was at least as heated as that over the notion of using American Indian chants for American symphonies. Ragtime's defenders in the white American press hailed it as an expression of the power, energy, and faster pace of the modern American city, and Europeans embraced it as a form of primitive modernism. Several European composers—Satie and Debussy, for example—used it to signal their own modernist breaks with tradition.[27]

That ragtime was becoming the international face of American music rankled a number of American critics, who, like Oscar Sonneck, head of the music division of the Library of Congress, were increasingly defensive about America's musical identity: "If our European critics merely contented themselves with stating the undeniable fact that we have not produced masters of the first rank, we should have no ground for complaint; but it is just a little galling to be told *ad nauseam* that 'commercial' America never can produce great creative musical artists, that even our best composers are but weak dilutions and imitations of an inferior European article, and that our only noteworthy contribution to music has been 'ragtime.'"[28] The critique of ragtime, then, hinged on several factors in conjunction with its racial associations: its "commercial" as opposed to artistic basis, its unfortunate advantage in representing American musicality abroad, and, not least, the very "curious effects" on the body and emotions that Johnson's "ex-colored man" celebrates.

This brief overview of American musical life at the turn of the century derives mainly from the discourse of critics and journalists writing about music at the time, or from historiography that itself relies on musical discourse recorded in newspapers, journals, and magazines. The chapters that follow deliberately relegate music criticism to the background, as a discursive context that will help establish fiction's resonance with and its *difference from* music's more official discourses. Rather than writing specifically or primarily about music, the novelists included here involve music in their fictional elaborations of personal and social dramas, approaching it not as a static and isolatable object of study but as a social activity that involves performers, social and material spaces, and listeners, and the relationships among them that shape, and are shaped by, the musical experience.[29] Their novels thus help us to think about music in specific contexts, times, and places; about the ways in which listeners as well as performers and composers create and revise music's meanings; about music's similarities and differences across genres, regions, and venues; and about the relationship between private musical experience and socially constructed conventions of performance, composition, and reception.

Chapter 1 places Theodore Dreiser's *Sister Carrie* in the context of the author's relationship with Tin Pan Alley, by giving close attention to his editorial writings as editor of *Ev'ry Month* (a Tin Pan Alley monthly) and other early journalistic treatments of music. As Dreiser's novel figures Carrie's urban experience and relationships as aural and more specifically musical, it registers a profound ambivalence about a new urban musicality that seems at once to emancipate Carrie from strictures of class and gender and to subject her more invisibly to emerging strictures of commodity capitalism.

Chapter 2 explores the remarkable similarity between the musical plots of Kate Chopin's *The Awakening* and Harold Frederic's *Damnation of Theron Ware*, both of which tell stories of young, married, musical Anglo-Saxon Protestants who "awaken" to a more authentic sense of themselves in part by listening to Catholic women pianists playing the music of Frédéric Chopin. I approach these novels as reflections on the musical contexts and issues they both invoke—Americans' reception of Chopin's music, new attitudes toward female professional pianists, and understandings of ethnic/regional musical subcultures.

The third chapter brings together two novels, Gertrude Atherton's *Tower of Ivory* and Willa Cather's *Song of the Lark*, that engage with the question of how American "folk" might inform a distinctly American operatic identity. Both novels give us American opera singers whose national origins, presumed a hindrance to their operatic ambition, in fact account for their success in both cases by virtue of their brush with "primitive" American subcultures.

As a counterpoint to the musical nationalist perspectives of Atherton and Cather, chapter 4 gives voice to an African American perspective on the possibilities of a cross-cultural American music at the turn of the century. Putting James Weldon Johnson's *The Autobiography of an Ex-Colored Man* in the context of the author's own experience writing popular songs for musical theater, I explore the ways in which the unnamed narrator's experiments with fusing African American and European musical traditions reflect upon the racial politics confronting black musical professionals at the time, as well as on the musical nationalist strategies of white American composers.

The final chapter turns to two little-known novels written by two early twentieth-century music critics: James Huneker's *Painted Veils* and William J. Henderson's *Soul of a Tenor*. That two of the most influential and well-known music critics in New York would write novels about the American opera scene suggests their own shared sense of the importance of fiction for articulating, and perhaps working out, the question of music's meaning and place in American culture. Furthermore, Huneker and Henderson both directly involve the figure of the critic in their novels, linking the problem of American musical identity with the problem of *writing* about music as an American. Like others in this study, they also grapple with the "problem" of modern American musical experience as it invites intimacy across boundaries of race and gender. I approach their novels as commentaries on the increasingly significant role of the American music critic in shaping and giving voice to musical meaning and argue that their portraits of embattled male writers underscore many of the issues—of race, ethnicity, and gender but also of representation and realism—that are of concern throughout this study.

The pages that follow, while opening up questions about the relationship between American music and the literary imagination, also underscore the limits of literature as a source of historical understanding of music's meanings. Indeed, writing about music—as I am not the first to acknowledge—tends to repeat the problematic relationships of ethnography, in which the very project of writing about an oral culture can do a kind of violence to the meanings and values of that culture.[30] While turn-of-the-century America is not generally characterized as an oral culture, it certainly included "subcultures" for whom text and writing were at least secondary to speech and music and whose music—particularly in the case of Native Americans and African Americans—was having a growing influence on the "mainstream." Novels reflect the perspective of the "literate"—a perspective, as we will see, that tends, at the turn of the twentieth century, to underscore and romanticize the difference between oral and textual literacy. Though limited in this way, the novels I have chosen to focus on are all themselves interested in the relationship between text and music, whether resigned to, confident in, or anxious about the limits of their own textual medium and realist/naturalist projects.

1
Not Just Looking
Sister Carrie's Musical Economy

In the voluminous critical discussion of Dreiser's first novel, which has long remained central to the canon of American realism and naturalism, a good deal of energy has gone into recognizing and analyzing its representations of the visual culture of commodity capitalism. Focus on the novel's "visual economy," as Bill Brown calls it, took off after Rachel Bowlby's provocative *Just Looking* (1985), which traces evocations of consumer culture in novels by Dreiser, Gissing, and Zola.[1] For Bowlby, *Sister Carrie* epitomizes the "new consumer capitalism" in which "'things' are inseparable from how they look," and Carrie herself exists as "an image *par excellence*."[2] While critics have since debated whether or not Dreiser's novel "endorses" the burgeoning consumer culture he so meticulously documents (the word is Walter Benn Michaels's), the assumption underlying Bowlby's title prevails: that vision remains separable from, as well as privileged over, other forms of perception in *Sister Carrie*.[3]

But Dreiser's characters, like most of us, are rarely "just looking." This chapter focuses on Dreiser's own quite remarkable, if undernoted, attention to the sounds of the new consumer capitalism and to the ways in which his characters imagine, as well as hear, their modern urban contexts as replete with sounds as well as sights. Rather than simply accompany the visual landscape of the modern city, like an added soundtrack, the aural interacts with and sometimes even subsumes the visual in Dreiser's novel. At times, it reinforces the idea that "things are inseparable from how they look," but as often suggests a gap between surface and interior, and invites characters, as well as readers, to imagine pockets of subjectivity and sociality that remain invisible, immaterial, ephemeral, and thus unavailable to vision and to a "visual economy."

In missing the aural register of *Sister Carrie*, critics have underappreciated the relevance of Theodore Dreiser's connections with the music business to his first novel. Scholars generally have approached his editorial stint with a Tin Pan Alley magazine as one part of his more general training in journalistic writing and have been less interested in what it says about Dreiser's attitudes about music and the music industry than in what it tells us about his vexed relationship with his brother, Paul Dresser, a highly successful writer of sentimental songs (who, like many in the entertainment industry, altered his name).[4] During the period when Dreiser edited *Ev'ry Month* for music publishers Howley and Haviland (1894–96), American musical practices were in the midst of dramatic changes and expansion, and his writings about those practices, in *Ev'ry Month* and elsewhere, offer a number of significant insights into music's presence and importance in American cultural life at this time.[5] His essays from the years just prior to the publication of *Sister Carrie* also help us to recognize the ways in which his first novel registers a fundamental shift in the way music is being experienced and understood in turn-of-the-century urban America.

While short on scenes of actual music making, *Sister Carrie* is in fact rich with what might be called musical *affect*. Traces of sentimental songs pervade this novel, from its chapter titles, which, as Sandy Petry notes, might be mistaken for Tin Pan Alley titles and lyrics,[6] to the language of the novel's many sentimental moments, to Carrie herself, as one particularly "affected by music" and at crucial moments both propelled and limited by her aural sensitivity. While some regret *Sister Carrie*'s occasional forays into sentimental rapture as lapses in Dreiser's more properly "realist" mission, others recognize them as significant expressions of his relationship with consumer capitalism.[7] But in their disparate readings of Dreiser's intentions, critics often assume a seamless link between sentimentalism and consumerism and reduce the novel's musical moments, along with the desires they arouse, to the profit-driven manipulations of commodity capitalism. In so doing, they effectively ignore Dreiser's interest in a resistance to consumerism that emerges from within sentimental moments, as indeed a crucial element of their appeal. As Amy Kaplan notes, *Sister Carrie* often gives sentimental voice to a form of desire that commodities appeal to but cannot fulfill within the social conditions of turn-of-the-century capitalism.[8] But the novel's musical moments, like Dreiser's turn-of-the-century essays about music and the music industry, suggest not only a tension between sentimental desire and the marketplace but also a tension within a commoditized musicality or within Tin Pan Alley songs themselves. Unlike the material items appealing to Carrie from the other side of department store windows and arousing her desire by remaining just out of reach, music comes to her, arousing her emotions and desires by crossing boundaries between self and other and between subject and object. The desire aroused by music, as Dreiser understands it, certainly resonates with consumer desire, but also suggests a longing for *social* connections that remain irreducible to market values and inaccessible to what, for Brown, is the "glass-mediated theatricality of everyday life"[9] often structuring Carrie's experience and relationships. What makes *Sister Carrie*'s musical moments so interesting, for our understanding of cultural history and of music in general, is the way they propel audiences both into and away from the marketplace, promising—and momentarily delivering—an ephemeral, invisible, and intangible experience that nonetheless depends upon, and is located within, an increasingly rationalized, depersonalized commodity capitalism.

Sister Carrie is the only novel in this study whose musicscape is dominated by the emotional register of Tin Pan Alley's sentimental song genre, to the virtual exclusion of all other styles and forms, including those generating the most heated debate—ragtime, Wagner, and nationalist art music. While Dreiser's journalistic writings on music at the turn of the century address a wider frame of musical reference than his first novel, they, too, demonstrate a decided preference for popular songs that evoked themes and emotions of nostalgia, loss, regret, and "far away" places over the more forward-looking, rousing modern music beginning to gain in popularity. What *Sister Carrie* does share, however, with the other novels in this study is its recognition of the changing place and function of music at the turn of the twentieth century. Musical experience, in this novel, even at its most sentimental, is associated with the spaces, relationships, opportunities, and dangers of the modern city. Music functions here, as in the other novels, equivocally, on the one hand promising to express otherwise inarticulable truths and realities and on the other threatening to remake what is true and real and thus underscore the impermeability and instability of modern American reality. Perhaps more than any other novel (except *The Awakening*, a focus of chapter 2), *Sister Carrie* gives us a musicscape that threatens to undermine the very project of realism, as both an object that defies representation and as itself a mode of representation that promises unmediated access to a hidden reality unavailable to words.

"Things Breath'd into the Unguarded Ear"

In the opening pages of *Sister Carrie*, Dreiser characterizes Chicago as "a blare of sound, a roar of life" and Carrie's initial relationship to it as that of an "unguarded ear" to a barrage of musical appeals.[10] He would echo this language twenty years later when recalling his own first encounter with the city, which he experienced as a "roaring, yelling, screaming whirlpool of life":

> It is given to some cities, as to some lands, to suggest romance, and to me Chicago did that daily and hourly. It sang, or seemed to, and in spite of what I deemed my various troubles I was singing with it. . . . How I loved the tonic note of even the grinding wheels of the trucks and cars of the Chicago of that day; the clang and the clatter of its cable and electric lines. Its great beer and express wagons, its lurching surge of vehicles in every street. All had a tonic, rhythmic, symphonic import. . . . Chicago, as I viewed it then, was symphonic. It was like a great orchestra in the tumult of noble strophes. I was like a guest at a feast, eating and drinking in a delirium of delight.[11]

As he represents it, a symphonic city immediately welcomed the young Dreiser into its music making, and offered his emerging urban selfhood a new kind of pleasure. Though inducing "delirium," Chicago's "noble strophes" do not threaten to undermine Dreiser's ambition or overwhelm his individuality. Carrie's Chicago, if similarly musical, is decidedly less "noble" in its invitation to the young female newcomer: "A blare of sound, a roar of life, a vast array of human hives, appeal to the astonished senses in equivocal terms. Without a counselor at hand to whisper cautious interpretations, what falsehoods may not these things breathe into the unguarded ear! Unrecognized for what they are, their beauty, like music, too often relaxes, then weakens, then perverts the simpler human perceptions" (4). The narrator's cautionary voice here warns against the effects of the city's sounds, which, "like music," might corrupt an "unsophisticated and natural mind" like Carrie's (4). While the novel quickly abandons a moralizing perspective (and any stable notion of "corruption"), it nonetheless remains focused on the beckoning musicality of urban experience, and in ways that remain "equivocal" about whether music is something to be celebrated or guarded against.

Dreiser's focus on the sounds of urban experience not only reflects the fact that cities were noisier places than the smaller towns from which he and his heroine traveled but also suggests music's changing presence in cities like Chicago and New York toward the end of the nineteenth century. Before writing *Sister Carrie*, Dreiser became familiar with some of these changes when rescued from unemployment during his first months in New York City by his brother's publishers. With Paul Dresser's encouragement, "Howley and Haviland" set Dreiser up as founding editor of *Ev'ry Month*, a women's magazine that would promote the company's sheet music by offering previews of three or four new songs with each issue. The magazine's principal writer as well as editor, Dreiser found himself both supporting and, in a sense, competing with the burgeoning sheet music industry that was coming to be known as Tin Pan Alley. Particularly at this early point in his career, before he had any real success as a journalist or fiction writer, Dreiser's enchantment with the immense popularity of his brother's songs was tempered by concern that his own more serious and important authorship still lacked any significant audience.[12]

While recording technology and radio would bring about dramatic changes for American musical experience after World War I—changes that have been the focus of much recent scholarship—Tin Pan Alley's modes of production, promotion, and distribution preceded these technology-driven changes and in many ways paved their way. Named for the cacophony of piano strains emanating from the windows of one block of 28th Street in New York, Tin Pan Alley centralized the work of composing, arranging, printing, and marketing popular music. Rather than wait for minstrel and vaudeville performances to generate a song's popularity and marketability, music publishers now worked strenuously to create instant collective demand and what might be called brand loyalty. Toward this end, publishers developed new strategies utilizing new venues of live performance on stage, as well as new uses of public space, to give the impression that a song had already "caught on" and thus was worthy of purchase in the form of sheet music. (The relationship between live performance and reproduced music continues to be at the center of the music industry, as each is presented as a necessary complement to the other.) Celebrity singers were paid to include new songs in their shows, while boys were hired to infiltrate audiences and join in at the song's refrain, to perform, in a sense, the song's irresistibility. Beyond the theater, publishers hired musicians to play and sing on street corners, from moving trucks, in music stores, department stores, and restaurants. Like the planted audience member, these performers would advertise a song's desirability by staging its irrepressible ubiquity, its already-being-part of the urban soundscape.[13] Charles Harris, whose "After the Ball" (1892) was the first multimillion copy hit, promised "Songs Written to Order" on the sign in his office window, thus announcing a shift from producer to consumer as songwriting's driving force. Magazines like *Ev'ry Month*, by including "free" sheet music with every issue (a strategy music publishers had, in fact, been using for decades), were perhaps the least conspicuous of marketing ploys, if still effective at creating a buzz, instilling loyalty to particular songwriters (and thus to Howley and Haviland) and, of course, increasing subscriptions to the magazine itself.

Tin Pan Alley's growing presence at the turn of the century must be understood in the context of a general transformation of popular music's place in urban life, including its ubiquity in the emerging venues and rituals of "nightlife." Offering new synergies of pleasure, cabarets, nightclubs, and restaurants combined popular tunes with alcohol and food. Musical theater was on the rise, benefiting from the influx of black composers and performers to the city, and with them new "ragtime" styles of music and dance. As Lewis Erenberg and Kathy Peiss have demonstrated, these urban sites of leisure afforded new forms of social experience that inspired new anxieties.[14] Of growing concern was the perceived threat to the innocence and virtue of young unmarried women, who in fact made up a majority of the new audiences. According to Erenberg, critics of nightlife "believed that too much expressive pleasure in a risqué environment endangered young women" and warned that women allowed to enjoy music in a public setting would be "easily led to prostitution and away from the traditional role of home and mother." Peiss recounts newspaper stories "filled with dramatic accounts of innocent daughters tempted by glittering dance halls, seduced and drugged by ruthless 'cadets' or pimps, and held against their will in brothels."[15] While such fears mostly centered on the working class, a similar kind of reaction to new musical environments was emerging within the more middle- and leisure-class world of classical music at this time, as will be discussed in chapter 2, with a main focus on the leisure-class woman's musical exodus from the parlor. Joseph Horowitz has described the "protofeminism" inspired by leisure-class women's growing passion for Wagner's opera, as it seemed to arouse and encourage female erotic experience not only outside the home but also in the company of other women.[16] No longer fixed within the private space of the parlor, where music once served, or was thought to serve, to strengthen the emotional bonds of family and the boundaries of bourgeois femininity, music's growing presence in public and anonymous arenas threatened no less than to remake women's emotional economies. That American musicians and audiences across the highbrow/lowbrow divide were beginning to embrace, more seriously than previous generations, the music of African Americans, fueled the perceived threat to white womanhood, and through them, to white America as a whole, as will be discussed in chapters 3 and 4.

Although Dreiser occasionally took note of the shifting racial dynamics of American music culture, he tended to collapse almost all of his observations about contemporary musical life into questions about the effects of its growing commercialization. His early journalism and first novel offer valuable and deeply ambivalent insights into the effects of the new relations of production and reception of music in America, as again and again he both celebrates and seems to regret the way music has been put into circulation along new social and spatial pathways, challenging conventional emotional economies of social life.[17]

"Words and Music": Writing for Tin Pan Alley

During his short tenure at *Ev'ry Month*, Dreiser only occasionally wrote essays that touched on the musical tastes of his readership, most of whom, he realized, were more interested in the magazine's bonus sheet music than its articles. In one *Ev'ry Month* column, Dreiser regretfully observes a waning interest in "newspapers, magazines, pamphlets and books" and goes on to suggest that people seem more interested in live voices than written text: "Everywhere, on every hand, come . . . signs of the but ill-suppressed excitement and desire to hear. Everywhere are those who seem half hungry to hear a man once more endowed as the orator; everywhere those who would gladly be thrilled by the sentiment of an impassioned voice."[18] In a short poem entitled "Words and Music," Dreiser conveys in no uncertain terms his sense of the secondary status of text and authorship to music and songwriting for his readers: "I being but the words and not the song, / None cares to hear, / Till wedded unto music sweet and strong / Divinely clear."[19] That his own audience was more interested in "music sweet and strong" than in his written words is echoed in a letter he received from his own sister (whom many consider the model for "Sister" Carrie): "I wish you would send me and Ed every month [*Ev'ry Month*] regular as Ed plays the violen [*sic*] and I would like it for the music there is in it. Sister Emma."[20]

As the purported lyricist of at least one verse of "On the Banks," Dreiser himself briefly experienced the powerful relationship to audience that he imagines both songwriter and orator to enjoy. In an introduction to his brother's songs, he describes (or, perhaps, imaginatively reinvents) his first hearing of the lyrics as they were sung in the street outside his New York apartment:

> At first I could not make out the words, but the melody attracted my attention. It was plaintive and compelling. I listened, attracted, satisfied that it was a new popular success that had "caught on." As they drew near my window I heard the words, "On the Banks of the Wabash" most mellifluously harmonized.
>
> I jumped up. A part of the words were mine—my careless, indifferent gift to him. But made by his melody and labor into something so much more appealing than I could ever have imagined. It was Paul's song. . . . And they were already singing it in the street. In three months more it was everywhere—in the papers, on the stage, on the street-organs, played by orchestras, bands, whistled and sung every place.[21]

In spite of his words, the song is "Paul's" at whose recognition he jumps, and its power of attraction is its "mellifluously harmonized" melody, which seems in turn to harmonize its mass audience.

While thus acknowledging music's power to reach a mass audience, and the diverse and ubiquitous marketing tools of Tin Pan Alley, Dreiser equivocated about the degree to which these tools, as opposed to the songwriter's talent, determined a song's popularity. At times he saw the two working in tandem, and at others, he saw the new song-production factory as a threat to good music. In *Ev'ry Month*, he argued that the future of Broadway musical theater depends on whether "our composers will come to understand that the people want the spontaneous mirth of the heart, and not mirth to order."[22] He accounted for the success of his brother's songs in the same terms, emphasizing Dresser's spontaneity and emotional authenticity. While Dreiser's relationship to his more successful brother proved rocky during these years, Dreiser eventually (twelve years after his brother's death in 1906) wrote a moving tribute that offers a romantic perspective on the nature of his songs' appeal:

> And what pale little things they were really, mere bits and scraps of sentiment and melodrama in story form, most asinine sighings over

> home and mother and lost sweethearts and dead heroes such as never were in real life, and yet with something about them, in the music at least, which always appealed to me intensely and must have appealed to others, since they attained so wide a circulation. They bespoke, as I always felt, a wistful, seeking, uncertain temperament, tender and illusioned, with no practical knowledge of any side of life, but full of a true poetic feeling for the mystery and pathos of life and death, the wonder of the waters, the stars, the flowers, accidents of life, success, failure.[23]

Written from the vantage point of a now-established writer of realist novels, Dreiser cavalierly dismisses his brother's sentimental lyrics as asinine and unrealistic, but he nonetheless acknowledges that their value rests outside the purview of literary realism. As it mysteriously "appeals" and "circulates," Dresser's music speaks a kind of truth about human experience in its very refusal to represent real life or offer "practical knowledge." Dresser's songs, of course, managed to satisfy the peoples' desire for spontaneity while also generating profit (and, some would insist, sticking with successful formulae).

In two articles written after he left *Ev'ry Month*, Dreiser delivers a more critical perspective on the music industry and attempts to account for the effects of the new methods of producing and marketing popular music on the songs and their audiences. What makes these essays interesting is their suggestion that the Tin Pan Alley factory, while exploiting talented songwriters like his brother and churning out songs "made to order," might also be creating new forms and routes of connection between songs and their audiences that transcend the confining social conventions of nineteenth-century American musicality.

Published in *Metropolitan Magazine* in 1898, Dreiser's article "Birth and Growth of a Popular Song" begins in a celebratory tone as it describes the "methods by which all songs are given publicity and an opportunity to appeal for the good favor of the public." But the several large photographs accompanying his text advertise a different story, showing stony-faced men and women laboriously translating songs into rows of "pins" at a piano-roll factory, and the article soon launches into sober descriptions of Tin Pan Alley's new division of labor, which turns even the songwriter into a kind of factory worker. After attracting the interest of a publisher, which requires the right connections more than anything else, the aspiring songwriter signs away most of his song's future profits upon relinquishing the manuscript to its new owners. It then travels to an arranger, who makes it "the best for general piano purposes"; to the printer; and finally to the marketing division, which disseminates it among a host of "pluggers," including the street organs whose own hierarchical business model Dreiser discusses in some detail. As his narrative progresses, the song which had seemed accessible to "almost every one" and romantically intangible in its appeal at the beginning of the article is revealed also to be an impersonal, reified commodity whose appeal seems entirely manufactured by the music industry.[24]

In "Whence the Song," published a couple of years later in *Harper's Weekly*, Dreiser dwells more specifically on the apparent contradiction between a popular song's romantic appeal and its Tin Pan Alley origins. He suggests, this time, not only that successful songs reflect the original, authentic spirit of the songwriter but that the mediations of Tin Pan Alley allow that spirit to become detached from particular human origins and relationships to create a more general *national* sense of community. He begins by describing the unstable life of the songwriter who, even after striking gold with a successful song, can never depend on continued success and typically returns to the obscurity from which he came (as would Paul Dresser himself). Highlighted in his cast of exploited talents is an African American songwriter whose catchy tunes are earning the company big profits while he himself seems content to forgo his own enrichment. Dreiser's stereotypically naïve, happy-go-lucky black songwriter here stands, in his exploitability, for all successful songwriters, whose success, he suggests, depends on their complete distraction from practical matters and thus renders them vulnerable to the very market forces that momentarily reward them. But rather than harness this observation of the unhappy fate of talented musicians to a critique of Tin Pan Alley or of capitalism, Dreiser goes on to rhapsodize over the music industry's remarkably effective dissemination of popular songs: "It seems wonderful that they should come to this [a pauper's burial], singers, authors, women and all; and yet not more wonderful than that their little feeling, worked into a melody and a set of words, should reach far out o'er land and water, touching the hearts of the nation." His sentimental language equates as "wonderful" Tin Pan Alley's exhaustive mode of distribution with the songwriter's undeserved impoverishment, as if the two are not in tension but collaborating to create a national arena of feeling, a kind of modern pastoral: "We have heard the street bands and the organs, the street boys and the street loungers, all expressing this brief melody snatched from the unknown by some process of the heart. Here it is wandering the land over like a sweet breath of summer, making for matings and partings, for happiness and for pain."[25] While one might, following Petry, read this sentimentalism as Dreiser's intentionally ironic exposure of false consciousness and commodity fetishism, Dreiser's rhetoric about music's power of transcendence nonetheless gives us a historically resonant image of music, even at its most reified, seeming to defy its commodity form and filling social spaces as immaterial, intangible, and spontaneous "breath."

While he doesn't directly invoke the emerging discourse of "folk" music, Dreiser's songwriter gestures toward the idea of "folk musician" that a number of ethnographers and music critics were beginning to celebrate as the potential basis for a new, authentic, and thus noncommercial American music. Henry Krehbiel, an important turn-of-the-century music critic who devoted much of his career to cultivating appreciation for the music of Native American and African American "folk," defined "folk song" as "not only the song admired of the people but, in a strict sense, the song created by the people. . . . as a spontaneous utterance, filled with characteristic expression of the feelings of a people."[26] Dreiser, as we have seen, also values the "spontaneous utterance" that informs popular song, even while he worries that Tin Pan Alley threatens to replace this spontaneity with "songs made to order." But unlike Krehbiel, who locates authentic American folk music primarily in rural African American culture, Dreiser remains more interested in the "folk" moments within Tin Pan Alley and within Carrie's mass cultural, urban context. His musical populism emerges not only in essays on popular music but also in his occasional reviews, at this time, of classical music, in which he tended to deride the dazzling virtuosi that drew growing audiences: "There is a difference between playing soul-stirring strains, and the rendition of flowery, classical passages which require ceaseless practice, lightening energy and a sort of wizard juggling of limbs and muscle, to perform. It is a far cry from a brilliant piano recital, to the rendering of a sympathetic melody. As a matter of fact, pure music has nothing to do with the instrumental performance of it. If it came borne upon some breeze from nowhere, it would be doubly sweet for then it would be freed of all earthiness and would have nothing to do with strings and keys and fingers."[27] Dreiser here gives us another sentimental paeon to "pure music," as something disembodied and free to travel as if "upon some breeze from nowhere." Dreiser is harder on the classical audience, who prefer a "brilliant piano recital," than the common listener, whom he trusts to know a good, truthful song (like Dresser's) when he hears it. He seems to consider those who flock to concert halls as disingenuous, pretending to enjoy music that they don't really understand and that doesn't, in fact, belong to them: "There is considerable evidence that the United States are largely superficial in their knowledge of music, and that as for their love of it, they have none—that is, none for the kind of music they profess to love."[28] In other words, Dreiser here implies, those paying high prices to hear the latest brilliant pianist would really prefer a sympathetically rendered Paul Dresser tearjerker. The problem is less that Americans lack musical "knowledge" than that they refuse adequately to value the music they do love in their efforts to appear cultured.

In one article, Dreiser reserves special praise for a concert singer, but in a way that reinforces his valorization of a kind of folk musicality over the mechanistic wizardry of the classical virtuoso. In a review of a recital by opera singer Sissieretta Jones (who was widely touted as "the Black Patti," after the famed Adelina Patti), Dreiser describes the African American singer's voice as inspiring "rhapsodies" and evoking "the beauty of nature." Infusing his review with a touch of plantation nostalgia—she "brings back visions of the still, glassy water and soft swaying branches of some drowsy nook in summer time"—Dreiser celebrates her voice as completely unmarked by the modern urban commercial context. It should be noted that his favorable review, though reproducing popular images of a benign Southern idyll, led rival newspapers to accuse his editor of being a "nigger lover."[29] Like the black songwriter and his own brother, Jones represents authentic musicality for Dreiser, naturally impervious to—if nonetheless exploited by—an increasingly commercialized industry. In both his journalism and *Sister Carrie*, Dreiser completely elided ragtime music, which was becoming the dominant genre of African American, and indeed American, music. He preferred the Tin Pan Alley of his brother's 1890s, as it nostalgically "brought back" visions of lost people and places, rather than drawing listeners forward into the rhythms of modern urban life.

While Paul Dresser wrote songs in some of the new popular genres—including ragtime songs and patriotic airs—he shared much more in common with Stephen Foster than with twentieth-century songwriters. Indeed, although he was one of the most popular songwriters in the early 1890s, his appeal would drop off sharply after the turn of the century, as he became one more victim of the brutal vicissitudes of the music industry, doomed to a "pauper's burial." Called the "weepiest willow of them all" by Tin Pan Alley historian Isaac Goldberg, Dresser's songs gave voice to the ambivalence of newcomers to the city in the late nineteenth century who, like himself, held memories—real or imagined—of a simpler, more knowable social world left behind.[30] Songs like "Just Tell Them that You Saw Me" and "The Letter that Never Came" derive their pathos not only from their sentimental recollections of "gray-haired mother" and abandoned "sweetheart" but also from the alienation of the songs' narrators, usually speaking from the position of urban migrants who, like Carrie, wistfully experience moments of "repentance" or regret and a "longing" for a past that can never be recovered.

When the narrator of "She Went to the City," for example, returns home to "the village, where [he] used to roam," he learns that his old sweetheart "went to the city, far, far away" and is thus lost not only to her mother, "hope ever burning in [her] breast," but also to himself, unless, of course, he happens to run into her in the more anonymous spaces of their shared new urban life. "The Letter that Never Came" more tragically describes a nameless melancholic, who waits in vain his entire life, and even after death, for a letter from a distant intimate. The absent letter seems to stand for the absent sociality of his past, something that the city, full of lonely souls like himself, cannot reproduce. Even Dresser's (and, purportedly, Dreiser's) most famous and celebratory song, "On the Banks of the Wabash," which became Indiana's state song, memorializes the brothers' home state from a perspective "far, far away" in space as well as time, as its narrator nostalgically recalls river, landscape, mother's face, and sweetheart, who died without knowing that he loved her. Sentimental songs of the 1890s like Paul Dresser's appealed so widely in part because they invite their audiences into an imagined community that shares both an irrecoverable provincial past and a lonely urban present. As Mark Booth argues, the genre's principal subjects are defined by both their lachrymose nostalgia and their implied urban heroism, as survivors of migration and its accompanying traumas, and as pioneers in a modern individualist world.[31] But Dreiser himself helps us to see how such songs function not only to represent feelings of loss and nostalgia and to describe modern heroes, but also to *produce* a modern form of shared emotional experience, one rooted in the city's anonymous, ephemeral musical spaces rather than in the small town's family parlors.

Dreiser clearly isn't a weepy sentimentalist like his brother; *Sister Carrie* harbors no nostalgia for "mother" or life "back home." Instead, I will argue in the pages that follow, Dreiser's first novel registers the ways in which a sentimental musicality creates new emotional bonds between city people, and between the city and its people, relocating, in a sense, the "feeling tone" of sentimental song's narrative referents—the parlor, the family, the countryside—to the musical spaces of the city: the theater, the apartment building, the department store, and, as we shall see, conversations between relative strangers.[32]

"She Went to the City"

On the novel's first pages, just after the narrator describes the potential hazards of the urban "blare of sound" to a young woman's "unguarded ear," Carrie finds her own ear appealed to by a more personal, though anonymous, voice on the speedy train to Chicago. The "masher" Drouet first enters the scene, in fact, as a "voice in her ear," an intrusion that challenges her "maidenly reserve" and undermines her "sense of what was conventional under the circumstances" (4–5). Drouet's bold display of "daring and magnetism" initiates Carrie into a new urban environment, one figured throughout the novel, particularly its Chicago section, as an aural relationship between Carrie's "ear" and the seductive "voices" not only of people but also of things. In this scene between Drouet and Carrie, the masher's hackneyed language and less-than-virtuous intentions are overshadowed in the narration by the ways in which their conversing voices create a sense of real connection between them: "How true it is that words are but the vague shadows of the volumes we mean. Little audible links, they are, chaining together great inaudible feelings and purposes. Here were these two, bandying little phrases, drawing purses, looking at cards, and both unconscious of how inarticulate all their real feelings were. . . . Now she felt that she had yielded something—he, that he had gained a victory. Already they felt that they were somehow associated" (9). As only "vague shadows" and "audible links," their words function not as signs but as conduits between pools of "real" feelings that nonetheless remain "inaudible" and "inarticulate." Rather than shared understanding (they are, indeed, "unconscious" of what's really happening to them), the pair's conversation achieves a shared sense of being "somehow associated." When Carrie later "relaxed and heard with open ears" his seductions, she "could not help but feel the vibration of force" emanating from his presence (78).

Carrie's relaxed, vibrating, and open ears point to Dreiser's elaboration of a significant difference between hearing and seeing, as both sensory experience and metaphor. While Dreiser's oft-noted attention to the visuality of Chicago—to the shop windows, the gaze, and Carrie's growing awareness of her own image—underscores a flattening of identity and experience, his continuous evocation of the sounds that inevitably accompany urban sights, and of the phenomenology of hearing, suggests the faint persistence of human interiority within this reflective, commoditized urban world. Dreiser's language here, and in subsequent scenes, resonates in interesting ways with emerging debates about the nature of American music and musicality. Krehbiel, whose definition of folk song was cited earlier, describes the musicality of everyday conversation in terms that resonate strongly with Dreiser's descriptions of Carrie's conversations with both Drouet and Hurstwood: "Music cannot lie, for the reason that the things which are at its base . . . are unconscious, unvolitional human products. We act on a recognition of this fact when we judge of the feelings of the one with whom we are conversing not so much by what he says to us as by the manner in which he says it. The feelings which sway him publish themselves in the pitch, dynamic intensity and timbre of his voice. Try as we may, if we are powerfully moved we cannot conceal the fact so we open our mouths for utterance. . . . The drama of feeling playing on the hidden stage of our hearts is betrayed by the tones which we utter."[33] If the "hidden stage of our hearts" smacks of Victorian sentimentalism, the idea that the pitch, dynamics, and timbre of our voices betray unconscious truths (and reveal the limited signifying power of words) turns a corner into a more modern perspective on linguistic and musical acoustics.[34] Dreiser distinguishes Hurstwood from Drouet not only by noting the visual register of his higher economic status but also by noting the superior qualities of Hurstwood's voice, qualities rooted in a greater tension between his "real feelings" and his surface being. He secures Carrie's affection, like Drouet, by emitting a "vibration of force" that resonates with her own self—and in this case "seemed to radiate an atmosphere which suffused her being." While the language of vibration and radiation might underscore the power of material things to attract Carrie's gaze, it here underscores the physical, bodily experience of both impassioned vocalization and of hearing. Hurstwood is "capable of strong feelings," we are told, and "his voice [is] colored with that seeming repression and pathos which is the essence of eloquence." As he declares his feelings for Carrie, "his voice trembled with that peculiar vibration which is the result of tensity [*sic*]. It went ringing home to his companion's heart." As Hurstwood begins to win her over, his voice "drop[s] to a soft minor," and Dreiser's language becomes more explicitly musical: "He was striking a chord now which found sympathetic response in her own situation" (128–29).

The narrator here reminds us, in language that seems both sociological and sentimental, that "words are, as a rule, the shallowest portion" of conversation and "but dimly represent the great surging feelings and desires which lie behind. When the distraction of the tongue is removed, the heart listens." Like a popular song that has "caught on," Hurstwood's voice shifts his listener's attention away from "mere words," and toward the same well of shared but inarticulable feelings evoked in Carrie's conversation with Drouet:

> In this conversation she heard, instead of his words, the voices of the things which he represented. How suave was the counsel of his appearance! How feelingly did his superior state speak for itself! The growing desire he felt for her lay upon her spirit as a gentle hand. She did not need to tremble at all, because it was invisible; she did not need to worry over what other people would say—what she herself would say—because it had no tangibility. She was being pleaded with, persuaded, led into denying old rights and assuming new ones, and yet there were no words to prove it. Such conversation as was indulged in held the same relationship to the actual mental enactments of the twain that the low music of the orchestra does to the dramatic incident which it is used to cover. (118)

It is worth noting the several ways that this moment stands both in and against the "visual economy" that critics persuasively identify throughout Dreiser's novel. While Carrie undoubtedly learns to internalize a ubiquitous "gaze" that makes her aware of how she appears to others and arouses her desire for the many goods on display but just out of her reach, she here enjoys a momentary abandonment of self-consciousness. The "invisibility" of her new association with Hurstwood eludes others' gaze as well as her own; there is no evidence of her seduction because it remains unavailable to representation. Dreiser underscores this invisibility by using a metaphor of theatricality to describe not, as one would expect, the performative surface but the hidden interior of human interaction. Just as Krehbiel suggested that the "tones which we utter" betray the "drama of feeling playing on the hidden stage of our hearts," Dreiser figures Carrie's and Hurstwood's conversation as theater music, which both "covers" and reveals their hidden "enactments."

If the musicality of their voices complicates the "visual economy" that critics identify with Dreiser's novel, it also undermines the accompanying idea that all desire, for this novel, boils down to consumer desire. That Carrie hears, while listening to Hurstwood, "the voices of the things which he represented" demonstrates, for Bill Brown, that she "doesn't love people; she loves things."[35] But this passage emphasizes the difference between *voices* and *representations* as much, if not more, than it emphasizes the difference between people and things. The unarguable fact that Hurstwood's material "things" are important to Carrie (and largely define for her his "superior state") shouldn't obscure the degree to which Carrie—and Hurstwood—value the feeling of being connected, of "being somehow associated," to recall Carrie's earlier seduction by Drouet.

Catherine Jurca writes that Hurstwood is drawn to Carrie largely as an escape from the "impersonal and interchangeable interior" of his home, which is full of artifacts bought at "the large furniture houses."[36] A "lovely home atmosphere" is created not by things, but by something akin to music, as Dreiser describes it in a highly sentimental passage that recalls his descriptions of Paul Dresser's songs: "Those who have never experienced such a beneficent influence will not understand wherefore the tear springs glistening to the eyelids at some strange breath in lovely music. The mystic chords which bind and thrill the heart of the nation, they will never know" (81). Dreiser's presumption, here, is that modern readers might no longer appreciate or even recognize such an atmosphere, and the fact that Hurstwood regrets its absence in his own home sets him apart from other modern men in this novel (such as Drouet), just as Carrie's emotional nature sets her apart from Mrs. Hurstwood's "cold, self-centered" (elsewhere described as "cold, commonplace") nature (112, 121). This difference in Hurstwood and Carrie, and what brings them together, is their shared sensitivity to musical voices, or, one could say, their shared musicality. Carrie promises to satisfy Hurstwood's longing for an "affectional atmosphere" just as Paul Dresser's sentimental songs re-create for their urban listeners cozy feelings of human relations before the conditions of modernity and re-create the "mystic chords which bind and thrill the heart of a nation" that thus seem both threatened and promised by the anonymous, individualistic, materialistic city. Underscoring the nostalgic and musical dimension of Hurstwood's desire for Carrie, as he leaves the scene of his conquest of Carrie's emotions, he "whistle[s] merrily for a good four miles to his office an old melody that he had not recalled for fifteen years" (120).

But Carrie, of course, does not end up sharing Hurstwood's desire for domestic bliss, and her sentimental responsiveness to musical voices is not limited to domestic spaces or courtship narratives. In a scene often cited for its evocations of the visual economy of commodity capitalism, Dreiser figures Carrie's relationship to department store displays in terms that echo her aural relationship to Hurstwood's and Drouet's voices: "Fine clothes to her were a vast persuasion; they spoke tenderly and Jesuitically, for themselves. When she came within earshot of their pleading, desire in her bent a willing ear. The voice of the so-called inanimate! Who shall translate for us the language of the stones?" (98). The aural metaphor here certainly supports commodity culture's visual economy, helping Dreiser to explain the magnetic appeal of objects that are, in reality, seen rather than heard. But the idea that commodities have animate voices nonetheless signals a phenomenology of hearing that differs from that of seeing: the "voice of the so-called inanimate," like the voices of Hurstwood and Drouet, can give cover to Carrie's desire because it remains invisible and untranslatable, something beyond explanation or representation. Whether or not Dreiser decries Carrie's desire as commodity fetishism, his language points up the interchangeability, for Carrie, of the power of fine clothes on display with the power of a seductive, vibrating voice. What her "willing ear" craves is the experience of being "caught," of being appealed to as someone with an inarticulable, unrepresentable, hidden selfhood, as much if not more than the ownership of material "things."

Later in the same chapter, a more literal auditory moment underscores this slippage between consumer desire and a more existential longing. As she sits "wistful and depressed" in her apartment after a day in the city, Carrie overhears her neighbor practicing the piano:

> Now Carrie was affected by music. Her nervous composition responded to certain strains, much as certain strings of a harp vibrate when a corresponding key of a piano is struck. She was delicately molded in sentiment, and answered with vague ruminations to certain wistful chords. They awoke longings for those things which she did not have. They caused her to cling closer to things she possessed. . . . As she contemplated her new state, the strain from the parlor below stole upward. With it her thoughts became colored and enmeshed. She reverted to the things which were best and saddest within the small limit of her experience. She became for the moment a repentant. (102–3)

The "wistful" piano music she overhears blurs distinctions between material and more abstract "things," as what might be called "consumer desire" (for the "things she did not have") gradually retreats from scenes of consumerism (the present) into memories of what she calls, oddly, both the "best" and the "saddest." Rather than awaken specific memories of childhood, family, or homestead, the music instead occasions her "reversion" to the highs and lows—the emotional register, one could say—of a different time and place. The music, in other words, brings, at least for this moment, the difference of past feelings into the present, interrupting both the "visual economy" and the desire for things that are defining Carrie's urban experience.

This moment also represents a distinctly modern scene of musical production and reception, one whose modernity contributes, paradoxically, to Carrie's "reversion" to past emotions. While her childhood might have featured a parlor piano around which the women of her family played sentimental songs for one another or for friends, sharing a "wistful" moment that intensified the "home atmosphere," Carrie here remains an isolated listener sitting in her rented apartment, resonating sympathetically to an unseen piano played by a young woman who has moved to Chicago to study. Prefiguring the solitary musical experience enabled by the record player and radio (and, later, the Walkman and iPod), this modern scene of listening divorces sentimental music from the domestic spaces and characters its lyrics often describe and puts it into counterpoint with the disembodied, seductive voices and "blare of sound" that permeate Dreiser's turn-of-the-century Chicago.[37] When Drouet enters this scene, he makes "his first great mistake" by exposing his inability to hear music in the same way that Carrie—who is distinguished as someone "affected by music"—hears it. Suggesting that they "waltz a little to that music," Drouet remains deaf to its sentimental qualities and thus "made clear to Carrie that he could not sympathize with her" (103). Drouet lives wholly in the moment, unlike Carrie and Hurstwood, who vacillate between desire and dissatisfaction, and are susceptible to "wistful" strains.

In what Bill Brown calls "one of the novel's most memorable scenes," Carrie concludes a day of shopping full of materialist desire in her rocking chair, gazing out her window and distraught over her emerging awareness of the expensive items that remains beyond her (and Drouet's) reach. For Brown, Carrie's "glass-mediated" gaze in this scene underscores the "dialectic of proximity and distance that perpetuates desire in *Sister Carrie*," but he fails to note (and indeed, excludes from his extended quotation) that Carrie's desire is mediated by music as well as by her window: "She was too wrought up to care to go down to eat, too pensive to do aught but rock and sing. Some old tunes crept to her lips, and, as she sang them, her heart sank. She longed and longed and longed."[38] Feeling as if "all her state was one of loneliness and forsakenness," she "hummed and hummed as the moments went by, sitting in the shadow by the window, and was therein as happy, though she did not perceive it, as she ever would be" (116). This depressing pronouncement at once posits music as the greatest source of happiness for this modern woman and as the sign of her entrapment in a largely joyless world.

Carrie's wistful humming also prefigures her eventual transformation from hearer of "certain strains" to the modern producer of her own "voice," and more specifically her own sentimental strains on the stage of musical theater. Her inspired performance in *Under the Gaslight* is often discussed as the culmination of her commercial self-construction, the moment when she most obviously becomes the "image" of herself. But her "innate taste for imitation" has found her not only "re-creating, before her mirror, the expressions of various faces," but also re-creating actresses' voices: she "loved to modulate her voice after the manner of the distressed heroine" (157). After a shaky start on stage before an audience, her moment of recovery is specifically tied to her finding just such a voice. Still nervous, Carrie initially delivers lines that "were merely spoken . . . in such a feeble voice" that "came out . . . flat" (181). Her talent reveals itself only when her voice becomes a conduit of a mysterious energy: "Carrie listened, and caught the infection of something—she did not know what," and, only then, "her voice assum[ed] for the first time a penetrating quality which it had never known" (184–85). She quickly overshadows her fellow cast members as she engages more with the play's musical accompaniment than its spoken lines: "Scarcely hearing the small, scheduled reply" of the other actor on stage with her, Carrie put "herself even more in harmony with the plaintive melody now issuing from the orchestra" (192).

Recalling the popular song that "catches on," the unnamable "something" that defined the appeal of Dresser's music, and the "vibration of force" expressed in Hurstwood's own penetrating voice, Carrie here assumes musical agency of her own, and joins the chorus of urban voices to which others' "willing ears" are drawn. Most importantly for the unfolding of Dreiser's plot, Carrie's voice now seduces a "listening" Hurstwood and sets into motion the chain of events that lead to his demise. After he too "[catches] the infection" that prompted Carrie's inspiration, he finds himself "almost deluded by that quality of voice and manner which, like a pathetic strain of music, seems ever a personal and intimate thing" (189), and ultimately, "deluded" or no, makes the decision to leave his wife for Carrie: "He forgot the need of circumspectness which his married state enforced.

He almost forgot that he had with him in the box those who knew him. By the Lord, he would have that lovely girl if it took his all. He would act at once" (193). The "infectious" emotionalism of this moment promises a kind of freedom from the hollow conventionality of his marriage and social position, in part by suspending his awareness of the gaze of those around him (who might police that conventionality).

Once Carrie and Hurstwood leave Chicago and arrive in New York, references to music and aurality virtually disappear. As a reminder of prior ways of feeling (or a suggestion that one used to feel differently), sentimental musicality in this novel seems most powerful for those characters—particularly Carrie—who are caught between dissatisfaction and desire. The newcomer to Chicago, as Dreiser's narrator told us on the novel's first pages, is easily overwhelmed by the modern city's musical "blare of sound," and by the time they move to New York, Carrie has become much better able to navigate her way through an urban setting, not least because she has learned to add her voice to the soundscape. Hurstwood, on the other hand, has become entirely passive after surrendering to Carrie's voice, and has given up any chance to use his own outside his relationship with Carrie. In the revised ending, however, Dreiser brings Carrie's musicality into new focus through the perspective of the visiting midwesterner, Ames, whom some take to be representative of Dreiser himself. In a conversation with Ames at a hotel dinner party, Carrie finds the young inventor sitting by the fire and listening to music being played in the background:

> "Isn't that a pathetic strain?" he inquired, listening.
>
> "Oh, very," she returned, also catching it, now that her attention was called. . . .
>
> They listened a few moments in silence, touched by the same feeling, only hers reached her through the heart. Music still charmed her as in the old days.
>
> "I don't know what it is about music," she started to say, moved by the inexplicable longings which surged within her; "but it always makes me feel as if I wanted something—I—"
>
> "Yes," he replied; "I know how you feel."[39]

By associating Carrie's musical responsiveness with the "old days"—which could equally refer to Chicago, now part of nostalgic memory after life in New York, as to the time preceding her migration to the city—music once again brings feeling tones of the past into the present, "catching" its listeners' distracted attention and drawing them into a confusion of nostalgic memory and desire. While Ames claims to "know" how Carrie feels, his own listening is something altogether different. Carrie experiences music's emotion "through the heart," while Ames seems more intent on analyzing the music's methods, and insists that music's emotional narratives remain unconnected to real life, or to the here and now: "It doesn't do us any good to wring our hands over the far-off things." He then, in this and a subsequent conversation, tries to get her to focus on her own power articulately to represent longing, rather than mutely submitting to it: "Sometimes nature . . . makes the face representative of all desire. That's what has happened in your case."[40]

Musical (and theatrical) performance, for Ames, should be understood as representational rather than experienced as vibrational force and infectious atmosphere; it should inspire thought rather than arouse emotion. Carrie has finally found that "counselor," cited in the novel's first chapter, to offer "cautious interpretations" of the urban blare as it appeals, "like music," to her "unguarded ear." But Ames's advice is not heard by Carrie in the way that he wishes—"the effect of his words was like roiling helpless waters"; indeed, Carrie remains to the end unable to wrest herself from her "inexplicable longings," longings that are given voice by music to a degree that mere words cannot hope to match. Dreiser, as a writer, has perhaps not yet decided whether he can succeed where Ames has failed with the common urban reader, to whom an exciting and growing array of popular songs and musical venues are beckoning throughout the spaces of the modern city.

According to Dreiser's close friend Richard Duffy, Dreiser struggled with the ending of *Sister Carrie* and would find relief during his breaks in talk and in song: "[Dreiser] always sat in a rocking chair, if he could find one. . . . If he was not talking he would be humming the refrain of 'On the Banks of the Wabash' or of some other popular song. He had hundreds in his head."[41] This image of Dreiser humming and rocking cannot but bring to mind the novel's final pages, with Carrie humming and rocking by her window, "as happy, though she did not perceive it, as she ever would be." While Duffy's anecdote underscores the difference between writing and music, between the work of writing a serious novel and the relaxation of humming popular songs, it also reminds us of Dreiser's own position as enchanted audience of the new popular songs coming out of Tin Pan Alley and thus his own possible identification with his inarticulate and perennially dissatisfied heroine. Perhaps his problem with writing an ending to his first novel reflected his own ambivalence about the status of writing in a world so increasingly permeated and influenced by musicality. Would his words, like those of Ames, have the effect of "roiling helpless waters"? Would he, like Ames, seem like an outsider to the world of his readers? Will music always seem more "real" than the most realist fiction? Dreiser's withdrawal into rocking and humming generates Carrie's own rocking-chair musings in the novel's final scene, which finds her "singing and dreaming" about "that radiance of delight which tints the distant hilltops of the world."[42] "The Way of the Beaten: A Harp in the Wind," the novel's final chapter suggests that, for the moment at least, sentimental song reigns supreme in this heroine's sense of self and of her place in the world.

The following chapters focus on novels in which music similarly unsettles projects of literary realism with the promise of access to deeper truths and more satisfying experiences than words alone can deliver. If the music in these novels—from Frédéric Chopin's piano pieces to Wagner's opera to Mexican folk song to ragtime—bears little resemblance to Dreiser's nostalgia-filled "pathetic" strains, it nonetheless similarly demonstrates a power to "infect" its listeners and draw them into new ideas of themselves and their relationship to the world around them. Music in these novels also promises, like Tin Pan Alley, to sound out and help produce modern social spaces that increasingly displace nineteenth-century musical settings—whether the "banks of the Wabash" or the parlor piano.

2

Listening to Women Playing Chopin

Chopin unsettles us.

—Jeffrey Kahlberg, *Chopin at the Boundaries: Sex, History, and Musical Genre*

With mock insistence that "the piano is passing and with it the piano girl—there really was a piano girl," James Huneker, one of New York's foremost music critics at the turn of the twentieth century, registers American women's musical migration from the parlor to the concert hall: "If she must have music, she goes to a piano recital and hears a great artist interpret her favorite composer."[1] But not all ex-piano girls ended up sitting in the audience. Acknowledging the growing presence of female pianists on public stages, Huneker ultimately arrives, in an essay published in 1902, at a question increasingly being asked within music journalism at this time of whether or not women were capable of being "great artist" interpreters of the Western musical canon.[2] Huneker specifically focuses his question on women's capacity to perform the music of a composer dear to his heart, about whom he had just written a definitive biography: "Can women," he asks, "play Chopin?"[3]

American women, in fact, were particularly drawn to Chopin's music at this time, a trend that Huneker mockingly refers to as "Chopinitis," thereby distinguishing women's fandom from his own presumably more healthy interest in the composer.[4] Musicologist Jeffrey Kahlberg, interested in the ways in which "Chopin unsettles us," has written about the particular challenges the Polish composer posed to nineteenth-century gender ideology by generating music whose expressive qualities and emotional associations crossed and blurred boundaries between private parlor and public stage and between constructions of masculinity and femininity.[5] As Kahlberg notes, Huneker was among a number of critics who defended Chopin against charges of effeminacy by urging unsentimental and "vigorous" performances of his music. Clearly anxious about the feminization of his favorite composer by both female pianists and audiences, Huneker finally concedes that at least two female pianists—Sophie Menter and Teresa Carreno—*can* play Chopin well, but only by virtue of their idiosyncratic masculinity—their "iron will and great muscular power."[6] And while he valorizes femininity as a crucial element of musical artistry—"all musical artists should [be] feminine in their temperament"—Huneker reserves the highest honors for feminine *men:* piano virtuoso Vladimir de Pachmann is "more feminine than any woman in his tactile sensibilities" and the great Chopin himself "infinitely more feminine than any woman."[7] Huneker, whose own fascinating novel about turn-of-the-century music will be a focus of chapter 5, thus embraces Chopin's unsettling effects in so far as he seems to recognize and value musical identities that blur the gender line, while nonetheless leaving us with the feeling he wished female pianists had stayed in the parlor.

This chapter examines two turn-of-the-century novels that feature women whose masterful performances of Chopin inspire no debate. Indeed, instead of comparing their talents with those of men, these novels explore the effects of their Chopin performances on the lives of particular listeners. Harold Frederic's *The Damnation of Theron Ware* (1896) and Kate Chopin's *The Awakening* (1899) invite us to think more carefully about the place of both Chopin's music and female performers within specific social contexts and spaces and to recognize musical experience as comprised of relationships between performers, composers, and listeners. Literary evocations of listening, as we have already seen so powerfully in *Sister Carrie*, can help us to understand how audiences made sense of and incorporated the music they heard in the context of their everyday lives, ideas, and values. Interestingly, scholars writing about music in these novels have focused almost entirely, like Huneker, on musical *production* as the sole nexus of musical significance. Critics have considered, for example, the musical natures of the pianist-characters Mlle Reisz and Celia Madden, or have explored the novels' thematic and structural relationships to the compositions or composers they cite. By missing the degree to which these novels focus on the phenomenology of listening, this body of criticism underscores a Western critical approach to music that all but ignores the social constructions of musical meaning.[8]

So what *do* these novels tell us about turn-of-the-century conventions of listening, listening to Chopin, and more specifically, listening to women playing Chopin? At first glance, Harold Frederic's remarkable and underappreciated narrative about a Methodist minister's "damnation" in a small

New England town seems to have little in common with Kate Chopin's depiction of a young woman's "awakening" amidst the sensuality of Gulf Coast Louisiana Creole culture.[9] To recognize these novels' shared attention to the relationship between female musicians and their responsive listeners, however, yields a startling set of parallels, which in turn highlight important differences that have much to tell us about music and gender in turn-of-the-century America. Both Theron and Edna are young married Protestants immersed in Catholic subcultures whose sensual, liberal, and musical atmospheres attract and disorient them. Both are particularly shaken by the experience of hearing unmarried female pianists playing the music of Frédéric Chopin. For both, listening to Chopin is, indeed, "unsettling," as it throws the emotional landscape of everyday life and the limits of their conventional social selves into intolerable relief. Both experience this awakening to self as, among other things, erotic, as an awakening to and of *desire.* And both, ultimately, find their new selves impossible to sustain within their given social worlds: Edna takes a suicidal walk into the sea, while Theron, after contemplating suicide, abandons his Chopin-inspired fantasy of self-fulfillment and spins a new, equally romantic but decidedly less musical, fantasy of a political career. As important as the similarities between these two novels' depictions of listening are their differences, which highlight tensions within turn-of-the-century discourses about music, particularly around questions of gender and sexuality, as well as tensions within the literary field of realism/naturalism.

By putting these two novels together, and reading them in terms of their central musical relationships, this chapter both builds on and challenges the scholarly conversations they have inspired, conversations that have so far been mutually exclusive. *The Awakening*, of course, has long been a focus, and indeed a register, of feminist literary scholarship, as earlier debates about Edna's choices have more recently been problematized by attention to the racial and class dimensions structuring Edna's and the novel's perspective. *Theron Ware* has occupied a very different, more marginal, and less coherent scholarly space, inspiring debate over its place in the American canon of literary realism and naturalism (with which it has had a rocky relationship), its approach to American religion, particularly its representation of the differences between Methodism and Catholicism, and its ambivalent vision of American modernity. By recognizing these novels' shared attention to particular musical figures and relationships, this chapter intervenes in both scholarly conversations by pointing out the degree to which the novels speak to one another—about gender ideology, religious and cultural difference, national identity, and the generic boundaries of literary naturalism—even if they ultimately draw very different conclusions.

One important index of their differences rests in their narrative voices and the relationship of these voices to the music and musicality they represent. In *The Awakening*, music emerges as a language of "the abiding truth" and Chopin's writerly voice seems everywhere informed by, and aspiring to, the rhythmic, melodic, and even harmonic contours of the musical elements it describes. *Theron Ware*, on the other hand, remains suspicious of music's "truth" claims, and, on the contrary, suggests that music, like other forms of social performance, is a kind of "fraud." Frederic's narrative voice, never what one would call musical, seems on the contrary to distance itself and the reader from Theron's musical experience, dissecting and describing rather than reproducing the music Theron hears. This difference of narrative style highlights an important tension within realism and naturalism's relationship to music, one already recognized within Dreiser's *Sister Carrie* as it vacillates between realist and sentimentalist narrative voices. This tension underscores music's equivocal and unsettled relationship to "the real" at this historical moment, while it also highlights a gendered experience of music's promise of unmediated and awakened subjectivity.

"That was his new birth—that marvellous [*sic*] night with the piano."

Theron's "marvellous night with the piano" has received surprisingly little critical attention, considering its transformative effect on the novel's central character and the remarkable detail of its narration.[10] Harold Frederic always prepared for writing his novels with painstaking research and prepared specifically for his Chopin episode by consulting with a "professional friend" who not only helped him understand the "technical musical stuff," but also played him a number of Chopin works while the author took notes.[11] This performance occasion, in which the author/listener actively consults and then scientifically records the musician's expertise, could not be further removed, in spirit or effect, from Celia's private recital for Theron. Rather than listening with a reporter's ear, and as preparation for the music's accurate representation, Theron listens and reacts emotionally, entirely at the mercy of music that dissolves his capacity to maintain any appearance of composure or self-control.

The novel implicitly explains Theron's response to Celia's performance not only as an effect of the combined power of Celia's performance and

Chopin's music (to which we will return) but also as one more episode in his seduction by the exotic foreignness and cultural sophistication of the Irish Catholic leadership of his upstate New York town. Theron first meets Celia, and experiences her musicality, in the context of Catholic ritual. During a walk soon after he has moved to Octavius as its new Methodist minister, Theron notices and follows a group of boys carrying a dying man through an Irish neighborhood and finally into a "dark and ill-smelling" working-class home. Here Theron finds himself witness to last rites, "sonorously" delivered in Latin by Father Forbes, the town's priest, who is accompanied by Celia Madden. Moved intensely—"no other final scene had stirred him like this" (67)—Theron notes that "the Irish, with all their faults, must have a poetic strain, or they would not have clung so tenaciously to those curious and ancient forms" (77). When he learns that Celia is a musician, his imagination immediately associates her musicality with this notion of archaic Irish culture, "having heard somewhere, or read, it might be, that they were a people much given to songs and music" (77–78).

As is evident across the novels in this study, listening to music can occasion intimacy and desire across boundaries—of race, ethnicity, and class—that otherwise remain inviolate. The intimacy occasioned by music seems to invite a confusion of desire and identification, as the listening self recognizes musicality as a sign of what he or she lacks and thus desires but also as a sign of what has been lost or repressed but might be restored (or "awakened"). Theron's inherited assumption about Irish identity leads him to contemplate his own identity and, by contrast, the relative absence of music in his own life lived within a Protestant culture suspicious of "songs and music": "Of all the closed doors which his choice of a career had left along his pathway, no other had for him such a magical fascination as that on which was graven the lute of Orpheus. He knew not even the alphabet of music, and his conceptions of its possibilities ran but little beyond the best of the hymn-singing he had heard at Conferences, yet none the less the longing for it raised on occasion such mutiny in his soul that more than once he had specifically prayed against it as a temptation" (78). As Aaron Urbanczyk notes, this scene introduces "the 'Catholic'" as "exotic other, the master trope and locus of [Theron's] most transgressive and self-destructive desires."[12] Exposure to the foreign musicality of this stirring Irish "final scene" represents, for Theron, a potential means of freeing his own repressed and mutinous interiority.

Prior to this encounter with Irish musicality, Theron is presented as having a relatively liberal attitude about music, one in keeping with his affiliation with the more modern branch of Methodism and at odds with the conservative Methodist church to which he is assigned at the start of the novel. In answer to the "archaic nasal singing" of an old-time preacher (14), Theron delivers sermons "with an alert ear, and calculation in every tone," thus demonstrating his potential to become a "great pulpit orator" (35). The more traditional Methodists have no interest in oratorical virtuosity, insisting instead on "the plain, old-fashioned Word of God, without any palaver or 'hems and ha's" (43). When Theron proposes including music in church services, the Octavius trustees reject such "new-fangled notions," associating "puttin' in organs an' choirs" with "deckin' our women-folks out with gewgaws, an' apin' the fashions of the worldly" (45). Theron encountered the Irish boys while asserting his own, modern Protestant version of rebellious musicality in making the decision, against the wishes of the tight-fisted trustees of Octavius's Methodist church, to purchase a piano for his wife Alice. While Theron's open-minded (and bourgeois) attitudes about music put him in the vanguard of Methodism, his encounter with the town's Catholics pushes his idea of a liberated musicality to a much darker, richer, and more dangerous horizon than the parlor piano.

Theron's second encounter with the town's Catholic leadership, during a visit with the intellectual Father Forbes and his scientist friend Dr. Ledsmar, challenges his fantasy of an ancient and musical Irish otherness: "For custodians of a mediæval superstition and fanaticism, the Catholic clergy seemed very much up to date" (99). Father Forbes's progressive theological ideas challenge the foundation of Theron's Methodism by inviting him to consider the Bible as metaphor and to question the moral absolutism underpinning his own faith. His intellectual and theological unsettling become inextricably linked with a subsequent experience of music that, unlike the ancient rites earlier witnessed and the bourgeois rituals anticipated in the purchase of a new piano, shakes his assumptions about what music is or does. At a pause in conversation, Theron becomes captivated by music that invisibly enters the scene as if by magic:

> There fell upon this silence—with a softness so delicate that it came almost like a progression in the hush—the sound of sweet music. For a little, strain and source were alike indefinite—an impalpable setting to harmony of the mellowed light, the perfumed opalescence of the air, the luxury and charm of the room. Then it rose as by a sweeping curve of beauty, into a firm, calm, severe melody, delicious to the ear, but as cold in the mind's vision as moonlit sculpture. . . .

> Theron found himself moved as he had never been before. He almost resented the discovery, when it was presented to him by the prosaic, mechanical side of his brain, that he was listening to organ-music, and that it came through the open window from the church close by. He would fain have reclined in his chair and closed his eyes, and saturated himself with the uttermost fulness [*sic*] of the sensation. (117)

Relishing this passive experience of listening to "sweet music" that is "delicious to the ear," Theron is "moved as he had never been before," drawn out of his everyday self and thoughts and seduced not by ethnic or racial otherness, in this case, but by an aesthetic "opulence" that strains to remain unmarked by reference to the social and material world. The question of what music is and does—and the idea that its meaning and value are, like the Bible, up for debate—comes into more explicit focus in this scene as Dr. Ledsmar proceeds to name, and then degrade, the source of this "sweet music," as none other than Celia Madden, playing unnamed music on the organ in the church next door. Coldly scientific, though somewhat authoritative, Dr. Ledsmar propounds his conviction that musicians, including Celia, "stand on the very bottom rung of the ladder in the sub-cellar of human intelligence" (122), a judgment that implicitly casts Theron's "vision of a moonlit sculpture" as mere sentimentalism and contributes to the undercurrent of irony that perpetually undermines Theron's perspective. Unswayed by Ledsmar's assertions (much as Dreiser's Carrie remains unswayed by Ames's scientific perspective on music late in *Sister Carrie*), Theron follows the overheard music to the church door, a boundary, like the "closed doors" of his career path, that the music beckons him to cross: "Through this wee aperture the organ-music, reduced and mellowed by distance, came to him again with that same curious, intimate, personal relation which had so moved him at the start. . . . It was as if it was being played for him alone" (125). From this moment onward, Theron's responsiveness to music becomes inextricably linked to his responsiveness to Celia herself, but it is important not to subsume the former entirely by the latter: Celia, to some extent, comes to represent music's promise of aesthetic saturation, desublimation, and open doors.

It is not until much later in the novel that Celia will invite him into her home and play an entire recital of Chopin "for him alone," and only after he encounters an entirely different perspective on music's value. (The number of perspectives on music in this novel alone gives us a sense of music's unstable place in the American imaginary at this moment.) Candace Soulsby is the other Chopin-performing woman in this novel and Celia's chief rival in the "damnation" of Theron Ware. A professional "debt-raiser" hired by Methodist churches to rouse their stingy congregations into a spirit of generosity, Sister Soulsby transforms misers into givers by casting a kind of "spell" on her audience, which she accomplishes in part with a clever musical trick: "The words were 'Rock of Ages,' but no one present had heard the tune to which she wedded them. Her voice was full and very sweet, and had in it tender cadences which her hearers found touching" (224). After a remarkably profitable session, Sister Soulsby reveals to Theron her secret: "I simply took Chopin—he is full of sixths, you know—and I got all sorts of melodies out of his waltzes and mazurkas and nocturnes and so on. . . . We take these tunes, written by a devil-may-care Pole who was living with George Sand openly at the time, and pass 'em off on the brethren for hymns. It's a fraud, yes; but it's a good fraud" (268). That the "melodies" of a Polish composer living with a woman out of wedlock would remain unfamiliar to this upstate New York Methodist congregation, particularly given its proscriptions against "fashionable" music, is not surprising. Their ignorance, combined with her musical savvy and skill, enables Sister Soulsby, as she puts it, to achieve a form of "passing" that is religious as well as musical: mazurkas passing as hymns, Catholic passing as Protestant, Polish passing as American, and sinner passing as righteous.

Sister Soulsby's musical charade both attracts and confuses Theron, whose religious faith and intellectual bearings have already been weakened by his exposure to Father Forbes's moral relativism. In response to Theron's continued insistence on notions of integrity and sincerity, Sister Soulsby urges him, in an oft-cited speech, to recognize the social world as a realm of performance, and to acknowledge "the machinery behind the scenes" (260). Her own "artistic" method, in Chopin-ized hymns as in everything else, moves (and manipulates) her audience through rhetorical, theatrical, and *musical* effect: "What Sister Soulsby said did not matter. The way she said it—the splendid, searching sweep of her great eyes; the vibrating roll of her voice, now full of tears, now scornful, now boldly, jubilantly triumphant; the sympathetic swaying of her willowy figure under the stress of her eloquence—was all wonderful" (230). When Theron asks her whether she and her husband have been "sincerely converted" to the Methodism they preach, her answer undermines the linearity implicit in his notion of "conversion": "Not only once—dozens of times—I may say every time. We couldn't do good work if we weren't. But that's a matter of temperament—of emotions" (267). Rather than signifying a one-time shift from a sinful to a righteous self, conversion signifies, for Sister Soulsby, nothing more than an endlessly repeatable emotional and performative effect, like the repeatable elation inspired by a Chopin mazurka.

Soulsby, we learn, has spent much of her life performing different roles, or "passing": as a vaudevillian, fortune teller, gambler, and, as it is hinted more than once, a white southerner disguising nonwhite antecedents. Theron raises the question of her race when, upon first meeting Sister Soulsby, he wonders about her "old Ethiopian name" (206) and then speculates "as to whether her yellowish complexion was due to that tea-drinking or came to her as a legacy of Southern blood" (208). (The question is raised again when Brother Soulsby archly addresses her as "white folks" [488].[13]) But rather than give us a stock scene of unmasking, the novel keeps her origins and "blood" inchoate and her identity fluid and changeable: Theron perceives her as at once young and old, thin and fleshy, feminine and masculine, in every sense defying conventional categorization (216). Performativity itself becomes the primary marker of her difference from and power over the ever-earnest and increasingly vulnerable Theron.

That Theron's exposure to Sister Soulsby's relativism has no apparent effect on his own "conversion" by Celia's performance of Chopin does not mean that the novel's readers aren't being invited to notice the degree to which both Sister Soulsby and Celia are musical performers able to "convert" others while themselves remaining invulnerable. Different as they appear from one another, their musical temperaments, I would argue, underscore (and mark) their shared difference from Theron's embattled Protestant masculinity. Both women enjoy freedom from the Protestant heritage of emotional restraint, musical repression, literalism, and religious "awakenings." By placing Chopin's music in both contexts, Frederic underscores the degree to which Celia and Soulsby wield similar kinds of musical power, if used for different ends: this music, if performed in the right way, and at the right moment, can cause people to do things they would not normally do, to at least temporarily experience a break from their everyday selves.

Theron's journey into Celia's private rooms at the center of her parents' large mansion (they are the richest family in town) reads almost like the beginning of an immersion narrative or a trek into the heart of darkness. Worlds away from the bourgeois parlor where women like Theron's wife Alice entertain their friends and nurture their families at the piano, Celia's space, and the piano within it, express and nourish only her own aesthetic sensibility. She invites Theron to recline on an "oriental couch," from where he gazes confusedly at neoclassical statues of naked women and paintings of the Virgin. Only when Celia begins to play the music of Chopin does he finally "[surrender] his senses to the mere unthinking charm of it all" (289) and allow himself to imagine a continuum between naked women and the Virgin, or between sexuality and religion: "In the presence of such a face, of such music, there ceased to be any such thing as nudity, and statues no more needed clothes than did those slow, deep, magnificent chords which came now, gravely accumulating their spell upon him" (291).

If Theron's melodramatic swooning before Celia and her music seems a bit ridiculous, Frederic gives this scene a definite gravitas with his extensive, well-researched description of eight different works by Chopin. As she plays Chopin's Fourth Prelude, Seventh Waltz, Sixth Nocturne, Second Sonata, the Berceuse, Ninth Nocturne, Third Ballade, and, finally, his Sixteenth Mazurka, Celia presents a Chopin tour de force (as if to prove, once and for all, that women can and do play Chopin). The narrative of this performance resonates with late nineteenth-century critical discussions of Chopin's music, when Chopin's piano music (composed a half century earlier) was still considered "modern" for its episodic, nonlinear tendencies, and shifting emotional registers.[14] Celia compounds the music's effects by juxtaposing dissimilar works, moving from waltz rhythms to "what might be church music"; from a "capricious" song to a "somber and lofty anthem" that makes Theron feel "most of all that one should kneel to hear such music"; and from a "weird, mediæval processional" whose "wild, clashing chords" affect him "like dizziness" to the "pure, liquid, mellifluous melody of a soft-throated woman singing to her lover," which interrupts a dancing "mockery of inconsequence" (291–96). The final mazurka refuses to add any resolution to this chaotic emotional narrative, ending with "an odd, unaccountable halt in what seemed the middle of everything" and "at last a few faltering ascending notes, making a half-finished strain" (297). In response to her announcement that the piece has ended, he insists, "'It *can't* be the end! . . . How *could* it be the end? . . . Things don't end that way!'" as he almost faints in "giddiness" and "fright" (298).

Celia's Chopin performance has not simply enthralled her listener but has entirely unhinged him from conventional emotional narrative and offered him a glimpse at an entirely different "structure of feeling." (Raymond Williams's term is, indeed, particularly useful for thinking about music's relationship to emotional conventions: "As firm and as definite as a 'structure' suggests, yet it is based in the deepest and often least tangible elements of our experience."[15]) When Celia explains to him her "Greek" philosophy, her determination to live only for pleasure and beauty and throw "moral bugbears" by the wayside, Theron awkwardly proclaims: "I want to be a Greek myself, if you're one. I want to get as close to you—to your ideal, that is, as I can. . . . you and the music have decided me. I am going to put the things out of my life that are not worth while" (301). As he struggles to distinguish between the desire to be near and to be *like* Celia he reveals a central tension in his experience of this exciting and unfamiliar music. As the gap between music, performer, and listener seems to dissolve in the moment of listening, the problem for Theron becomes how to maintain this intimacy beyond the invisible walls of the musical performance and how to name and embody his new sense of self in isolation from the particular circumstances of the musical occasion. While Celia can casually name her aesthetic philosophy just as she can wield the aestheticized language of Romantic music, Theron remains trapped in inarticulable experience.

His downfall is, in effect, his naïve belief that he can remain, in society, who he felt himself to be while listening to Celia play Chopin. He fails to recognize what both Celia and Sister Soulsby know well: that aesthetic effect is at least in part produced by "machinery behind the scenes" and by what remains unknowable to the naïve listener. This machinery includes not only Chopin's compositional skill and Celia's talent as a performer, but also Theron's attraction to Celia, his emotional and intellectual confusion, his unfamiliarity with Chopin's music and, not least, the rich and sensual atmosphere of the performance space. Instead of heeding Sister Soulsby's advice, Theron defers facing the impossibility of his desire by latching onto two ready-made narratives of liberated masculine subjectivity through which he can both *have* and *be* Celia: he will have an affair with Celia (which he never fully articulates to himself but clearly anticipates), and he will become an independent, Emersonian, free American determining his own reality. "It was apparent to the Rev. Theron Ware, from the very first moment of waking next morning [after the evening of Chopin], that both he and the world had changed over night. The metamorphosis, in the harsh toils of which he had been laboring blindly so long, was accomplished. He stood forth, so to speak, in a new skin, and looked about him, with perceptions of quite an altered kind, upon what seemed in every way a fresh existence. He lacked even the impulse to turn round and inspect the cocoon from which he had emerged. Let the past bury the past. He had no vestige of interest in it" (303). By thus naming this experience of ontological rupture as rebirth, Theron fails to see that there is no future for this new Theron within the existing social spaces of Octavius. This failure spells out his disempowerment within those social spaces; like Hurstwood, he becomes a victim of his own responsiveness to a musical woman, able neither to woo her nor to extricate himself from his already existing web of responsibilities and relationships.

While this scene participates in elaborating the terms of an American reception of Chopin, and more specifically of an American male reception of a woman playing Chopin, it also invites consideration of the relationship between music and literary realism. When Theron protests, after the Mazurka's abrupt ending, that "things don't end that way," he registers his surprise that Chopin's music not only fails to conform to more familiar musical conventions, by which melodic strains would "finish" with decisive endings resolving prior conflicts and tensions, but also fails realistically to represent *social* conventions, the way "things are," by refusing to mirror the contours of real life which have definite beginnings, middles, and endings. Frederic clearly, and especially at this moment of Theron's fateful submission to Celia's charms, invites us to believe that things do sometimes "end that way," that narrative conventions, like musical conventions, are not writ in stone but subject to change and revision. But while granting Chopin's music a kind of realism, Frederic's prose style does not, like Dreiser's in his more sentimental moments and like Kate Chopin's throughout *The Awakening*, aspire to the condition of music. On the contrary, he maintains an ironic voice, as Scott Donaldson and others have pointed out, from the beginning of his novel to the end, that he compounds in this Chopin scene by supplying as much "technical stuff" as possible, naming each and every piece, and giving us a blow-by-blow account of their different emotional qualities. Furthermore, by giving us Sister Soulsby's Chopin "fraud" prior to this scene, Frederic has planted the idea, in his reader's mind if not Theron's, that performers and composers operate within particular social situations, not simply "representing" a static reality but influencing, shaping, constructing, and sometimes disguising that reality. What Chopin's music means and does in one context might be very different from what it means and does in another.

Making reference to the gendered discourses about ministers in nineteenth-century America, Lisa MacFarlane compellingly reads Frederic's novel as an "allegory about the social constructions of gender" driven by Theron's anxious attempts, as an increasingly feminized man in the company of unconventionally powerful women, to recover his masculinity. She notes that Celia's sexuality "disconcerts and disorients Theron," and that it remains "a sexuality beyond his control, beyond his capacity to move it, except in his fantasies." The disorienting force of Celia's sexuality is expressed, for MacFarlane, in the unconventional juxtapositions of her character—"sisterly, sensual, virginal, passionate."[16] While MacFarlane's analysis does not focus at all on the musical scenes, which are a primary means through which Celia expresses her character, she helps us see how this novel reveals and reproduces, more obliquely than Huneker but perhaps more powerfully, the veiled threat experienced by men listening to women playing Chopin at the turn of the twentieth century. Grounding his narrative voice in a scientific realism that remains safely unmoved by the musicality it narrates, Frederic distances himself, like Huneker, from Chopin-playing women whose power he acknowledges but also might resent. Both Celia and Sister Soulsby, as "new women" whose musical expressiveness has abandoned the fixed moral purpose of domestic womanhood, are capable of using their musical talents for their own ends—which, whatever they may be, have little to do with protecting the virtue, or maintaining the authority, of Protestant ministers.[17]

One could argue that Frederic's realist voice allows him both to acknowledge a changing American social landscape and to remain (as Frederic remained, living in England most of his adult life) invulnerable to its potential threats. The novel, as already noted, associates anxieties about women freed from domesticity with anxieties about the encroachment of immigrant others on American culture and society at the turn of the twentieth century. Theron's embattled masculinity is established, in part, by his openness to and desire for new, foreign ideas, sounds, and contexts. That he ultimately meets an impassable wall between his selfhood and the seemingly freer, more sensual, more vital world of these "others" might be (and has been) read as Frederic's warning against such cross-cultural contact and, by extension, his assertion of a nativist anxiety about a multicultural America. Celia's brother, rendered authoritative on his deathbed, might speak for Frederic as he cryptically warns Theron late in the novel: "Keep among your own people, Mr. Ware!" (442). But at least one critic sees in Theron's romance with Irish Catholicism a more resigned assertion of "the inevitability of cross-cultural encounters and intermingling." Carrie Tirado Bramen argues that, through Theron's encounters, the novel indeed "destabilizes regional, cultural, and national identities" and then proceeds to replace an outdated sectarian American identity with a more modern, Rooseveltian "broad Americanism" rooted in "heart and soul, in spirit and purpose" rather than religion or region. Bramen thus reads Michael Madden's warning as "anachronistic, inappropriate for a modern age of contact and mobility," and Theron's final gesture of lighting out for the West as a move toward this more abstract, secular, modern Americanism, albeit one that is itself already becoming a cliché.[18]

The musical threads of the novel, to which Bramen like MacFarlane gives little attention, both support and complicate her reading of the novel's conclusion. To recognize music as a central "space" in which Theron experiences "cross-cultural intermingling" is to see the degree to which this novel affiliates music with a difference marked by both religion/ethnicity and gender. When produced by women, music liberates the American Protestant male from *both* a repressive masculinity and a repressive religious doctrine but leaves him drifting in a liminal and relatively powerless position within American culture. Whether Frederic and his novel ultimately rescue Theron from this drift with a Rooseveltian fantasy of "broad Americanism" depends on whether, upon reading the rather abrupt ending, we believe in its possibility given all that has preceded it. As Bramen herself admits, it's very difficult, in the end, to pin Frederic down: perhaps, she writes, "the West and Americanism function less as a form of narrative resolution and more as a strategy of evasion."[19]

What we can note, however, are the terms of this "strategy of evasion," which involves not only a clichéd image of the West as rebirth but also an extended image of Theron once again taking up the role of orator, this time as a senator before his constituency. As MacFarlane observes, this crowd echoes his congregations with a crucial difference: his audience is now entirely male. Theron's vision of a future political success recovers both his masculinity and his national identity in part by eliminating from view, or from hearing, any vestige of women playing Chopin. Instead, he has now, one could argue, usurped the role of Sister Soulsby or Celia Madden, his "difference" defined not by gender or religion or race but by his own performative agency: "They were attentive faces all—rapt, eager, credulous to a degree. Their eyes were admiringly bent upon a common object of excited interest. They were looking at HIM; they strained their ears to miss no cadence of his voice. . . . The audience rose at him, as he dropped his hand, and filled his day-dream with a mighty roar of applause, in volume like an ocean tempest, yet pitched for his hearing alone" (511). This passage calls to mind an *Ev'ry Month* editorial, cited in chapter 1, in which Dreiser observes growing demand among Americans for live voices: "Everywhere are those who seem half hungry to hear a man once more endowed as the orator; everywhere those who would gladly be thrilled by the sentiment of an impassioned voice."[20] But even as Theron imagines himself a performer before a rapt, admiring male audience, the final words of the passage once again position him as listener, this time to "a mighty roar of applause, in volume like an ocean tempest, yet pitched for his hearing alone." Just as he imagined Celia's organ music to be "played for him alone," he remains here drawn to an eroticized experience of being immersed in an ocean of sound that strips away social boundaries and hierarchies to leave an entirely personal and sensual experience of release. Further qualifying Theron's recovery of masculine agency, Frederic ends not with Theron's fantasy of oratorical glory, but with Alice's much drier, savvier, and more realistic observation of the enabling limits of her husband's vision: "Oh, it isn't likely I would come East. . . . Most probably I'd be left to amuse myself in Seattle" (512). Realism, one could argue, remains with Alice in Seattle (as it does with Frederic in England?), while the musically impassioned voice and its desiring audience carry on the "good fraud" of shaping America's cultural and political future.

"[T]he music penetrated her whole being like an effulgence, warming and brightening the dark places of her soul."

Kate Chopin did not require any special research for the musical scenes of her novel.[21] An accomplished pianist and composer who once considered becoming a professional musician, Chopin remained involved with music and musicians throughout her life, regularly hosting salons and musicales at her home, and counting among her friends many significant European and American musical artists. Her biographer Emily Toth writes that in her childhood diary, "Kate seemed truly interested only when she wrote about music."[22] Her very first published story, "Wiser than a God," centers on the figure of a female pianist who chooses a musical career over marrying the man she loves. *The Awakening* gives us two female pianists in Mlle Reisz and Mme Ratignolle, both arguably more realistic characters than Harold Frederic's Celia Madden, and focuses our attention specifically on these pianists' effects on a *woman* listener. The unmarried Mlle Reisz, like Celia Madden, deeply moves her listener with her masterful performances of Frédéric Chopin's music, and in so doing presents an alternative to domestic musicality, but she otherwise shares very little with Frederic's Irish siren. Misanthropic, asexual, physically unattractive, and living simply in a stark apartment on the margins of respectable society, Mlle Reisz seems to represent Kate Chopin's deliberate rejection of

Theron's conventional fantasy of female musicality as erotic, seductive, and performed primarily (or even exclusively) for male ears.

Like *Theron Ware*, Chopin's novel affiliates its female pianist and the music of Frédéric Chopin with a larger zone of musicality in *The Awakening* that seduces, intoxicates, and "awakens" a listener whose prior musical experience had remained contained within the boundaries of Protestant bourgeois propriety. If Chopin avoids reproducing the gendered stereotypes of the siren, she joins Frederic in allying musicality with a Catholic subculture whose *difference* (from the perspective of the central character and implied northern reader) is thrown into relief by its musical expressivity. The musicality of ethnic others in *The Awakening*—whether white French Creoles, "mulattoes," or Acadians—promises, like Celia Madden's performance of Chopin, to revitalize an enervated and repressed white, middle-class Protestant subjectivity.

But *The Awakening*'s musicscape is much larger than its Catholic subculture. While music at first seems metonymically to underscore the sensual allure of southern Louisiana local color, it eventually elaborates, for Edna, a more absolute horizon of difference, unmarked by ethnicity, language, custom, or even the demands of biology. The scenes of music in the novel progress from bourgeois parlor to professional studio to this more abstract space, as the music itself moves from unspecified parlor music to Chopin to a hazy combination of Chopin and Wagner, and ultimately (back and forward) to the open space of the sea and its chorus of remembered, disembodied voices. Edna hears Mlle Reisz's musical performances as akin to a force of nature, to an "abiding truth" as omniscient and abstract as the sonorous and ever-beckoning sea, whose all-encompassing musicality finally envelops Edna like an untranslated opera. With no Sister Soulsby to unmask them as "fraud," this novel unironically allies certain musical performances with a realm of "truth." The different fates of Edna and Theron and the novels' different fields of musical resonance are, finally, attributable to two very different worldviews, which, among other things, suggest to us ways in which music might have meant very different things for a man than it did for a woman at the turn of the twentieth century. For both Edna and Theron, music's erotic and liberatory promises are real, powerful, and illuminating; and both inevitably come up against social strictures that, outside the concert hall or music studio, offer no respectable place for awakened subjectivity. But while Theron can imagine himself re-emerging from the abyss of intolerable isolation, Edna's imagination can find no such escape, choosing, instead, the solitary abyss as the only possible avenue of fulfillment.

Unlike scholarship on *Theron Ware*, which rarely addresses the novel's musical dimension, the voluminous critical discussion of *The Awakening* has generated many comments on and several more sustained examinations of music's role in the novel. Almost all of these focus on either Mlle Reisz's character or the relationship of Frédéric Chopin's compositional style to the novel's aesthetics. The pianist's character has been a focus of significant disagreement among the novel's critics, only one of whom reads her in relation to the historical circumstance of new female professional musicians at the turn of the century. Lynda Boren considers her a "thinly disguised witch," who "violates Edna's very soul with her musical machinations."[23] Melanie Dawson reads her as a type of the "late romantic" performer, akin to Liszt and Paganini who were themselves often cast as demons or devils.[24] Elaine Showalter argues that Reisz "seems to speak for the author's view of art and for the artist. It is surely no accident," she continues, "that it is Chopin's music that Mademoiselle Reisz performs."[25] Doris Davis introduces a more properly historicized dimension to this discussion by illuminating the ways in which Mlle Reisz's character engages with nineteenth-century discourses about female concert pianists and about the gendering of musicality. She concludes that the novel incorporates in its characterization of Reisz common conceptions of female professional pianists as masculine and unnatural (recall Huneker) while unsettling the notion that female musicality lacks authority or creativity. Davis importantly grants the relationship between Edna and the pianist an underappreciated centrality, but in reading Edna less as a listener than as a potential artist herself, she misses a crucial dimension of *The Awakening*'s engagement with contemporary musical discourses and its elaborations of the phenomenology of listening.[26]

Melanie Dawson does focus specifically on the historicity of Edna's reception of music by considering the novel's engagement with what she calls the "tradition of listening," by which she means the prevalent lamentations in nineteenth-century European culture of romantic music's feminizing effects on listeners, and of its potentially dangerous effects specifically on women. While her sources remain oddly removed from the American debates of Kate Chopin's era (she cites Kierkegaard and Nietzsche), her point is valid, and one could easily make an analogous case with reference to critics like Huneker—recall his "Chopinitis"—and the debates about female Wagnerites (to which this chapter will return to below, and which is a focus of chapter 3). Like Davis, Dawson seems intent to rescue Edna from the perils of listening by seeing in her reception a direct route to her own "artistic self-expression" as a painter. But Edna's painting does not displace her listening; indeed, music and painting remain distinct cultural forms in the novel, as modes of both production and reception.[27] The privileging of musical production over reception also informs scholarship that considers the status of composers, particularly Chopin but also Richard Wagner, in the novel's composition and concerns. Nicole Camastra, for example, considers Chopin "integral" to the novel's form and style and also to its characterizations of Mlle Reisz, who "personifies Chopin's artistic talent and disposition," and Edna, who "embodies the composer's tortured soul."[28] Intent on proving Chopin's "influence on" the novel, Camastra introduces the very important idea that music provides a unique "emotional and intellectual space" for Edna to experience and reflect on her social predicament.[29]

But rather than emphasize how *The Awakening* reflects or is influenced by its musical referents, I am more interested here, and throughout this study, in how the novel participates in constructing music's meanings and values by situating it in specific social, material, and narrative contexts. While the novel certainly resonates with discursive contexts beyond the text (including those in other novels), it should, first, be adequately examined as itself a discursive field that puts performers, composers, listeners, and spaces into dynamic relationships with one another and with other sounds and forms of aural experience. Such an approach allows us to recognize music as, indeed, elaborating a "space" that both enables and limits Edna's capacity to see beyond the social conventions of her position in the world as a white leisure-class woman. More specifically, it helps us imagine the musical occasion as providing the space for a kind of covert—because it is internal, invisible, inchoate—rebellion against the social role expected of women like Edna.

The first specifically musical occasion in the novel—as opposed to the more general diffusion of musical sound that inflects Grand Isle from the novel's first page—is Mlle Reisz's invited performance at an evening get-together at Mme Lebrun's hotel. While not a formal concert, or even an informal "soiree" such as those Kate Chopin herself hosted in St. Louis and New Orleans, Mlle Reisz's performance brings into focus the elements of Said's "extreme occasion," elements that are, in fact, thrown into relief by what her arrival on the scene interrupts. The evening had involved, until then, a series of amateur entertainment pieces mainly showcasing the children's talents to a room of proud parents and otherwise tolerant, if not particularly engaged, spectators/listeners. The Farival twins played their signature "duet from 'Zampa'" (which they'd been practicing in the background of the first scene of the novel), followed by the overture to "The Poet and the Peasant," both somewhat frivolous works of comic opera.[30] The parrot, shrieking "Allez vous-en! Sapristi!" (also echoing the novel's first pages), underscores the unremarkable, and somewhat tiresome, conventionality of this scene, as "the only one present who possessed sufficient candor to admit that he was not listening to these gracious performances for the first time this summer" (69). After these performances, the group begins to dance to unspecified waltz music played on the piano by Mme Ratignolle. Her skill—"she played very well"—represents one of her many strengths as an impressive "mother-woman" of this family-centered Creole community: "She was keeping up her music on account of the children, she said; because she and her husband both considered it a means of brightening the home and making it attractive" (69). After the children are sent off to bed, however, Robert requests that Mlle Reisz play for the group, and her acceptance changes the entire mood of the scene, replacing a casual and amateur gaiety with silent, focused attention on a true artist: "A general air of surprise and genuine satisfaction fell upon every one as they saw the pianist enter. There was a settling down, and a prevailing air of expectancy everywhere" (71).

During this moment of anticipation, the narrative zooms in on Edna's particular expectation that the piano playing will, as music has in the past, "evok[e] pictures in her mind." We learn here that when listening to Mme Ratignolle practicing her piano in the mornings (a more private kind of musical space and moment), Edna has found herself translating what she heard (unnamed parlor music) into images—of a naked man standing in "hopeless resignation" on the seashore watching a bird in flight, of a young woman "taking mincing dancing steps" between tall hedges, of a "demure lady stroking a cat." Mlle Reisz's performance, while satisfying what the majority in the room expects, completely upends Edna's prior and anticipated relationship to music:

> The very first chords which Mademoiselle Reisz struck upon the piano sent a keen tremor down Mrs. Pontellier's spinal column. It

> was not the first time she had heard an artist at the piano. Perhaps it was the first time she was ready, perhaps the first time her being was tempered to take an impress of the abiding truth.
>
> She waited for the material pictures which she thought would gather and blaze before her imagination. She waited in vain. She saw no pictures of solitude, of hope, of longing, or of despair. But the very passions themselves were aroused within her soul, swaying it, lashing it, as the waves daily beat upon her splendid body. She trembled, she was choking, and the tears blinded her. (71–72)

This musical experience affords Edna no room to create visual metaphors for what she hears or to translate the sounds into anything at all beyond the simile (produced not by Edna but by the narrator) of ocean waves. Mlle Reisz's performance of Chopin (not yet identified as such) means or refers to nothing outside itself but instead *acts* on Edna, arousing her passions and reverberating within her body. But this musical effect rests not only on Reisz's performance. Importantly, Edna herself contributes to the music's impact in being "ready"—"tempered" to receive a "truth" represented by Reisz's performance of Chopin's music. While the others in the room respond vocally with heartfelt truisms—"'What an artist!' 'I have always said no one could play Chopin like Mademoiselle Reisz!' 'That last prelude!'"—Edna remains mute when the pianist asks how she liked the music: "The young woman was unable to answer; she pressed the hand of the pianist convulsively" (72). Edna's muteness compounds her difference from those around her and from her own prior listening self: she finds herself without a verbal or visual language with which to express, represent, translate, or create distance from her experience.[31]

Edna's ability to "understand" the music on its own terms (rather than rush to displace it with clichéd praise or familiar images) is what sets her apart from the others and makes her "the only one worth playing for" to Mlle Reisz, who sees in her muteness the very sign of her understanding. What makes music problematic for this novel, however, and perhaps feeds the critical tendency to vilify Mlle Reisz, is the condition of the musical occasion's extremeness, namely, the power differential between performer and listener, determined by the skill and expertise required of the professional musical artist. We saw this differential between Celia and Theron, and the foolishness revealed in Theron's presumption that he could somehow close the gap between them with romantic love. Although she cultivates her talent as an artist, Edna recognizes that she will never sit on the other side of the relationship, as, indeed, Kate Chopin would recognize the limits of all but the select few who choose to dedicate themselves to the exacting career of music. But while she accepts her place in the musical relationship, as passive listener enthralled by an accomplished performer, Edna nonetheless experiences, through her relative passivity, an otherwise impossible *language* of expression that breaks free of bourgeois, patriarchal convention.

As it produces a moment of rupture in Edna's ability to represent what she hears by exceeding what can be said, Mlle Reisz's performance instantiates what Patricia Yaeger has called the novel's "extra-linguistic zone of meaning," by which the novel struggles to free Edna from the limited possibilities imaginable (and articulable) for a leisure-class woman. Yaeger joins the anti-Reisz critics, however, in finding the pianist "complicitous in limiting Edna's options," particularly in what she sees as her efforts "like a manic cupid" to cement Edna's relationship with Robert by, later in the novel, playing music while letting Edna read Robert's letters (and, according to Yaeger, submit to his "voice"). But I would argue that, as in this first performance, Mlle Reisz's piano playing encourages, rather than forecloses, Edna's struggle to escape the linguistically encoded limits of her social reality.[32]

Rather than limiting Edna's options, this music draws her at least temporarily outside of those limits and expands her range of experience. After her vacation ends, Edna compulsively seeks the pianist out in spite of certain "disagreeable" memories of her: "She nonetheless felt a desire to see her—above all, to listen while she played upon the piano" (109). The pianist's musical relationship with Edna, as it continues in New Orleans, takes on certain new qualities that demand our attention. At Grand Isle the pianist's music took Edna by surprise, but Edna now anticipates what the music will do to her and seeks it out when she feels the need once again to feel her "passions" aroused and—like Sister Soulsby, who enjoys conversion "every time"—to relive the experience of awakening: "There was nothing which so quieted the turmoil of Edna's senses as a visit to Mademoiselle Reisz. It was then, in the presence of that personality which was offensive to her, that the woman, by her divine art, seemed to reach Edna's spirit and set it free" (133). Like an addict anxious for her next fix, Edna goes to great lengths to find the pianist, first traveling some distance to the Bienville Street address listed in the directory, only to find that house now occupied "by a respectable family of mulattoes" who, along with the nearby grocer, have no idea where she now lives. By making the pianist difficult for Edna to locate, the novel underscores both Mlle Reisz's marginality to New Orleans society (as an artist, unmarried woman, xenophobe) and Edna's desire for her music, which thus becomes more valuable and more of an "extreme occasion": "Edna's desire to see Mademoiselle Reisz had increased tenfold since these unlooked-for obstacles had arisen to thwart it" (110).

Once she does find her, in a small rooftop apartment near the river, Edna regularly visits her for a series of now entirely private concerts, more akin to Celia's private performance for Theron than to Mlle Reisz's first performance on Grand Isle. But rather than a scene of seduction, or even of matchmaking, which critics variously see in Mlle Reisz's musical "machinations," the pianist's intimate recitals are more a refusal of such a scene, or a deliberate unsettling of its conventional contours. While we know the unmarried pianist is uninterested in conventional, heterosexual romance, her desires and motives remain difficult to read. Her musical performances tell us nothing about her interior selfhood, veiled throughout the novel, while they bear nothing in common with her visible surface, on which false hair and artificial flowers only contribute to an "appearance of deformity" (116). In making Reisz inscrutable and unattractive, Chopin not only draws attention to the anomaly of female artistry in a society that celebrates "mother-women" and to the eccentricity of artists more generally, but she also gives Edna a source of powerful music that does not, at the same time, implicate her in erotic entanglement. When the pianist states, "I really don't believe you like me, Mrs. Pontellier," Edna replies, "I don't know whether I like you or not," the "candor" of which "greatly please[s]" her companion (114). To Adele's suggestion that the pianist come stay with Edna to keep her company while her husband is away, Edna replies: "No; she wouldn't wish to come, and I shouldn't want her always with me" (153). More like the sea that invites Edna into an abstracted and solitary "maze of inward contemplation," Mlle Reisz's music abstracts Edna's emotions from the dynamics of actual social relationships, whether domestic or extramarital, conventional or scandalous.

To some extent, the pianist does mediate Robert and Edna's relationship by providing a musical space in which Edna can read Robert's letters, but the novel does not support Yaeger's claim that, in so doing, she helps displace Edna's "own particular sonority" with Robert's discourse. While the music represents Robert's desire (the pianist plays a Chopin impromptu that Robert has requested she play for Edna) and affiliates Edna's listening with both his words and her desire for him, it ultimately serves to disengage her from them. Instead, the music stimulates Edna's growing attention to her own inward being: "The music penetrated her whole being like an effulgence, warming and brightening the dark places of her soul. It prepared her for joy and exultation" (135–36). Furthermore, Mlle Reisz's performance does not simply reproduce Robert's wishes but nestles the impromptu within her own amalgam of improvisation and a highly resonant moment from Richard Wagner's opera *Tristan und Isolde*:

> Mademoiselle played a soft interlude. It was an improvisation. She sat low at the instrument, and the lines of her body settled into ungraceful curves and angles that gave it an appearance of deformity. Gradually and imperceptibly the interlude melted into the soft opening minor chords of the Chopin Impromptu.
>
> Edna did not know when the Impromptu began or ended. She sat in the sofa corner reading Robert's letter by the fading light. Mademoiselle had glided from the Chopin into the quivering love notes of Isolde's song, and back again to the Impromptu with its soulful and poignant longing.
>
> The shadows deepened in the little room. The music grew strange and fantastic—turbulent, insistent, plaintive and soft with entreaty. The shadows grew deeper. The music filled the room. It floated out upon the night, over the housetops, the crescent of the river, losing itself in the silence of the upper air.
>
> Edna was sobbing, just as she had wept one midnight at Grand Isle when strange, new voices awoke in her. She arose in some agitation to take her departure. "May I come again, Mademoiselle?" she asked at the threshold. (116)

This performance resonates with the larger musicscape of the novel in multiple ways, while having little to do with Edna's desire specifically for Robert, or with Robert's voice. As the "ungraceful curves and angles" of the pianist's body dissolve into sound, she produces a "strange and fantastic" musical pastiche that both recalls and prefigures the "voice of the sea" in its string of adjectives ("turbulent, insistent, plaintive and soft") that parallel the string of present participles attributed to the sea ("whispering, clamoring, murmuring, inviting") and in its gradual, fluid, permeation of space. As it "fill[s]" the room and then "float[s]" beyond human habitat to the "silence of the upper air," the music "los[es] itself" (just as the sea invites one to "lose oneself") in this silence beyond the confines of physical space and temporality.

The pianist's brief quotation of Wagner in this scene has largely escaped the attention of critics, who understandably focus mainly on the novel's more frequent and explicit references to Frédéric Chopin. At least two scholars of music, however, have mentioned it in their discussions of Wagner in ways that bear on our discussion here. Lawrence Kramer mentions *The Awakening* during a discussion of "musical form and fin-de-siecle sexuality" in his well-regarded monograph *Music as Cultural Practice*. After reproducing the text of Isolde's final song, he notes: "Both this text and Wagner's music for it certainly came to Kate Chopin's mind when her novel *The Awakening* (1899) needed a central image of 'höchste Lust.' Chopin exploits the vital ambiguity of Wagner's final term—'Lust' being capable of meaning both bliss and longing." He goes on to note the parallel between Kate Chopin's and Wagner's identification of female desire with the sea: "Beginning with Wagner's own program note to the concert version of the Prelude, *Tristan und Isolde* has always been understood to represent desire as an endless ebbing and flowing, 'forever renewing itself, craving and languishing.'"[33]

Joseph Horowitz, in his cultural history of Wagnerism in America, cites a passage from Nietzsche that, like Wagner's program note, describes the experience of listening to Wagner in terms that could easily have been taken from Chopin's novel: "One walks into the sea, gradually loses one's secure footing, and finally surrenders oneself to the elements without reservation: one must swim." Horowitz joins Kramer in noting *The Awakening*'s "oblique . . . Wagnerian" moment, which he puts in the context of what he calls the "protofeminism" of Wagner reception among American women who were drawn in great numbers to the composer's intense emotionalism. Resembling Edward Said's more general discussion of the "extreme occasion" of modern musical performance, Horowitz describes a "dialectic of submission and liberation" in women's relationship to Wagner's music, which seemed at once to free them from parlor pieties and enthrall them to an all-encompassing musical experience. At the time that Chopin wrote her novel, American critics were deeply involved in discussion and debate over the merits and effects of Wagner's operas. Critics were particularly agitated by the "thrill and alarm of emotional surrender" occasioned by *Tristan und Isolde*, which had its US premiere in 1886. Henry Krehbiel, one of New York's most respected critics, advised listeners to attend to the music's formal elements to protect themselves from its emotional effects, whereas William J. Henderson, an equally influential New York critic (to whose own novel we will turn in chapter 5), confesses: "I find it difficult to proceed coolly and systematically. There is a witchery in this marvelous drama of fatal love that masters my mind."[34]

To recognize *The Awakening*'s participation in this American Wagnerian moment is to appreciate the degree to which Edna's crisis of identity engages with the terms of Americans' reception of Wagner as well as Chopin. Mlle Reisz's brief inclusion of Isolde's song not only highlights the novel's central focus on "bliss and longing" but also suggests certain intertextual resonances between the novel and Wagner's opera. Most obviously, Edna and Isolde share the same fate, choosing death over a life that would be limited by social obligation; as Kramer notes, *Tristan und Isolde*'s evocation of feminine desire resonates deeply with Edna's experiences of desire: as oceanic, as ebbing and flowing, as unquenchable. Beyond these analogies of theme and effect, one could describe *The Awakening* more generally as Wagnerian in style and tone, a quality that distinguishes it starkly from *Theron Ware*, which attends to aurality only in its musical scenes. Like Wagner, Kate Chopin uses "leitmotifs" to structure and propel her narrative, with a host of recurring images and phrases that move away from more conventional linear narrative structure. From the whistling of a parrot and a mockingbird at the opening, the repetitive "voice of the sea," and the "strange" and "indistinct voices" of French Creole and Acadian culture, to the final "hum of bees" in the last paragraph, *The Awakening*'s evocations of musical sound, and specifically of voice, are pervasive.

This brief Wagnerian moment also underscores the degree to which Edna's musical experience offers her the possibility of emotional intensity outside the constraints of human relationships. Music historian Bryan Magee describes the effects of Wagner's music as "like being in love" without the burden of an actual lover: "It makes possible a passionate warmth and fullness of emotion without personal relationships."[35] (Theodor Adorno, in the context of a very different argument, asserts that Wagner's music functions to "warm up the alienated and reified relations of men and make them sound as if they were still human."[36]) Music's significance to Edna's "awakening" lies in its ability to elaborate a "space" of authentic emotion that has no "real" social space in which it can become trapped or fixed. Edna's awakened passion for music seems consistently to require her distance from those she claims to love, a distance both poignantly emphasized and imaginatively bridged by music. The displacement of Robert by music is a case in point. During Robert's absence in Mexico, Edna not only seeks out Mlle Reisz's music making, but she also finds herself "haunted" by a song Robert once sang: "While Edna worked she sometimes sang low the little air, 'Ah! si tu savais!' It moved her with recollections. . . . A subtle current of desire passed through her body weakening her hold upon the brushes and making her eyes burn" (109). Interrupting her efforts at painting (and obscuring her vision), the music, like Reisz's Chopin, marks the absence of her lover, and rather than displace her voice with his, I would argue it substitutes his musicality for his presence. When Robert finally returns to New Orleans, Edna meets him for the first time in Mlle Reisz's apartment, seated at the now silent piano. Rather than celebrate his return, Edna feels that "some way he had seemed nearer to her off there in Mexico" (161). (Edna similarly feels closer to her children when they are away with their grandparents; on her way home from a visit with them, she "carried away with her the sound of their voices," as "their presence lingered with her like the memory of a delicious song" [152].)

Indeed, Edna's most significant moments of arousal and satisfaction come not in the bodily presence of others but when she is alone with their disembodied voices, as if listening not simply to music but more specifically to opera. When she and Robert make a trip to the Chenière Caminada to attend Sunday mass, she becomes ill during the service and recovers alone in a room at a hotel run by a local Acadian woman. Lolling in bed after a luxurious nap that feels like a retreat into another time and place, Edna finds herself listening to voices outside her window whose vagueness and incomprehensibility intensify a sensual pleasure of dreamy sedation: "Tonie's slow, Acadian drawl, Robert's quick, soft, smooth French" become musical sonorities that make up "only part of the other drowsy, muffled sounds lulling her senses" (84). Recalling the parrot that, in its polyvocal mimicry, speaks "a language nobody understands" on the novel's first page, these voices, including Robert's, derive their power not by their discursive authority but as part of a multilingual, disembodied, and, indeed, extralinguistic tapestry of "muffled sound."

Edna's pleasure in disembodied foreign voices is, of course, made possible by the fact that the Acadians in this scene exist to serve leisure-class Americans in the tourist economy of the Gulf Coast islands, and in the imagination of the novel's presumed readers. Several critics read *The Awakening*'s feminist politics as limited by, and bound up with, the class, race, and colonial hierarchies that structure the novel's social world and Edna's perspective. Michele Birnbaum reads the "indistinct voices" in this scene as inviting Edna "to be both 'in' and yet not implicated in a culture which she finds appealing only to a point," thus demonstrating the degree to which Edna instantiates the "imperial self who appears to rule while being herself ruled."[37] Wai Chee Dimock similarly notes that Edna's heightened sense of her own reality has a "de-realizing effect" on those around her, particularly the working-class African Americans who—doing the work that might otherwise impinge on Edna's autonomy—assume a phantom-like presence.[38] Music, as we will explore more directly in the following chapters, is an important medium for this kind of limited, disembodied cross-cultural identification, particularly around the turn of the century when African American music—both in popular and classical musical spaces—was becoming identified as a "voice" of American musical distinction. Recognizing the ethnic dimension to Edna's musical experience helps us to see her own musicality as engaged with these discourses of "American" music.

While Irish otherness ultimately remains beyond Theron's reach, Edna's sensual absorption of the "strange voices" of these others (and her disinterest in actual social relationships with them) leads her to cast away convention and fully embrace her newly aroused desires in ways that emphasize her incorporation of otherness into herself. The powerful image of her "tearing" a piece of crusty brown bread "with her strong, white teeth" after awaking from her nap at Madame Antoine's is echoed in New Orleans with a series of food-oriented scenes (85). First, she begins to abandon her wifely duty of overseeing the cook in her home and instead spends her time exploring the back roads of New Orleans and eating out: "She liked then to wander alone into strange and unfamiliar places. She discovered many a sunny, sleepy corner, fashioned to dream in" (109). One of these wanderings leads her to food prepared by "an old mulatresse" who "slept her idle hours away in her chair at the open window" until a customer calls: "There was no one who could make such excellent coffee or fry chicken so golden brown as she" (163–64). In contrast, a dinner with the bourgeois Highcamps leaves her wanting; the food, "though of excellent quality, lacked abundance." The requisite after-dinner piano music also fails to inspire Edna. Miss Highcamp's selections from Grieg "seemed to have apprehended all of the composer's coldness and none of his poetry. While Edna listened she wondered if she had lost her taste for music" (129). Later that night she renews her "taste" for both food and music with a compensatory snack: "She rummaged in the larder and brought forth a slice of Gruyere and some crackers. She opened a bottle of beer. . . . She vacantly hummed a fantastic tune as she poked at the wood embers on the hearth and munched a cracker" (129).

Fantastic tunes and impulsive appetites here join the imagined otherness of Mme Antoine, strange foreign voices, sleepy mulatresses, and Frédéric Chopin as primitive eruptions of authenticity in a world otherwise entrenched in bourgeois, white, northern convention (reflected by Grieg's "coldness"). They provide an important context for understanding Edna's growing addiction to late-romantic music, played by an "artist" unbound by domestic responsibilities. One familiar with New Orleans's musical culture at the turn of the century may be tempted to imagine Edna, on one of her walks, wandering up Canal Street into a nearby but altogether different neighborhood, and stumbling upon the early jazz of Buddy Bolden. But such an exercise in imagination underscores its historical impossibility: the only "others" Edna vicariously enjoys seem to be at her special service, whether making her food, providing her with a clean bed, or playing for her on the piano. Hers is a prewar, leisure-class, white woman's fantasy, catered to by workers at the margins of her proper sphere, but not beyond them.

But Edna's fantasy, of course, remains impossible in other ways as well. The musical spaces of this novel are, like its women, ultimately circumscribed and limited by the professional men who pay the bills. Edna's openness to and readiness for music puts her in particular contrast with her husband, who, unlike Theron Ware, is in no danger of submitting to music or of losing his social authority even if the island's feminine aurality momentarily frustrates his composure. The very first scene of the novel centers on M. Pontellier, during his weekend visit to Grand Isle, attempting with great frustration to read the newspaper's business page in the midst of a cacophony of musical sounds. The vociferous interruptions of the multilingual parrot and a mockingbird "whistling his fluty notes out upon the breeze with maddening persistence" make reading impossible and, indeed, unsettle linguistic coherence itself (43). M. Pontellier invokes his sense of the order of things by insisting that although the birds have "the right to make all the noise they wished," being the "property" of Mme Lebrun, it is nonetheless his own "privilege" as a paying guest to walk away and seek quiet. Quiet, however, is not easily found on Grand Isle, whose spaces are both owned and populated primarily by women: "There was more noise than ever over at the house. . . . The chattering and whistling birds were still at it. Two young girls, the Farival twins, were playing a duet from 'Zampa' upon the piano. Madame Lebrun was . . . giving orders in a high key to a yard-boy . . ., and directions in an equally high voice to a dining-room servant" (44). This musical pastiche causes M. Pontellier to abandon altogether the "task of reading" the paper's market reports and other "bits of news" that promise succinctly to represent the important facts of daily life, and become temporarily drawn instead into the noisy vitality of female work and play (44).

His point of view, however, returns to a visuality that asserts its presumption of authority by framing Edna's first appearance in the novel as he shifts his eyes from the newspaper and "fixes his gaze upon a white sunshade" in the distance. Initially as abstract as the noise, this image eventually comes into focus as his wife on her slow return from the gulf with Robert Lebrun. At her arrival he casually scolds her for, in effect, eluding his gaze and, by association, his "rights" of ownership: "'You are burnt beyond recognition,'" he declares, "looking at his wife as one looks at a valuable piece of personal property" (44). But Edna's own way of seeing challenges his proprietary gaze: "She had a way of turning [her eyes] swiftly upon an object and holding them there as if lost in some inward maze of contemplation or thought" (45–46). Unlike her husband's objectifying gaze, which translates abstractions into tangible exchange values and known quantities, Edna's vision retreats back into herself, her eyes refusing either to know or be known.

Highlighting a gendered tension between vision and hearing, Edna's way of seeing seems modeled on aural rather than visual experience. The "inward maze of contemplation" in which her eyes seem lost recurs twice more, in fact, in reference to her aural relationship with the "voice of the sea," this novel's absolute horizon of disembodied vocality: "The voice of the sea is seductive; never ceasing, whispering, clamoring, murmuring, inviting the soul to wander for a spell in abysses of solitude; to lose oneself in mazes of inward contemplation" (57, 174). This leitmotif (repeated verbatim) figures the island's oceanic soundscape as sirenic voice, promising a retreat from sociality (and social structure) into a solitude characterized by the absence of limits or legible order. Edna's initial resistance to her husband's gaze frames the feminist narrative thread of this novel and should be understood as an assertion of an aurality—literal and metaphorical—that at least momentarily frustrates M. Pontellier's ability to exercise his "privilege" as a husband. It is, however, a zone of resistance that remains inarticulable, interior, rooted in aesthetic experience rather than social reform, and circumscribed within certain social spaces, particularly the vacation island and the musical event.

Edna's final walk into the sea is a walk into that zone of resistance that promises no return to its enabling social contexts. The oceanic element, in this final scene, weaves social voices—of father, children, beloveds—into a decidedly sonic aesthetic medium, as the "voice of the sea" becomes another tapestry of disembodied voices and "muffled sounds": "Edna heard her father's voice and her sister Margaret's. She heard the barking of an old dog that was chained to the sycamore tree. The spurs of the cavalry officer clanged as he walked across the porch. There was the hum of bees, and the musky odor of pinks filled the air" (176). As it moves from "Edna heard" to the "spurs . . . clanged" to "there was the hum," this final sentence effectively dissolves Edna's body and being into hearing itself, as sound/smell itself becomes the agent and subject of the sentence, giving us the ultimate version, one could say, of Said's "extreme occasion."

These two turn-of-the-century novels, as we have seen, embody quite different points of view on music, musicians, and musical experience. Harold Frederic's musical women, finally, are still constructed in the siren mold, although both are sirens of a modern order. Sister Soulsby, the pragmatist, sees all of society as a matter of performance and persuasion and recognizes music's power to shape listeners' behavior and to give them a thrilling "conversion" that can be repeated *ad infinitum.* Celia Madden, the aesthete, similarly dismisses the idea of any single truth or reality and preaches instead the values of beauty and impulse. But while they both insist on their freedom from creeds and fixed realities, these musical women also know that they are limited by and to the social worlds in which they live; it is only Theron that imagines otherwise, much to his peril. Harold Frederic leaves us guessing, at the end of his novel, whether we should decry these powerful musical women as Satan's allies or accept them as icons of a brave new American world.

The Awakening similarly unsettles any fixed notion of reality and suggests that music, and musicians, have the power to draw listeners out of conventional ways of seeing and into a more fluid sense of self and context. But rather than focus on the "damning" effects of this epistemological and ontological rupture on professional, well-meaning men with repressed desires, Kate Chopin's novel traces its emotionally liberating effects on a married, leisure-class woman. Chopin draws her readers into Edna's growing dissociation from the social world that has long defined her and leaves us understanding her choice to walk into the sea and away from her children even if we disagree with it. Unlike Theron, Edna does not fall in love with the musician along with the music: music for her is an alternative to romantic love, a substitute for human relationships, and liberation from marriage of any kind. Mlle Reisz, unlike Celia Madden, is no extension of male fantasy but a serious artist, who, like Edna, remains uninterested in sustained human relationships. The modernity of Chopin's novel, unlike Frederic's, is located less in the idea of a new social order—in which power lies with pragmatic and charismatic leaders controlling the "machinery behind the scenes"—than in an aesthetic sensibility shared by artists and certain sensitive audiences. Leonce Pontellier, Adele Ratignolle, and the Highcamps, we readily assume, will carry on with business as usual, enjoying the music they hear in New Orleans concert halls and salons with the proper degree of emotional response, no more, no less.

But what makes Edna sensitive is what finally reconnects her with Theron and with questions about modern American culture and power. As white, Protestant, middle- or leisure-class subjects, Edna and Theron are susceptible to music and, particularly, to music that seems an extension of the "otherness" of cultures imagined to be more sensual, performative, and free. For both of them, however, listening to these others does not give them entry into a new social world but instead isolates them entirely: from both their origins and the otherness they desire. As Adele warns Robert, Edna "is not one of us; she is not like us" (26) just as Celia's brother warns Theron to "keep among [his] own people" (442). Common to both Edna and Theron is their final paralysis, their experience of being unable to go back to the society they fled, while remaining unable to move forward, except in fantasy. Which returns us to their difference: while Theron's fantasy frees him from any vestige of feminine musicality, Edna's submits entirely to its utopian, oceanic embrace.

3

Opera's "Impossible Country"

Figuring the American Diva

> In their rude forcefulness and freedom from restrictive conventions they might be said to be representative of the American people. They are so full of that vital energy which made us a nation.
>
> —Henry Krehbiel, in Joseph Horowitz, *Classical Music in America*

Clara Louise Kellogg, one of the nation's first home-grown opera stars, begins her *Memoirs of an American Prima Donna* (1913) with a new kind of origin story for nineteenth-century white American operatic identity. Recalling how often she "slept and waked" as her slave nurse sang "Jim along Josy" while rocking her, Kellogg claims that her "first musical efforts," before she could even speak, "were to sing this ditty in imitation of my negro mammy." She then boasts that in her youth she became "the first American girl who ever played a banjo. . . . I watched and studied the darkies until I had picked up the trick of playing it, and soon acquired a real negro touch."[1] Highlighting the distance she has traveled from the antebellum American South to the high cultural enclaves of New York and Europe, and from singing Negro "ditties" to the Italian and French operas that marked her greatest successes, Kellogg's memoir asserts her distinction from European operatic identity, as an American who had imbibed "real negro" musicality at the source. By the time Kellogg wrote her memoir, long after the peak of her career in the 1880s, American operatic identity had become associated with a new musical repertoire as well as a new discursive terrain. Rather than the operatic fare of Gounod and Rossini, the new American diva distinguished herself in the mythical and highly demanding roles of Richard Wagner. In place of Kellogg's domesticated plantation scenes, the modern American diva's musicality would be associated, more abstractly, with the "rude forcefulness and freedom from restrictive conventions" that, according to New York music critic Henry Krehbiel, made Wagner roles "representative" of American identity.

Two novels written around the same time as Kellogg's memoir—Gertrude Atherton's *Tower of Ivory* (1910) and Willa Cather's *Song of the*

Lark (1915)—contribute to this new association of Wagner with American identity by imagining origin stories for American divas who sing Wagner. Resonating with Krehbiel's pronouncement, these novels give us singer-characters who embody a "vital" American spirit that seems specifically to suit them for Wagner's roles, but unlike Krehbiel, and the many other critics opining at this time about the special relationship between Wagner and America, they explore the origins of this vitality in particular American scenarios. The origin stories proffered by these novels take us not to the antebellum South and scenes of encounter with black musicality but to new scenes of encounter that remain, nonetheless, defined by cross-racial intimacy. Both novels figure the diva as a product of her experience in the frontier West, and, among other things, of her intimacy with Native Americans. Bringing to mind the new American composers discussed in the introduction, these novels participate in constructing a modern American musicality by appropriating the primitive "vitality" of the nation's most "native," and most mythologized, peoples.

Cather claimed to have taken inspiration for her diva character from the life of Olive Fremstad, one of the great Wagnerian sopranos of the era who, though born in Stockholm, was raised in and "adopted by" America as one of its own. In an essay entitled "Three American Singers," Cather had called Fremstad "the most interesting kind of American" who was "a great and highly individual talent, unlike any that had gone before it," invoking Roosevelt's idea that "Americanism is not a condition of birth, but a condition of spirit."[2] But in spite of the existence of numerous prominent American singers at the time they were written, these novels register the degree to which American origins were still considered obstacles to musical success at the time their characters were beginning their careers. Atherton's *Tower of Ivory* introduces her diva's nationality as, indeed, a problem: "Origin in America [does not count] with Europeans in the least," her narrator tells us, and to ward off such prejudice, her diva-heroine Margarethe Styr has revealed little about her past: "Beyond the bare assertion that she is an American she has barely alluded to her impossible country."[3] Cather's fiction, including *Song of the Lark*, is peppered with European immigrants alienated by the superficial values, and particularly the commercialism, of American music culture. About Maine-born Lillian Nordica, Cather wrote: "Could a singer have been born in a worse place?" and decries those American opera-goers who would claim Nordica as "America's pride" in the same voice as "certain soap advertisements."[4] Both novels, however, ultimately ground the musical greatness of their white American divas in a primitive, American spirit—which, in both cases, represent more modern versions of Clara Kellogg's black mammy—that serves to authenticate the opera singers as both musicians and Americans. Taking a close look at Cather's and Atherton's constructions of American operatic identity, this chapter considers specifically how their novels explain "impossible" origins in America as, ultimately, an asset rather than an obstacle.

As Joseph Horowitz's remarkable study of American Wagnerism demonstrates—to a degree that has not been sufficiently acknowledged in scholarship on this period—Americans of many different stripes, and particularly white American *women,* were quite passionately drawn to Wagner's music and music dramas around the turn of the twentieth century.[5] Indeed, the story of the emergence of American opera singers is inextricably linked to the story of Wagnerism in America. Wagner's works enjoyed a privileged place in American performing arts institutions; the Metropolitan Opera programmed only German opera (or opera translated into German) and many of Wagner's music dramas while under the directorship, during the late 1880s and early 1890s, of Anton Seidl, who would then go on to conduct the premiere of Dvořák's "New World" Symphony as conductor of the New York Philharmonic. Born in Budapest and a protégé of Wagner himself, Seidl joined German opera diva Lilli Lehmann in claiming the United States as their adoptive home in large part because of Americans' embrace of Wagner, an embrace they attributed to the nations' "unbiased" hearing and "peculiar sense of freedom."[6]

Much of the scholarship on music in these novels (and almost all of the scant recent scholarship on Atherton's novel) focuses particularly on their revisions of conventional depictions of the diva. Instead of amoral sirens or the vacuous instruments of plotting Svengalis, Cather's and Atherton's singers are independent and assertive women who choose professional careers over marriage and family without regret, who display their bodies and splendid voices on public stages without punishment, and who claim the siren's power without shame.[7] But in giving us literature's first *American* divas, these novels harness their feminist imaginations in ways, as yet underappreciated, to the project of imagining and narrating what it means to be musical as an American—more precisely, as a white American performing European music. While their attention to national, as well as gender, identity does not necessarily qualify their feminist projects, it does involve a construction of female musicality as a privileged site of national "spirit."

As professional female performers, the women singing Wagner in *Song of the Lark* and *Tower of Ivory* beg comparison to the women playing Chopin considered in the previous chapter. Like Harold Frederic's Celia Madden and Kate Chopin's Mlle Reisz, Thea Kronborg and Margarethe Styr both have powerful, visceral effects on their listeners, inspiring certain of them to wrest themselves from the trappings of convention; and both forego marriage and motherhood in favor of the self-fulfillment promised by the practice of their art. As singers, however, Kronborg and Styr occupy quite different symbolic and associative fields, as well as different historical counterparts, than the pianists playing Chopin. While these pianists represent modern or "new" women who reject the bourgeois parlor and its requisite "piano girl," they nonetheless remain associated with interior domestic spaces (the apartment, the studio, the hotel room) and with pianos. Their artistry is mediated by Chopin's compositions and by the piano itself, which draw our attention away from the performers' bodies and social identities and toward the abstract, disembodied, emotional experience of their listeners. Kronborg and Styr, on the other hand, are represented as fully embodied in their musicality: their instruments *are* their bodies, and they embody, on stage, Wagnerian characters that seemed themselves to embody a "vital energy" associated with the "American people." In important ways, however, the fictional singers considered in this chapter are also analogous to Edna Pontellier and Theron Ware, the American *audiences* of the Catholic and somewhat foreign pianists of Frederic's and Chopin's novels. Indeed, both Kronborg and Styr undergo what could be called "awakenings" that hinge on their own receptiveness to American subcultures, with pockets of authentic, primitive, "native" energies that, like the Catholics in Chopin's and Frederic's novels, remain isolated by region, religion, language, and culture. These singers embody the agency and independence of new female performers largely as a result of their prior receptiveness to powerful and primitive musical energies that promise release from the constraints of nineteenth-century domesticity.

From Coal Mine to Gold Mine: The American Voice of Margarethe Styr

In their reading of Atherton's *Tower of Ivory*, Susan Leonardi and Rebecca Pope single out one scene that particularly underscores the novel's participation in a feminist project of revision. Invoking the most foundational of "masculinist" diva narratives, Odysseus's encounter with the Sirens, Atherton's Margarethe Styr ties herself to a ship's mast in a desperate effort to survive a raging storm off the Oregon coast. But instead of identifying with

Odysseus, she "takes to herself the role of siren, here divine rather than demonic,"[8] as she experiences a kind of rebirth into opera: "I was Brünhilde, awaking from a sleep, not of a generation, but of the centuries that had gone since she rode into the funeral pyre" (91). But as this scene appropriates Homeric myth and Wagnerian legend to recuperate the siren as a version of modern female artistry, it also mythologizes the birth of an American diva. Distant in time and place from the European present of Atherton's novel, the primitive and stormy American West Coast represents a fitting setting for Styr's awakening as a more authentic Wagnerian than her European counterparts.

What it means for this diva to be American becomes a central question for the novel, which takes place entirely in Munich and a stiflingly class-conscious England, with American spaces existing only in hazy flashbacks or speculative gossip. Set in the 1880s, before American opera singers had gained much of an international footing, the novel introduces Styr's Americanness as anomalous and mysterious: because "origin in America [does not count] with Europeans in the least," and because rumor has it she was once on the vaudeville stage and led the promiscuous life associated with it, the singer presumably has kept her story as brief as possible "to stifle curiosity in her origin" (20). The novel's plot is driven by the relationship between Styr and Ordham, the second son of a British aristocrat, whose financial survival depends on his marrying well. Just before he decides to propose to another American in Europe, the vacuous (though rich and beautiful) Mabel Cutting, Ordham falls desperately in love with Styr, with whom marriage is impossible not only because she lacks the wealth his failing estate requires but also because she, herself, has vowed never to marry, having devoted herself entirely to opera. When Ordham, after first seeing Styr sing in Munich, asks a well-connected friend about the singer's origins, he only learns that, beyond the town gossip that Styr is the king's mistress, almost nothing is known about her past: "But where did she come from? Who is she? Why has she no credentials?" (19).

Just as Styr's artistry sets her apart from the more typical American women in Europe (of which Mabel Cutting is the prototype), Ordham's genteel reserve distinguishes him from the typical obsequious fan and earns him special audience with the singer, who tells him a few fragments of her story first hand. She reveals to him, in what becomes the first version of her origin story, that she was born "Peggy Hill": "I deliberately tried to make myself over into a German, put myself into the rôles, as one does on the stage. I succeeded for a time, but all that is past. Once an American always an American, I fancy. And the longer I live in Europe the more American I become. Don't ask me to define this. It is merely an instinct—perhaps a jealousy of birthright. I may never return to the United States. I know nothing of her affairs. But—well, my essence was compounded in that great country" (32). In asserting a difference between her performing and authentic selves—a difference between role-playing and essence—she initiates this novel's discursive construction of the American diva as authentic, as owning a depth of spirit that bespeaks the "greatness" of her country, even if that essence remains intangible. Hers becomes, in effect, a rags-to-riches story, one that begins with a scene of abject poverty, and that to some extent belies the idea of "essence" as something distinct from performance. Before she made herself over into Margarethe Styr, it seems she had to become Peggy Hill first: "I did not know even the English alphabet until I was fifteen. Nor did any other child in the wretched coal-mining district where I first saw light. It was peopled wholly by the poorest class of immigrants from eastern Europe—brought over wholesale by enterprising and not too honest mine owners. My clothes were made of hop-sacking. I had not the faintest idea that I was good-looking, for the simple reason that I was never clean or half fed" (45). These lowly origins function, for Styr's origin story, in several ways beyond establishing the distance she has traveled in her rise to success. They establish her as the daughter of immigrants raised in a language other than English—and thus, perhaps, owning a deeper affinity for Old World culture than more assimilated Americans. They give us an image of her family as not only working-class and poor but virtually enslaved by unscrupulous capitalists and thus establish her affinity with the country's lowliest peoples. Although Styr periodically insists that her talents have no relationship to these origins—"Whence I inherit my tendencies and talents I have no idea. From nowhere, most likely. Some mysterious disarrangement of particles" (46)—the novel encourages us in other ways to believe that her origins at the bottom of American society, as well her experiences climbing her way out of those origins, have everything to do with her "tendencies and talents," which could not otherwise have been imagined in an American. "All my life," she states, "seems to have been but a schooling for my art" (189). It is the mystery, in part, which invites two nationalist interpretations at once: that she inherited her talents "from nowhere" (as an American with no history); and that she earned them through the blood, sweat, and tears required to pull herself up from abject poverty.

Most of her life's story comes through apocryphal gossip that nonetheless gives us the only images, scenarios, and storylines with which to fill in the gaps of her own confessional narrative. What comprised Styr's "schooling" is never precisely named as such but only hinted at as a hard-scrabble American life filled with promiscuity, interracial dalliance, and raw ambition:

> The favorite story ... was that "Peggy Hill" had deserted her starving and consumptive mother in the native mining town to become the squaw of an Indian chieftain, and had worn paint and feathers and carried papooses on her back until a western millionnaire had chanced along, offered her sealskin and diamonds, fought a duel unto death with the chieftain—who, wearing only feathers, had many vulnerable points—and carried the heartless mother to New York. There she promptly deserted him for a horse jockey, and after having figured as co-respondent in innumerable divorce suits, had opened a disreputable resort, over which she had presided affluently (when not in jail) until ordered once and for all out of New York by the police. Then she had cultivated her voice, and, finding it a gold mine, conserved it with a fairly consistent exercise of virtue. (377)

Even as this story is told with tongue in cheek, it reproduces an imaginative link between female promiscuity and public singing familiar to the nineteenth-century imagination, while challenging readers to rethink its aesthetic as well as moral implications. Most importantly, this gossip understands Styr's musicality as a kind of sublimation of her sexuality, and of her sexual agency. Her unruly desire, like that of an uncivilized savage, leads her to the unthinkable acts of abandoning her mother, and then marrying an Indian and becoming, in effect, a "squaw" herself. Epitomizing the anxious patriarchal fantasy of unbridled female sexuality and an endlessly mutable female identity, she is not, in the end, punished for her promiscuity, as Victorian narrative convention would require, but ends up taking control of it by cultivating her "gold mine" of a voice, an American natural resource much more profitable than coal, and of which she is the owner and miner both. The gap between Styr's banishment from New York and the discovery of her voice remains outside this gossip's purview but can be filled in by the reader, at least in part, with the mythical story of the Oregon storm, which, joining her Indian marriage, becomes her second Western scene of transformation and escape from the East Coast.

While never confirming or denying this gossip, Styr later ambiguously notes that she has "lived with more men than I pretend to remember" (436) and that the decade preceding her transformative moment in the Oregon storm was indeed the stuff of scandal. Indeed, we are led to understand Styr's rise from the coal mines to the opera stage as an idealized process of sublimation, that at once reforms the primitive, illiterate, and underfed coal miner's daughter and then the promiscuous courtesan into an artist and, at the same time, preserves her primitive roots *through* artistry. Upon hearing her story, Ordham reflects "with a sudden access of vision" that she "had it in [her] to become all bad" (189). But as Styr puts it, in her own moment of truth at the novel's conclusion, it is precisely her potential "bad"-ness that accounts for the "vitality" of her ultimate artistry: "The natural passions of an uncommonly lusty and highly organized woman were turned back upon themselves by the accumulated disgust and horrors of those thirteen years, with all their vitalities unimpaired; rather were they recuperated, and rushed into the channels of art the moment the sluices were opened." The convolutions of this passage tell us much about how Atherton imagined musical talent. Rather than learned through training or inherited through culture, Styr's artistry is here figured as fluid, "natural passions" that are channeled, rushed, and "recuperated" by circumstance. That she owns such "natural passions" sets her at the opposite end of the emotional spectrum from Mabel Cutting, who cares only about her appearance and status, has only enough "culture" to make small talk at parties, is self-righteously puritanical, and seems incapable of strong feeling in any form: "It was patent," Ordham learns, too late, "that Mabel was not to be permitted to furnish any of her vacant cells in the primal colours" (240).

Styr's most effective performances are echoes of the Oregon storm, in which Wagnerian characters arouse and channel her "natural passions," giving them an outlet on stage if not in her social life. When she learns of Ordham's marriage to Mabel, for example, she pours "the blind primitive fury of a jungle beast deprived of its mate" (283) into her performance of Wagner's Isolde. Wagner's opera, in this novel, is as far removed from the vacant, performative American leisure class as is Styr herself and finally represents a more appropriate "ending" for Styr than marriage to the waffling Ordham or any man. Styr believes that Wagner's operas require that she "live the part"—"you abandon yourself deliberately . . . and are not your own self for one instant" (41–42). By living rather than merely performing her roles, Styr inspires fear in her European colleagues: "Everybody on the stage was uneasy, half fearing that this terrifying creature, always an alien in their midst, but awaited the final moment to wreak her vengeance" (275). It turns out that European singers, who "managed to convey the impression of deep intense emotion, artistically repressed," are themselves lacking in primal colors as well: "As a matter of fact [they] had nothing to repress" (442). The American—the "alien" among Europeans—thus becomes the ideal performer of Wagner, owning a "deep intense emotion" that can be entirely given over to "the part."

As Ordham's future becomes increasingly untenable—trapped as he is in a loveless marriage and in love with a diva whom he cannot marry—Styr's Wagnerian performances begin to open the sluices for his "primal passions" as well. Unlike Odysseus (but echoing Dreiser's Hurstwood and Frederic's Theron Ware), Ordham willingly succumbs to the siren's song, disregarding obligations to society and family (including his pregnant wife about to go into labor), when he chooses to travel to Munich to hear Styr's *Gotterdämmerung* one last time. Awaiting the performance, Ordham "felt as primitive as the characters in the drama about to be presented, as he sat there, frowning, dogged, almost growling, in the cavernous darkness" (451). In a bit of over-the-top melodrama, Ordham's wife dies in childbirth in the instant that Styr immolates herself before him on stage, literally enacting the fictional self-immolation of Brünhilde, the very character that marked the stormy Oregon birth of her operatic identity now enshrining it in death. But while Styr's death claims her for Wagner in eternity (and thus, in a sense, echoes *The Awakening*'s ending), Ordham remains trapped by social obligation and convention. He preserves his own scandalous passions literally in a closet, a private room in his home devoted to "the Styr" and hidden from view of his public life as a British politician. Styr's difference, her "alien" identity, might be read, as critics have read it, as evidence of her "sapphonic" subversion of gender conventions.[9] But her unconventional sexuality also leads us to, and indeed preserves, the difference of her American origins; her artistry channels and redirects the primitive instincts she has both inherited from and absorbed in her American past. By having her heroine die on stage as Brünhilde, Atherton not only betrays her "middlebrow" penchant for spectacle and melodrama but also, perhaps, indicates her unwillingness or incapacity to imagine such a passionate white American woman as anything but operatic, safely contained by the boundary between stage and audience, diva and fan.

It is interesting to note the ways in which Atherton's only diva character mirrors some of the attributes she gave to her other heroines. As historian Kevin Starr has noted, Atherton's California novels (for which she was most famous) tended to mythologize an old California population of mixed Spanish and Indian origins—"aristocratic blood laced with a touch of the exotic"—and to imagine, in retrospect, what might have been had the "vigor" of "California savagery" been "endow[ed] . . . with civilization," rather than subdued by American progress.[10] Atherton's American diva, who finds herself at least at one pivotal moment on the far reaches of the American West, might be imagined as a displaced version of this idealized hybrid Californian. But it is Willa Cather who would give us a more explicit narration of operatic identity rooted in the "savagery" of the West, one that refuses simply to romanticize the social and cultural dimensions of her diva's musical relationship to national identity, instead putting them at the novel's center.

"Something on the Inside": Willa Cather's New World Diva

In a letter to Dorothy Canfield, Cather claimed to have chosen an opera singer for her semi-autobiographical novel about the struggles of a female artist because "her artistry was concrete; people saw and heard a living voice before them . . . and could not help being captured by a Jenny Lind." She also claimed that "a singer was the only artist who could impress Moonstone," the fictional Colorado town in which her novel is set, recalling that people from her own childhood town of Red Cloud "would go to Kansas City to hear Geraldine Farrar."[11] Much more than the writer, Cather's female singer is capable at once of "artistry" and of popularity, of using her "living voice" to "capture" both Moonstone and the Metropolitan Opera House audience.

While Gertrude Atherton devoted only one of her many novels to a musician, Willa Cather could not seem to let go of musical characters. Indeed, one could argue that no American fiction writer has so elaborately explored the social and aesthetic phenomena of classical music as Cather, whose musical fiction registers, along with her own passion for music, much about the changing presence of music and musicians in America around the turn of the twentieth century. Certainly, as Leonardi and Pope assert, she was "the writer most obsessed with the diva," having produced at least twelve narratives centered on a female singer.[12] (Her other principal musician characters are violinists, pianists, and one composer.) Richard Giannone, who has written the only book-length study of music's role in Cather's fiction, argues that music "serves a central purpose" in her literature that is "not accidental to technique, not simply an extension of personal interest in musical art, not merely ornamental to her achievement," but "a distinctive quality of Willa Cather's mind and creation; and it is a univocal index to her loyalties." Music particularly registers Cather's loyalties, Giannone notes, to the rural immigrant folk and to urban high culture, two distinct social and cultural realms that *Song of the Lark*'s Thea Kronborg manages to integrate with "the combined passion of the folk artist and the educated intelligence of the professional."[13] As we have seen, this "combination," much as it reflected Cather's idiosyncratic "mind and creation," also comprised a central trope of national musical style emerging in Cather's America (and, one might add, of regional fiction, as it brings high literary perspective to rural American communities).[14] What distinguishes Cather's version of this trope, however, is her interest in its inner workings and conflicts, her refusal, in other words, to simply romanticize the relationship between artist and folk material. While Atherton raises the question of American operatic identity and answers with only vague suggestions of a connection between her diva's musicality and her origins in the American "abyss," Cather devotes her entire novel, one could argue, to understanding the role of American contexts in the formation of her diva's musical artistry.

Many of Cather's early stories use music to underscore an unbridgeable gap between "old" and "new" world values, giving us immigrant musicians shocked to discover that their new country values music as a commodity or spectacle rather than a rich language for human expression. In "Peter" (1892), her very first published story, the eponymous old German immigrant treasures his violin as a symbol of the musical life he left behind, only to have the instrument stolen from him by his Americanized son, who thinks only of its exchange value. Peter's ensuing suicide leaves us in the world of "doom without hope" that Giannone associates with many of her early stories about musicians.[15] Indeed, from her earliest stories to her penultimate novel, *Lucy Gayheart* (1935), Cather's musical characters seem either to suffer tragically in their alienation from American commercialism or, like Eden Bowers in "Coming, Aphrodite," sacrifice their musical ideals by submitting to their country's more superficial values and to their own commoditization. If we read Thea Kronborg as able to bring old and new world values, "folk" and "professional" musical traditions, together into one musical nature, she represents a decided anomaly in Cather's fiction. She is certainly Cather's only diva whose American origins can be said to contribute positively to her artistic greatness.

But *Song of the Lark* nonetheless highlights the disjunctions in Thea's experience as she struggles to "combine" her heterogenous "passions" for city and country, for folk culture and high art. And rather than represent some kind of triumphant synthesis, Thea's final arrival at operatic stardom and Wagnerian triumph remains deeply unsettled by her exhaustion, her social isolation, and by the gap between her life on stage and off. In her preface to the 1932 reissue of the novel, Cather distanced herself from its ending, lamenting particularly her decision to dwell on the uninspiring nature of an artist's success: "Her artistic life is the only one in which she is happy, or free, or even very real" and her "personal life becomes paler as the imaginative life becomes richer."[16] But while Cather retrospectively deems this "paling" of personal life inevitable for any artist, the novel itself suggests otherwise, in the two crucial moments when Thea steps out of the conventional narrative of diva training into the spaces of Mexican and Native American society. Thea, in fact, is the only white musician in Cather's fiction who sings with Mexicans and communes with the imagined drumbeats of dead Indians, two "native" cultures whose musical values triangulate the "Old World"/"New World" binary otherwise structuring her musical fiction.

Born into a large minister's family in Moonstone, Colorado, Thea begins her path towards greatness with the combined musical influences of the diverse group of immigrants who have settled in this frontier railroad town, and for whom music retains its value as a central aspect of social life. Her devoted mother, whose father was an oboist in Sweden, her German piano teacher who pines for the Old World, and a Mexican mandolin player living on the outskirts of town all recognize her musical talent as a precious vestige of Old World culture threatened by a provincial American musical culture that would reduce Thea to playing for church functions and teaching piano lessons. Their support, as well as some money left to her by an admirer killed in an industrial accident, frees her from the limits of small-town musicality, sending Thea to Chicago where she can train with real professionals. In Chicago, her Hungarian piano teacher discovers her singing voice and, in turn, sends her to a famous voice teacher who can prepare her for the concert world. Before beginning this training, Thea vacations in Moonstone for the summer and experiences a kind of musical awakening while singing for and with the Mexican community there. When she returns to Chicago, Madison Bowers, her first non-immigrant music teacher, quickly succeeds in dampening her spirit with his slick professionalism and cynical, commercial attitude. Her German American boyfriend, who is both musical and extremely rich, funds another retreat from a limiting American music culture, this time to the prehistoric Indian Cliff Dwellings in Arizona, where she finds herself profoundly inspired and rejuvenated by a kind of spiritual communion with the Indians who once lived there. This experience gives birth to her artistic mastery and leads directly in the text (which mentions her subsequent European training and early career only in passing) to her Wagnerian triumphs at the Met.

Early in the novel, Herr Wunsch, the German immigrant who teaches Thea piano in Moonstone, names the problem of American musicality as a problem of American identity: "For a singer there must be something in the inside from the beginning," he tells Thea; "*Aber nicht die amerikanishcen Fräuleins.* They have nothing inside them" (71). The singing "amerikanischen Fräuleins" that Thea encounters along her way all substantiate this idea of Americans as hollow shells, lacking, like Atherton's "vacant" Mabel, any substance "inside." Lily Fischer, who sings "Rock of Ages" at the Moonstone Christmas pageant, "looked exactly like the beautiful children on soap calendars. . . . She sang all songs and played all parts alike" (62). Jessie Darcy, the popular Chicago "semi-professional" singer, is "only Lily Fisher under another name" (236). Mrs. Priest, another Chicago singer who studies with Bowers, gives "the impression of wearing a cargo of splendid merchandise" and exudes a "glowing, overwhelming self-satisfaction, only to be found where human society is young and strong and without yesterdays" (229). Bowers himself epitomizes the shallow, commercial values of American musical "semi-professionalism" by cynically advising Thea to hide the depth of her talent under a veneer of "smoothness": "When you come to marketing your wares in the world, a little smoothness goes farther than a great deal of talent sometimes. If you happen to be cursed with a real talent, then you've got to be very smooth, indeed, or you'll never get your money back" (228).

Like Cather's earlier stories, *Song of the Lark* contrasts this American commercialism with the integrity of immigrant Europeans, whose memories protect them from the leveling influence of their American circumstances. In Moonstone, the Kohlers keep their German heritage alive by, against all odds, creating a "Rhine village" garden in the Colorado desert; they cannot, however, instill this German culture in their sons, who "forgot the past" (22), living like Mrs. Priest "without yesterdays." But Moonstone's immigrant musicians are unable to recreate their musical pasts as easily as planting a garden, and their memories remain painful reminders of what they have lost. Herr Wunsch lives in tormented and usually drunken alienation from his adopted country. Spanish Johnny, Thea's Mexican friend, similarly longs for the "Old World," a longing he periodically indulges during "crazy" singing sprees: "He would go on until he had no voice left, until he wheezed and rasped. Then he would play his mandolin furiously, and drink until his eyes sank back into his head" (39). On particularly desperate occasions, he would travel southward "from saloon to saloon until he got across the border," where he would play his mandolin and sing in bars until he finally dragged himself back to Colorado and to his patient wife. Excluded from the emerging classical musical culture of the United States, in which the alienated European immigrants can at least find work, Johnny's musicality betrays both his "craziness" and his foreignness, pulling him back "across the border" to Mexico. Immigrant America occupies a privileged place in Cather's national imaginary: memory and alienation give voice to not only immigrants' loss but also their unrealized potential for constructing a new American culture independent of commercial values. With her capacity to hear and be influenced by immigrant music and musical values, while remaining free from the burden of Old World memory and the stigma of racial difference, Thea becomes the vehicle of that new American musical identity.

It is immigrant America that informs Cather's ideas about Dvořák's "New World" Symphony, which she praised once (in a review of a concert by the Pittsburgh Symphony) for its evocations not of "slave songs and Indian chants" but of "the empty, hungry plains of the Middle West . . . full of the peasantry of all the nations of Europe."[17] In *Song of the Lark*, Thea hears Dvořák's controversial American symphony at a pivotal moment at the end of her first year in Chicago, a moment that explicitly ties this novel to contemporary discourses of musical nationalism. For Thea, Dvořák's symphony expresses "the amazement of a new soul in a new world; a soul new and yet old. . . . A soul obsessed by what it did not know, under the cloud of a past it could not recall" (181). Much vaguer than Cather's Pittsburgh review, Thea's language calls to mind less the immigrant Middle West than her own as yet inarticulable relationship to both the Old and New Worlds, removed as she is by a generation from the immigrant's memory and longing, but nonetheless resisting the new generation's assimilation into a memoryless American culture. Instead of memory, this music arouses in Thea a desire for memory, for "a past [she] could not recall." As a daughter of immigrants with no direct memory of the Old World, Thea's musical identity has no obvious national roots, no given heritage, but her musicality clearly marks her as different from the "americanischen Fräuleins" who happily refrain from any connection with the past.[18]

Like Margarethe Styr, Thea's American musicality lacks a discourse available to describe it, and stands, in a sense, as the novel's central mystery: Where does it come from and what place can it have? Thea's immigrant teachers understand her as a kind of wild or natural being, free of both culture and history, and immune to the "civilizing" forces of modernity. Herr Wunsch hears Thea's voice as "a nature voice . . . breathed from the creature and apart from language" (70). Her Hungarian piano teacher is reminded by Thea's singing that he "loved to hear a big voice throb in a relaxed, natural throat" (171) and notes that "she came to me as a fine young savage, a book with nothing written in it" (185). A fellow student echoes this image when he coyly gives her the nickname "savage blonde" (162). This language of savagery and nature helps to construct Thea's difference as essential and vaguely racial. But the fact that this "savage" voice belongs to a "blonde" puts the visual and aural markers of Thea's identity into a titillating contradiction and marks her difference from the *real* "savages," whose bodies remain unwelcome in American high culture.

In her own imagination, Thea understands her difference as something that both sets her apart from modern society and potentially defines an alternative modern American community. As she notices that some people respond to her singing more than others, she muses, "perhaps each of them concealed another person in himself, just as she did. . . . What if one's second self could somehow speak to all these second selves? . . . How deep they lay, these second persons, and how little one knew about them, except to guard them fiercely." Echoing Wunsch's insistence that a musician has something "on the inside," she concludes, "it was to music, more than to anything else, that these hidden things in people responded" (197). A number of critics associate Thea's secret interiority with the unnamable homosexuality suggested by so many of Cather's alienated characters, but it is important to recognize the ways in which Thea's "hidden" musical self evokes a more generalizable notion of authenticity and authentic sociality (even as it certainly invites us to imagine her queerness).[19] "Second selves," freed from standardizing social distinctions, and from the "merchandise" that reproduces them, can truly "speak to" one another.[20] The novel gestures towards this alternative sociality not only in immigrant memories and in Thea's own imagined community of musically connected "second selves" but also in Moonstone's "Mexican Town," whose musical expressions are not confined to concerts and church but permeate everyday social life.

The novel articulates Moonstone's cultural identity in multiple and contradictory ways: as provincial and unsophisticated; as peopled by immigrants; and as a segregated society, with distinct white and Mexican communities. On the train home after her first year in Chicago, Thea struggles to account for the relationship between her budding musical artistry and her Colorado origins. Like the "home" she'd heard in Dvořák's symphony, she imagines Colorado as a place defined by the immigrant experience: "This earth seemed to her young, and fresh and kindly, a place where refugees from old, sad countries were given another chance." Although still convinced it was not the best starting place for a future opera singer, "Thea was glad that this was her country; even if one did not learn to speak elegantly there." Indeed, rather than frame this unrefined country as lacking in musicality (as she has done previously), Thea now associates it with a new kind of music: "It was, somehow, an honest country, and there was a new song in that blue air which had never been sung in the world before. It was hard to tell about it, for it had nothing to do with words; it was . . . intangible but powerful" (199). Recalling Styr's Pacific coast storm, Thea's West here represents a musical frontier whose narrative only such participant observers as herself will be able to write. Thea goes on to associate this figure of Colorado's powerful "new song" with a "feeling of empire" and assumes a kind of musical ownership over this empty and unsung landscape, like an artist or composer discovering new material to develop.

Once she arrives, however, Thea's sense of propriety is complicated by her reunion with an actual, historical musical community that her train-ride fantasy had occluded. The moment she encounters her old friend Spanish Johnny, Thea tries to assert a kind of ownership over his musicality and just as quickly meets Johnny's resistance to her presumption of mastery. "I want you to write down the words of that Mexican serenade you used to sing," she states, immediately invoking the ethnological act of transcription that gave classical composers access to "folk" sources; "you know, '*Rosa de Noche*.' It's an unusual song. I'm going to study it. I know enough Spanish for that" (205). But rather than send Thea down the road of the new musical nationalist who sings concert versions of "folk" music or composes new American song cycles based on "folk" themes, Cather spends the rest of this chapter complicating Thea's relationship to Johnny's musicality. Johnny proceeds, playfully but stubbornly, to resist her appeal and to emphasize what might be lost of the song's particular historical and cultural reality were it to become one more work studied and performed by a white opera singer in Chicago. He suggests, first, that Thea is too young and her voice too high for the song, which was written for "married ladies" (a fact that has not prevented him from singing it). He then politely corrects her imprecise labeling of the song as Mexican: "'It come from farther down; Brazil, Venezuela, may-bee. I learn it from some fellow down there, and he learn it from another fellow. It is a—most like Mexican, but not quite.'" The slippery origins of the song and Johnny's insider knowledge of the fine distinctions between Mexican and other musical traditions challenge Thea's desire to name its origins, fix it on the page, and thus take it out of its fluid passage among the distinct but mutually constitutive musical cultures south of the border. After Thea's inflexible response—"she did not release him, but pointed to the paper"—Johnny playfully acquiesces but not before asking, "How you accompany with piano?" (205). The question is important: to adapt the song to the concert stage will bring it into an entirely different frame of reference, one centered around the piano, that immobile modern fixture of the bourgeois parlor and concert stage, rather than the portable and more accessible mandolin or guitar.

After meeting her request, Johnny tells a story that draws Thea back into his own oral culture and situates her as *his* audience, both of, and in, his story:

> When you was a little girl, no bigger than that, you come to my house one day 'bout noon, like this, and I was in the door, playing guitar. You was barehead, barefoot; you run away from home. You stand there and make a frown at me an' listen. By 'n by you say for me to sing. I sing some lil' ting, and then I say for you to sing with me. You don' know no words, of course, but you take the air and you sing it just-a beautiful! I never see a child do that, outside Mexico. You was, oh, I do' know—seven year may-bee. By 'n by the preacher come look for you and begin for scold. I say, "Don' scold, Meester Kronborg. She come for hear guitar. She gotta some music in her, that child. Where she get?" Then he tell me 'bout your gran'papa play oboe in the old country. I never forgetta that time. (206)

Beyond flattering his old friend, Johnny's story answers the question of "where she get" the music that she reveals to be "in her"—the question of this novel, I am arguing—by offering a version of Clara Kellogg's story of learning to sing by listening to and then imitating her Negro mammy. Whatever debt she owes to her grandpa's "old country" oboe playing, Thea's openness to and affinity for Mexican music, rooted in song, and learned by ear, sets her apart from the European immigrants of Moonstone as much as it sets her apart from their Americanized children. Johnny's story not only constructs an origin for Thea's musicality but it invites her, in the present, to revisit the source. When he finishes speaking, she acknowledges that she indeed "liked [the Mexicans'] music better than the church music" and then asks, "When are you going to have a dance over there, Johnny?" (206). The chapter that began with Thea's effort to draw Mexican music into the rituals of urban opera culture leads to her own reimmersion in a ritual of Mexican culture.

Thea's experience at the ball continues this dialectic between Euro-American and Mexican perspectives. Initially, Thea stands apart from the scene occupying the ethnological role of fascinated observer, contrasting what she witnesses with the loud railroad men's dances she grew up with, where "the boys played rough jokes and thought it smart to be clumsy and to run into each other on the floor": "This Mexican dance was soft and quiet. There was no calling, the conversation was very low, the rhythm of the music was smooth and engaging, the men were graceful and courteous. . . . There was an atmosphere of ease and friendly pleasure in the low, dimly lit room, and Thea could not help wondering whether the Mexicans had no jealousies or neighbourly grudges as the people in Moonstone had. There was no constraint of any kind there to-night, but a kind of natural harmony about their movements, their greetings, their low conversation, their smiles" (208). Thea emphasizes, here, the collective experience of this event that includes the entire community; musicality and sociality define each other as young and old, men and women, come together to dance and sing in an expression of "natural harmony." The homogeneity of this scene gives way, however, to a spectacle of difference as Thea becomes the observed rather than the observer: "The Ramas boys thought Thea dazzlingly beautiful. They had never seen a Scandinavian girl before, and her hair and fair skin bewitched them" (208–9). Cather then dwells on the Mexican boys' point of view, as they discuss Thea's beauty among themselves and then invite her to dance: "When they were not dancing with her, their eyes followed her, over the coiffures of their other partners. That was not difficult: one blonde head moving among so many dark ones" (209). Although Thea is drawn into the "harmony," she remains an honorary guest, whose whiteness warrants special attention and treatment.

Thea moves from observer and observed to the role of participant observer only after she is invited to sing. While her blondness attracted the Ramas boys for its starkly visible difference from themselves (and their women), her voice, as Johnny has already indicated, is like one of their own, albeit of rare quality. While Thea sings, her perspective once again takes over the narration as she begins to imagine a total collapse of boundary between herself and her audience: "She had sung for churches and funerals and teachers, but she had never before sung for a really musical people, and this was the first time she had ever felt the response that such a people can give. They turned themselves and all they had over to her. For the moment they cared about nothing in the world but what she was doing. Their faces confronted her—open, eager, unprotected. She felt as if all these warm-blooded people debouched into her. . . . In an instant [they] seemed to be within her instead of without, as if they had come from her in the first place" (210). While Thea has experienced a musical connection with select individuals before this moment, including Spanish Johnny, this is the first time—and, indeed, the only time—she sings for a group of people who are *all* musical, for whom being musical is a common way of being. The language here oddly underscores the ways in which listening can be figured as both analogous to and yet different from looking. As this "really musical" audience "turned themselves" to her, and their "faces confronted" her, they embody a kind of aural gaze that does not fix its object but rather flows into and fills up that which it hears, while also remaining itself "unprotected." This flow of Mexicanness into Thea's interiority initiates a kind of rebirth or awakening of her musical self.

Of course, upon "debouching" into her, these "warm-blooded people" become aspects of *her* self, their separate histories and origins obliterated in her feeling that they have "come from her." While Cather initially seemed critical of the imperialistic overtones of transcription, of a white American writing down and then performing the music of a Mexican folk singer, she here seems uncritically to celebrate Thea's appropriation of Mexican musicality for her own. Indeed, the narrative makes one more shift in perspective that reminds us of the status of Mexicans bodies and voices in the Wagnerian opera world for which Thea now seems destined. As several of the Mexicans later join her in singing a sextette from Donizetti's "Lucia," moving from South American serenade to Italian opera, the narrative enters the perspective of the German immigrant Kohlers, Moonstone's only other "really musical people" now that Herr Wunsch has left, who overhear the singing through their open window: "Johnny's reedy tenor they knew well, and the bricklayer's big, opaque baritone; the others might be anybody over there—just Mexican voices. Then at the appointed, at the acute, moment, the soprano voice, like a fountain jet, shot up into the light. . . . How it leaped from among those dusky male voices! How it played in and about and around and over them, like a goldfish darting among creek minnows, like a yellow butterfly soaring above a swarm of dark ones" (213). By imagining Thea's voice as a "fountain jet" reaching for the light, the Kohlers effectively reassert European hegemony, reducing the dusky Mexicans and their voices to an undifferentiated supporting role in the white diva's story. This is the last time Mexicans sing in the novel, as their silence becomes, or so the novel implies, an inevitable consequence of Thea's operatic emergence.

While the Kohlers enjoy hearing Thea sing at the Mexican ball, as one might enjoy a night at the opera, the rest of white Moonstone hear it as a blatant disregard for and transgression of the town's color line. The general attitude of white Moonstone about Mexican music making had earlier been summed up by Thea's sister, who could not understand why Thea spent so much time on the other side of town: "Thea pretended, of course, that she liked the Mexicans because they were fond of music; but everyone knew that music was nothing very real, and that it did not matter in a girl's relations with people." The narrator—and, clearly, Cather herself—responds, "What was real, then, and what did matter? Poor Anna!" (120). Moonstone's and particularly her own family's reaction to her participation at the ball—one brother mocks, "High society, that" (214), while Anna laments, "We all hoped that going away would improve you" (215)—initiates a turning point in Thea's relationship to her origins and in her sense of self. Feeling "as if everything inside her had solidified and grown hard" (215), she concludes that "nothing that she would ever do in the world would seem important to [her family], and nothing they would ever do would seem important to her" (217). While she utterly rejects her family's racist attitude toward Mexicans, their reaction has effectively shut down her own desire to be with them: "Mexican Town, somehow, was spoiled for her just then" (218). In a conversation with her only other friend in town, Dr. Archie, she proclaims in agitation that she now "only want[s] impossible things" (219), deciding to leave Moonstone "for ever," and thus to preclude any further attempt to draw its landscape or people into her own musical future (222).

Cather's novel might have ended, like her later diva stories, with her diva hardened and cynical, trapped in an opera culture that ultimately wants material rather than "impossible" things.[21] But Cather instead chooses, at this late point in the novel, to introduce the character of Fred Ottenburg, son of a successful German beer brewer in St. Louis and with him a series of new possible futures—as well as possible origins—for Thea's operatic self. Besides opening up the prospect of marriage, he also importantly establishes himself as an authority on the hidden enclaves of authentic musicality in Chicago: "We may have a musical public in this country some day, but as yet there are only the Germans and the Jews. All the other people go to hear Jessie Darcey sing, 'O, Promise Me!'" In an effort to draw Thea out of her growing cynicism, he has her sing for the Nathanmeyers, who are "the finest kind of Jews." Hearing that Mrs. Nathanmeyer would have no interest in another "Jessie Darcey," Thea remarks, "that's the kind of people I want to find" (247).

The Nathanmeyers' Jewishness serves as a kind of bridge, in this novel, between the threatened cultures and memories of the novel's European and Mexican immigrants and a more primordial, and historically abstracted, "native" cultural identity. Fred represents Mrs. Nathanmeyer's perspective as fundamentally immune to contemporary fashion, with musical standards that "have nothing to do with Chicago," as Cather invokes what one critic has called her "romantic sense of Judaism's long past."[22] Instead of being shaped by her environment, Mrs. Nathanmeyer's "perceptions—or her grandmother's, which is the same thing—were keen when all this was an Indian village" (247). While Thea finds herself feeling "at home" in the Nathanmeyers' house, it is not until Fred offers to send her to an actual "Indian village" that she finally can envision her musical future as rooted in a "long past" she can call her own.

Thea's visit to cliff dwellings in Arizona, in a chapter entitled "Ancient People," invokes Indianness as both a figure for and means of connection with a fundamental American identity. The absence of actual, live Indians at Panther Canyon allows Thea to imagine herself stepping entirely out of history and modern social space and into an unmediated relationship with a spirit of Indianness still rooted in the landscape. Music plays a central, if silent, role in her imagination of Indianness and of her relationship to it, as she finds herself possessed by forms of musical experience: "She was singing very little now, but a song would go through her head all morning, as a spring keeps welling up, and it was like a pleasant sensation indefinitely prolonged. It was much more like a sensation than like an idea, or an act of remembering. Music had never before come to her in that sensuous form" (269). Thea begins to imagine this sensation as the transmission, across time, of Indian feelings: "Certain feelings were transmitted to her, suggestions that were simple, insistent, and monotonous, like the beating of Indian drums. They were not expressible in words, but seemed rather to translate themselves into attitudes of body, into degrees of muscular tension or relaxation" (272). As she traverses the land, she "found herself trying to walk as they must have walked, with a feeling in her feet and knees and loins which she had never known before—which must have come up to her out of the accustomed dust of that rocky trail." Echoing the gossip surrounding Atherton's Styr, who purportedly married an Indian and "carried papooses on her back," Thea imagines that she feels "the weight of an Indian baby hanging to her back as she climbed" (271). In language that blurs the line between imitation and reincarnation, she eventually seizes upon another metaphor for her new identification with these "ancient people," one that more directly connects her *singing* body with the Indian "feelings" that are flooding her experience. Taking her cue from the fragments of pottery she finds among the dwellings, Thea imagines that, like the women making vessels for water, "in singing, one made a vessel of one's throat and nostrils and held it on one's breath, caught the stream in a scale of natural intervals" (273). This stream of natural music, "the shining, elusive element which is life itself," connects her, through her body and particularly her singing throat, to "a continuity of life that reached back into the old time" (273). In short, "the Cliff Dwellers had lengthened her past" (276).

This final repositioning of Thea's voice into continuity with "the old time" authenticates her American artistry by giving her "something on the inside" that distinguishes her from both "americanischen Fräuleins" and first generation immigrants. It also specifically prepares her for Wagner. "Instead of inventing a lot of business and expedients to suggest character," we are told about Thea's seamless performances of Wagner's roles: "she knows the thing at the root, and lets the musical pattern take care of her. The score pours her into all those lovely postures" (367). Fred notes "You're as much at home on the stage as you were down in Panther Canyon," and Thea, in response, claims that what she learned in the Cliff Dwellings that she has carried with her to the stage is "an animal sort of feeling" that you can't know "with your mind"; instead you must "realize it in your body; deep" (398). Dr. Archie, hearing her sing Elsa on stage for the first time, begins "to feel the exhilaration of getting free from personalities, of being released from his own past as well as from Thea Kronborg's" (360). Like Indian drum beats, Thea's Wagner releases her and her audience from history and the "first selves" of social identity.

For Theodor Adorno, who devoted much of his writing to the problem of music in modern capitalist culture, Wagner's music dramas epitomized music's nascent commodity character; their mythical insistence on the "universally human" required "the dismantling of . . . the relative and contingent in favor of the idea of an unvarying human nature."[23] Wagner's promise of musical transcendence obscures, like commodity fetishism, its own social and historical being. But while Cather perpetuates a romantic notion that Wagner, like Indian artifacts, can connect white Americans to a common, "unvarying" human nature, her novel's ending remains marked by its own efforts to exclude and forget present-day American contexts that have both enabled and limited Thea's musical achievement. Cather singles out one person hearing Thea sing at the Met who "got greater pleasure out of that afternoon" than anyone else (410). Spanish Johnny has buried his wife in Moonstone and come to New York with Barnum and Bailey's circus, a manager of which "had traveled about the Southwest, signing up a lot of Mexican musicians at low wages" (410). The final words of this scene are given to Johnny, and, I would argue, ask us to think about the ways in which Thea's success in Wagnerian opera join Barnum and Bailey's circus in exploiting, and obscuring, darker-skinned American musicians. When she rushes from stage door to car after her performance, and fails to notice him waiting, Johnny "walked down Broadway with his hands in his overcoat pockets, wearing a smile which embraced all the stream of life that passed him and the lighted towers that rose into the limpid blue of the evening sky. If the singer, going home exhausted in her car, was wondering what was the good of it all, that smile, could she have seen it, would have answered her. It was the only commensurate answer" (411). It is tempting to dismiss this conclusion as patronizing, with Johnny passively accepting his own lowly anonymity, pleased merely to be in the presence of Thea's greatness. But as "the only commensurate answer" to Thea's still cynical and "exhausted" question of the value of her performance, Johnny's musical pleasure, itself a receptacle for the elusive "stream of life," highlights the degree to which the American musical establishment still lacks something "on the inside." But Johnny's sympathetic audition here also reinforces the idea of Thea's distinction as an American: as a Mexican he reminds us of the non-European roots of her musicality, and as an uncomfortable and marginalized participant in modernity, he emphasizes her connection to a "stream of life" that is outside history.

Like those composers invested in basing musical nationalist styles on Native American and African American music, *Song of the Lark* and *Tower of Ivory* gesture toward the ethnic margins of American society as a source of musical "vitality" that can be channeled, translated, or transmitted into the forms and practices of American classical music. Unlike composers, however, these fictional singers absorb musical "otherness" through their own ears and bodies and reproduce it through their own embodied performances of Wagner. In channeling their vitality into Wagnerian opera, these narratives ultimately confine both their divas' unconventional femininity and the "otherness" of their American sources to the rarified opera stage, as their divas move promiscuously through the musical cultural spaces of American society only as steps on the way to that stage. Indeed, the only relationships that either novel can imagine between "second selves" freed from limiting determinations of class, race, gender, and sexuality are between singer and audience, or diva and fan, within a delimited highbrow opera culture.

But while Cather limits Spanish Johnny and Indian spirits to the role of inspiring muse, and Atherton can only imagine the Indian "other" as a mythologized origin, the following chapter considers this moment of musical nationalism from the point of view of a more problematic "participant observer," who comes to somewhat different ends. The biracial narrator of James Weldon Johnson's *Autobiography of an Ex-Colored Man* also struggles to voice an authentic American musicality but in so doing refuses to render its "native" sources invisible or to collapse their cultural and historical particularity into a universalizing and transcendent musicality.

4
James Weldon Johnson's Ex-Colored Musician

> [Ragtime] is an evil music that has crept into the homes and hearts of our American people regardless of race, and must be wiped out as other bad and dangerous epidemics have been exterminated.
>
> —"Our Musical Condition," *Negro Music Journal* 1

> As you walk up and down the streets of an American city you feel in its jerk and rattle a personality different from that of any European capital. This is American. . . . No European music can or possibly could express this American personality. Ragtime I believe does express it. It is today the one true American music.
>
> —Hiram Moderwell, "Ragtime"

If *Song of the Lark* revises Antonin Dvořák's idea of a national art music built upon "Indian chants" by locating American musicality in a female performer's body rather than the male composer's Indian-inspired musical texts, Willa Cather's American diva succeeds at the expense of both the modern bodies and the actual musical production of her "native" sources. Indeed, for Dvořák and the American composers he inspired, "plantation melodies" and "Indian chants" worked as source material for a national musicality only by virtue of their disembodiment and by their enclosure in a mythologized American past cut off from modernity by the Civil War and Indian Removal. But more popular than either the "plantation melodies" or "Indian chants" with turn-of-the-century audiences, and a more controversial contender for the status of "American music," was a song and piano style created and performed by modern, urban, and often African American musicians, whose bodies and modernity could not be so easily erased.

Named for its "ragged" syncopated rhythms, ragtime originated with African American bands and pianists in the Midwest who turned popular American band music into dance music through syncopating its regular marching pulse. While the style's originators typically did not transcribe and market their ragtime pieces as sheet music, ragtime eventually became a written music for piano solo or for singer and accompaniment, entering into mainstream popular music across the color line. Even as a composed, texted form, ragtime was consistently described, by its celebrants and critics, in terms that emphasize the *embodied* experience of its listeners, who found themselves spontaneously and even involuntarily "jerking" along with its rhythms. Disagreement between those defending and those decrying ragtime hinged on competing reactions to this embodied response, which reflected competing notions of national identity: what for some expressed the modern, American "jerk and rattle" that one might feel walking down the streets of New York City, was for others an "evil" infiltrator of American homes and hearts, and a "dangerous epidemic." Anxious attention to ragtime's effects on the body and spirit reached a sometimes hysterical pitch, as critics hyperbolically characterized its syncopated rhythms as "commotion without purpose" and "virulent poison" that would "infect" America's youth with immoral impulses.[1] The modern, urban, sounds of ragtime, depending on one's point of view, either threatened or promised to displace a reigning metaphor of the nation—and of American musical experience—as a space of moral and, for some, racial purity.

This chapter considers James Weldon Johnson's *The Autobiography of an Ex-Colored Man* as in part an effort to understand the place of African American musicians in this urban musical landscape in which both ragtime and "plantation melodies" vied for representation in and as American musical identity. Published in 1912, the same year Irving Berlin's "Alexander's Ragtime Band" became the most commercially successful ragtime song to date, Johnson's novel is set at the turn of the century, a moment when African American songwriters and performers still could claim primary authorship of the style. Teamed up with his brother J. Rosamond Johnson and their partner Robert Cole, Johnson himself wrote ragtime songs for Broadway musical theater and lived in New York amidst a diverse community of African American performing artists that included classical composers, popular songwriters, performers, lyricists, actors, and poets. The new attention of those in the musical establishment to questions of musical nationalism joined the new vogue for "ragtime" to create unprecedented opportunities for black musicians to claim a voice in mainstream American musical culture. As embodiments of one significant "source" material for the new American musicality, these musicians found themselves invited to participate not only in musically representing the nation but also in influencing the musical representation of their race. Like

Scott Joplin and other early composers of ragtime, the musicians in Johnson's circle were what one scholar has termed "bi-musical": trained in European classical music as well as in African American musical styles, forms, and performance traditions.[2] The ex-colored man's various bimusical innovations—he is, within the world of the novel, the first to "rag the classics" and the first to conceive of classical music based on African American themes—decidedly echo the collective innovations of the circle of African American musicians among whom Johnson worked and lived before writing his novel.

Much of the scholarship addressing music in Johnson's novel (sparked, in part, by an earlier version of this chapter) focuses specifically on the novel's approach to differences between European and African American musical forms and styles.[3] In spite of the long critical discussion of the novel's unsettling of fixed notions of racial identity, scholars have nonetheless tended to see music in this novel as asserting an essential difference between European and African American music. Some have argued that the novel celebrates the subversive power of ragtime and black spirituals, while others read the novel as too Eurocentric and thus failing adequately to appreciate ragtime's subversive power.[4] In either case, a critical insistence on the difference of black musicality obscures the degree to which Johnson's novel refuses to extricate musical difference from the different social conditions of musical production, reception, and performance. Music's power and its relationship to identity, in this novel, depend as much on the listener's point of view, and on the relations of power between musicians and listeners, as it does on the music itself. The narrator's bimusicality constitutes a specific form of agency within the social and musical landscape of the narrative and exists, ultimately, as a condition of entry into and influence on musical discourse within that landscape. For Johnson, the fundamental question for the trained black musician living in Jim Crow America is, finally, a question about his relationship to his audience: How can music speak to an audience that hears music, and a marketplace that packages it, as either black or white? Can music speak across the color line?[5]

Johnson began his novel, which he would publish anonymously as nonfiction, in the midst of making his decision to leave songwriting, and completed it while working as US Consul in Latin America. While abroad, he received letters from his brother and his wife urging him to return to songwriting and to New York. In one, Rosamond assures him that there "is easy money in vaudeville" and insists "there is no future for you in the consular service compared with your possibilities in putting up some good musical plays."[6] It is not surprising that Johnson's novel dwells, if somewhat obliquely, on the struggles of the world he had only just left behind in a departure he later described, in his memoir, as "an escape." As Joseph T. Skerrett Jr. has noted, the ex-colored man similarly "escapes" the New York entertainment scene. While Johnson's narrator is clearly no simple mouthpiece for Johnson himself, both "escape" their efforts to write African American music or to write American music that draws upon African American musical traditions, only to write "autobiographies" that remain preoccupied with those efforts.[7] One could argue that the slippery generic status of the novel—which would not be published as fiction, with Johnson's name attached, until 1927—highlights its author's struggle to convey the truth about race in America. Indeed, the text's internal generic inconsistencies, as it vacillates between narration and what one critic calls "intrusively didactic speeches and gratuitous remarks on black culture," underscore a tension between fiction and nonfiction that could also describe the tension between representation and expression or between what Johnson would call "conscious imitation" and "originality," in the former songwriter's sense of his own African American musical production.[8]

In its focus on the perspective of a modern African American musician, Johnson's *Autobiography of an Ex-Colored Man* offers an important counterpoint to the musical narratives I have discussed so far, even as it resonates with their central motifs. Like Theodore Dreiser's Carrie, Johnson's "ex-colored man" comes to New York with nothing and discovers there a market for his musical talents, which bring him significant financial and social reward but leave him aesthetically frustrated and personally unfulfilled.[9] Like Kate Chopin's and Harold Frederic's pianists, the ex-colored man performs on the piano (and, indeed, performs Frédéric Chopin's music) to white audiences, who crave the difference of his musicality. And like the fictional American divas discussed in chapter 3, he imagines himself channeling the native energies of the American "folk" to produce an American classical music.

But these parallels also highlight the difference of Johnson's representation of American musical life. More than any other novel in this study, *The Autobiography of an Ex-Colored Man* understands musicality as a form of agency, as a marker and producer of social identity, and as a mediator of relationships. As an adolescent, Johnson's narrator earns money for college by playing Beethoven's *Pathétique* sonata to a white Connecticut audience. While living in Jacksonville, he supports himself in part by giving piano lessons that also introduce him to "the best class of colored people" and initiate his "entrance into the race."[10] In New York he supports himself playing ragtime renditions of classics on the piano, a practice that eventually opens "more doors and made [him] a welcome guest than [his] playing of Beethoven and Chopin could ever have done" (115). And, after aborting his idea of composing classical music based on African American themes, he finally encourages a white woman to marry him largely through a convincing performance of Chopin. Music mediates virtually all of the ex-colored man's primary relationships, each of which involves not only a particular musical form, but a particular musical setting that carries with it particular conventions, hierarchies, expectations, and enabling limits. The narrator's versatile musicality allows him to enter both white and black society, to pass as both white and black, and to earn a better living than he could otherwise imagine. His musicality is crucial to the narrative's capacity to reveal the color line with such authority and detail, while it also underscores the degree to which the color line itself constitutes, and thus limits, music's capacity to speak.

"The one true American music"

To fully appreciate the novel's implicit engagement with Johnson's experiences while writing songs with his brother, it is worth devoting some of this chapter to those experiences and to the possibilities and limits faced by Johnson and his colleagues. His entrance into professional music came late in life and marked a dramatic turning point in his social and financial circumstances. In the summer of 1899, while Johnson was working as a high school principal in Jacksonville and studying for the Florida Bar exam, he received a royalty check for a song he and his brother had recently sold. With little hesitation, the thirty year old abandoned the stable professional life he had long worked toward in Jacksonville and rushed to join his brother at the black-run Marshall Hotel on New York's West 53rd Street. Johnson claims he was drawn to this community by its emerging status as a "new centre" for black entertainers that, as he later wrote even as he erased himself from the story, "brought about a revolutionary change in New York artistic life" two decades before the "Harlem Renaissance."[11] Black songwriters, composers, and performers flocked to Manhattan around 1900, drawn like Johnson by a sense of new opportunities: to make good money and, as importantly, to define a central place for black musicians and black musical traditions in mainstream American music.

These opportunities depended on the two emergent musical trends in mainstream culture that promised to involve African American music, and African American musicians, in new definitions of American music in the 1890s.[12] Tin Pan Alley publishers and musical theater producers began to see large profits in the syncopated rhythms of "ragtime" at virtually the same moment that American composers, eager to define a national style, began to appropriate and develop whatever they could claim as native "folk" traditions. While most of these composers turned to Native American music as their source, many were inspired by the "plantation melodies" of slavery that had been transcribed by nineteenth-century music-ethnographers and popularized by black college groups like the Fisk Jubilee Singers. Coming out of different musical spheres, both ragtime and "plantation melodies" were celebrated at this moment as distinctly American and welcome departures from European influence. A decade before Hiram Moderwell proclaimed ragtime as "the one true American music," able to express the "American personality" as "no European music can or possibly could," Dvořák described the "plantation melodies and the slave songs" as "the most potent as well as the most beautiful" examples of "the voice of the people," and the most promising basis for a new national musical style.[13] However, the slave songs, like ragtime, also became the focus of anxious disavowals, and in terms that pointed much more explicitly to a discomfort with their racial significations than did warnings against ragtime's infectious rhythms. Popular as the slave songs became with white Americans, many felt uncomfortable with the idea that they could or should speak for all Americans. Music historian Rupert Hughes, for example, dismissed African American slave music as "in no sense a national expression" and "as foreign a music as any Tyrolean jodel [*sic*] or Hungarian czardas."[14] (The debates over ragtime and slave songs are more thoroughly discussed in the introduction.) In his *Souls of Black Folk*, W. E. B. Du Bois directly contradicts such pronouncements by devoting his final chapter entirely to the new American appropriations of slave songs, which he insists are the "sole American music." As Ronald Radano has suggested, Du Bois's chapter underscores the threat this music potentially represents to white America, by giving music no less than the power to "put into motion a 'transformation' destabilizing the whiteness and oneness of American life."[15] Where white musicians and audiences might have seen novelty, "national" spirit, or "foreign" sounds, black musicians saw an opportunity to redefine, through music, the very idea of what it means to be "American."

The career of Harry T. Burleigh, a musician in Johnson's circle and one of the best-known black composers of this moment, reveals some of the consequences for black musicians of this emerging interest in slave music.

Widely held to be the first black composer to incorporate black musical forms in "classical" works, Burleigh considered Dvořák's own use of a "slave song" in his "Symphony of the New World" to be a milestone in music history: "[The 1893 premiere] was the first time in the history of music that a Negro's song had been a major theme in a great symphonic work." Burleigh earned a scholarship to the National Conservatory in 1892 where he befriended Dvořák and claims to have influenced the composer's conception of the "slave songs": "I feel sure the composer caught this peculiarity [a flat seventh] of most of the slaves songs from some that I sang to him; for he used to stop me and ask if that was the way the slaves sang."[16] Burleigh received training in both African American and European musical traditions, learning spirituals from his mother and grandmother and studying classical voice and piano through the encouragement of his mother's white employers. After moving to New York, Burleigh maintained and combined these paths, composing works based on African American music and performing as singer in, and then director of, the choir at St. George's Episcopal Church (a predominantly white congregation). Burleigh's acceptance into this white community seemed to rest, according to biographer Anne Simpson, on his mastery of European musical conventions as well as his capacity and willingness occasionally to perform "Negro songs." Though he spent many of his evenings with the Johnsons and others at the Marshall Hotel, Burleigh established himself outside musical theater, which was clearly the more remunerative route, although he purportedly composed popular songs under a pseudonym, thus reaping financial rewards without damaging his emerging reputation as a "serious" musician. Like the ex-colored man, Burleigh's career was boosted by a white millionaire's interest in his particular musical style. J. Pierpont Morgan, a member of St. George's, found himself "so immediately and completely smitten" with Burleigh's voice that he hired him for private parties in his home and the homes of his friends.[17] Burleigh was famous for his numerous instrumental and "art song" arrangements of spirituals, as well as for his settings of African American texts such as Paul Lawrence Dunbar's "An Antebellum Sermon." All of this work helped to carve out a central place for African American traditions within the highbrow forms and venues of classical music.

Unlike Burleigh, however, most of the crowd on West 53rd had moved from the conservatory into musical theater as opportunities arose. Their training in composition and classical styles and forms allowed them to take ownership of, and to market, their songs at a moment when the publication of sheet music was a burgeoning industry closely tied to the growing popularity of Broadway musical theater. While black performers were for the most part constrained to working for little pay in black clubs, a number of black musicians with skill in notation and an ear for the mainstream began to find work as both songwriters and performers in musical theater. Many of these musicians were drawn to New York and to musical theater by the several new all-black variety shows suddenly popular in the late 1890s. By hiring the "best-trained Negro singers and musicians then available" and by diversifying their minstrel repertory with such novelties as a "cakewalk jubilee" and "operatic kaleidoscope," all-black shows like *Oriental America* and *A Trip to Coontown* started a new wave of black musical theater and, at the same time, brought more African American musicians to the attention of white producers, publishers, and audiences.[18] One of these musicians was Johnson's brother Rosamond, who joined *Oriental America* after six years of studying composition at the New England Conservatory of Music.

Rosamond Johnson's early career, as his brother describes it, demonstrates his facility across different musical traditions and his awareness of the benefits this facility afforded a black musician. After a year with *Oriental America*, Rosamond returned for a brief stint as a "classical" musician back in Jacksonville, working as choirmaster, teacher, and organist. According to his brother, his students' recitals at that time "set a new standard" in Jacksonville musical performance and "started local white music lovers coming to concerts by colored people." During this period, James, then a high school principal, joined Rosamond to write a comic opera in the style of Gilbert and Sullivan, which brought further notice from local whites. Rosamond played through the opera on the piano at a party that James describes as "the first inter-racial artistic party in our experience." In 1899 the brothers took their opera to New York, where they found that their songs, if not the opera as a whole, seemed to "open doors by magic" and very quickly plunged them into the limelight of an increasingly "inter-racial" musical sphere.[19]

Eventually, the Johnsons, like most songwriters at this time, were producing songs that "ragged"—that used syncopated rhythms—and that often depicted black characters speaking dialect in scenarios rooted in the still-popular conventions of blackface minstrelsy. Trained in European-American forms of composition and songwriting and able to claim a privileged relationship to the black "source" of the genre, the Johnson brothers found themselves with both the opportunity and the burden to "represent" black music and identity by pushing against the boundaries of minstrel conventions. The ragtime of black culture was, of course, already a "hybrid" form, combining the rhythms and harmonies of African American expressive culture with the Euro-American march form. While the "line" between white and black might have been heard within the music as an implied tension between downbeats and syncopated off-beats, it persisted more dramatically among musicians as a difference between "trained" musicians who wrote down their songs, marketing them as sheet music, and those for whom music remained an oral practice, inseparable from performance. (Chapter 3 noted how a similar line gave Cather's Thea Kronborg a kind of power over Spanish Johnny's musicality, when she proposed writing down his song so she [not he] could perform it in the concert hall.) Like their white counterparts, black songwriters seeking mainstream success crossed *this* line by producing notated versions of what had been a vernacular, and largely improvised, practice. By crossing this line, black musicians expressed their "blackness," whether or not this was, in fact, their goal, through the musical technology of white culture. They also were in a position, whether dark- or light-skinned, to pass as white, since their music was now detachable from their bodies. Indeed, the Johnsons, whose sheet music covers often featured photographs of the white performers who popularized the songs rather than the black songwriters, occasionally were presumed to be white, particularly by audiences outside New York.[20] Since their songs were heard and purchased by white audiences/amateurs and, in the case of the Johnsons and and their partner Bob Cole, performed for the most part by white singers, these black songwriters had in effect infiltrated an institution central to the production of racial ideology.

The majority of "rag" songs being published in the 1890s and early 1900s were referred to as "coon songs," which—like most of the dialect fiction also popular at this time—promoted a very narrow, racist set of stereotyped plantation scenarios and "happy darky" characters. In their many contributions to this genre, the Johnsons and Cole might be said to have achieved mainstream success by wearing a black mask, just as Jewish performers like Al Jolson and Irving Berlin, as some scholars suggest, achieved their success (and their "whiteness") by donning blackface.[21] But the Johnsons saw themselves neither as recuperating some kind of black authenticity nor as simply performing an inauthentic blackface and instead worked quite seriously to transform racial stereotype from within one of its most popular and powerful media. Their strategies from "within" were several, and, indeed, Johnson recalls many heated discussions about how much assimilation to the white mainstream was desirable or necessary to achieve their goals. While at least one scholar has identified a pronounced strain of irony and parody in many of the "coon songs" composed by blacks at this time, the Johnsons adhered primarily to the more genteel idea of "elevating" stereotypes through "artistry."[22] Johnson lamented the "crude, raucous, bawdy, often obscene" elements of this song genre and wrote that even though such qualities "frequently are excellencies in folksongs," they "are rarely so in conscious imitations." Rather than simply imitate the already popular "imitations" of "crude" "folksongs," his team instead tried to imitate the genre with a "higher degree of artistry."[23] In effect, they approached their task in much the same terms as Dvořák or Burleigh, as artists transforming the raw material of the folk into a higher aesthetic form. The black press celebrated the Johnsons' songs in just these terms; one critic praises their ability to "blend . . . the music of the Negro enslaved [with] the intellectual strivings of a newer life, prompted by study of purely classical lore"; this "blend," he continues, bespeaks a "new spirit, peculiarly American."[24] The fact that the Johnsons' music relied less on "the music of the Negro enslaved" than on the minstrel tradition of mainstream white popular culture seems less important, here, than the "peculiarly American" spirit of a hybrid musicality.

Indeed, Johnson remained well aware of the degree to which he and his companions were all engaged in some kind of "conscious imitation," whether composing popular song or art music. The problem, for these musicians, was how best to complicate their audiences' narrow assumptions about black identity with these representations, which would *inevitably* remain something very different from the music produced by the black "folk." It is this awareness of the problem of musical representation, I will argue, that becomes a central preoccupation of *The Autobiography of an Ex-Colored Man*. Johnson's veiled, fictionalized gesture toward this moment in American music gives voice to the efforts of his group, and surely to his own investment as songwriter in their ambitions, while it ultimately represents their efforts at producing "hybrid," newly "American" music as an impossible task within early twentieth-century American culture. This impossibility, the novel suggests, lies in the color line that persists not only in the music industry's ongoing investment in racial stereotypes but in the very project of "blending" a tradition that is rooted in notation and imitation with one that is rooted in oral performance. Critics have noted the degree to which *The Autobiography* exposes all identity as a matter of "imitation"—and thus exposes "race" as a learned rather than inherited set of characteristics—but the novel nonetheless upholds a distinction between original and copy in its insistence on a modern black musicality whose *meanings*—whose values, effects, and significations—cannot be reproduced outside of its original social and material context. The black musicality of the vast majority of black people, for whom music speaks in the context of social ritual rather than disembodied text or stage performance, can only, for Johnson's novel, be represented as that which cannot be represented and thus cannot participate in a hybrid, national musical voice.

"Something they've never had before"

Like Rosamond Johnson and Harry Burleigh, the ex-colored man receives formal training as a classical musician, training that prepares him for his ragtime performances as well as his compositional ambitions. But Johnson is careful to include in his narrator's youth a different form of training that precedes and qualifies his piano lessons: the distinctly African American style that the ex-colored man hears in his mother's piano playing and singing. "When she was not sewing" for the white women of the neighborhood, we learn, and as an alternative to her Sunday practice of playing "hymns from the book," the ex-colored man's mother would sing "old Southern songs" in the performance of which "she was freer, because she played them by ear" (8). By setting her "freer" style of singing "by ear" against both her labor and "the book," Johnson suggests a complicity between her white employers and their musical practice, both of which work, however subtly, to confine her.

The source of these alternative and freer musical impulses is not explicitly named at this point in the narrative, which precedes the narrator's "racial" consciousness. But Johnson makes sure to gesture toward an invisible, absent black cultural referent enigmatically coloring the mother's performance and pathos: "Always on such evenings, when the music was over, my mother would sit with me in her arms, often for a very long time. She would hold me close, softly crooning some old melody without words, all the while gently stroking her face against my head. . . . I can see her now, her great dark eyes looking into the fire, to where? No one knew but her" (8). In imagining her point of reference as private and solitary, the narrator (if not the author and reader) remains unaware of the social context of her musical memory, its basis in a southern black community that he will only encounter for the first time later in his life, as an outsider. His own musical impulses, influenced by his mother, will find expression through the instruments, institutions, and genres of the north, a world, in his experience, predominantly white and middle class. But before taking piano lessons from the local white teacher, Johnson's narrator recalls how he responded to his mother's playing by joining her in a kind of "call and response": "I used to stand by her side and often interrupt and annoy her by chiming in with strange harmonies. . . . I remember I had a particular fondness for the black keys" (8). His "chiming in" carries on, more aggressively than his mother would like, an oral tradition, whose racial basis is, perhaps, symbolized by his preference for "black" keys.

The narrator eventually asserts this style learned, and perhaps inherited, from his mother at his first piano lesson where, in response to his teacher's attempt at "pinning [him] down to the notes," he chooses instead "to reproduce the required sounds without the slightest recourse to the written characters" (9). Similarly eluding convention, the narrator approaches the piano as a "sympathetic, singing instrument," a manner he attributes "to the fact that I did not begin to learn the piano by counting out exercises, but by trying to reproduce the quaint songs which my mother used to sing, with all their pathetic turns and cadences" (26, 27). Resistant to printed "notes" and to "counting out exercises," the narrator learns by ear, thus inserting himself into an oral tradition even in the midst of his training in the text-based tradition of European classical music. This scene highlights the narrator's tendency, to be repeated several times in the novel, toward a hybridizing musicality, while it also, already, suggests the inherent contradiction between oral and textual musical practices. Understood as "natural" rather than disciplined, vocal rather than instrumental, oral rather than textual, and improvisatory rather than composed, his mother's southern songs invoke a black space of freedom that seems rooted in its difference and separation from white cultural practices. (The narrator also unsettles the boundary between piano and voice—which, as we've seen, carry with them different sets of associations and symbolic possibilities at the turn of the twentieth century.)

The narrator's youthful impulses to blend musical traditions, and to thus resist silencing his mother's voice in his performances of European piano music, go largely unnoticed by his white audiences, who simply hear him as a talented black boy worthy of financial reward. Early in the text, the narrator's white father offers his only display of emotion toward his son upon hearing him play Frédéric Chopin: "My father stepped across the room, seized me in his arms, and squeezed me to his breast. I am certain that for that moment he was proud to be my father" (35). While far removed from the scenes of Catholic women playing Chopin to vulnerable Protestant audiences (the focus of chapter 2), this Chopin performance is similarly structured by the difference between performer and audience, which momentarily dissolves in the emotion the music arouses. Their intimacy, however, quickly dissipates as his father returns to his white family and rewards his son's performance with the gift of an upright piano, which, the narrator notes, is "not a grand" (40). This gift sends a familiar message to the black artist aspiring to succeed in "European" cultural practices: however talented he might be, the pianist will never surpass the level of amateur. Furthermore, by rewarding his son's performance with a gift rather than any sustained supportive relationship, his father underscores what will become an increasingly problematic condition for the ex-colored man's performances: the reward of success in white America is also its cost as music's expressive value becomes overshadowed and indeed displaced by its exchange value on a market determined by white audiences.

Ragtime holds much greater promise in this novel for, as Radano puts it, "destabilizing the whiteness and oneness of American life"—and, indeed, most of the critical focus on music in this novel attends to its representations of ragtime. On the narrator's first night in New York City, he finds himself in a black nightclub "dazzled and dazed" not only by gambling, alcohol, and the "brilliancy" of the atmosphere but also by a music that is new to him: "I stopped talking to listen. It was music of a kind I had never heard before. It was music that demanded physical response, patting of the feet, drumming of the fingers, or nodding of the head in time with the beat. The barbaric harmonies; the audacious resolutions, often consisting of an abrupt jump from one key to another; the intricate rhythms in which the accents fell in the most unexpected places, but in which the beat was never lost, produced a most curious effect" (98–99). It was this "curious effect"—the music's irresistible and seemingly "barbaric" arousal of the body—that inspired anxious debate and many urgent calls for ragtime's suppression mentioned earlier. By its aggressively syncopated beats and "abrupt" changes of key, ragtime broke with the dominant rhythmic and harmonic conventions of European music and, in so doing, "demanded" new ways of hearing. It also potentially accorded black musicians a new kind of power over white bodies.

Through his narrator, Johnson proceeds to underscore the significance of ragtime as a black contribution to American culture in a long passage that has been excerpted more than once in histories of black music. In insisting upon the African American origins of this music, Johnson's narrator casts white ragtime performers as "imitators" and "adulterators" who, in effect, have stolen both the music and its rewards (99–100). These imitators, the narrator insists, are doomed to mediocrity by virtue of the very skills that allow them to reproduce what they hear as notation. The pianist in the "Club" achieves the status of originator and rightful owner precisely because he *can't* write his music down, being untrained in a skill that, according to the narrator, might allow him to better market his music but would destroy its authenticity. The narrator introduces the ragtime pianist as "just a natural musician, never having taken a lesson in his life," whose relation to music is, in other words, entirely unlike his own:

> He had, by ear alone, composed some pieces, several of which he played over for me; each of them was properly proportioned and balanced. I began to wonder what this man with such a lavish natural endowment would have done had he been trained. Perhaps he wouldn't have done anything at all; he might have become, at best, a mediocre imitator of the great masters in what they have already done to a finish, or one of the modern innovators who strive after originality by seeing how cleverly they can dodge about through the rules of harmony and at the.same time avoid melody. It is certain that he would not have been so delightful as he was in ragtime. (101–2)

This moment articulates a line between "untrained" and "trained" that, if not racial, nonetheless suggests—like his mother's musical difference from his piano teacher—a line between black and white musical traditions. For the ragtime pianist as for the narrator's mother, both "natural" musicians who play "by ear," music remains inseparable from the moment of its performance and the body of its performer. The "trained" musician, on the other hand, is doomed either to "imitate" or to "strive after originality" in an artificial, and ultimately sterile, manner.

As a trained musician, the narrator seems inevitably to occupy the scurrilous position of "imitator," though Johnson reserves a privileged place for the *black* imitator who, like his circle at the Marshall Hotel, is in a position to bring "a higher degree of artistry" to black music's place in mainstream American culture. "Through continually listening to the music at the 'Club,' and through my own previous training, my natural talent and perseverance, I developed into a remarkable player of ragtime. . . . I brought all my knowledge of classic music to bear and, in so doing, achieved some novelties which pleased and even astonished my listeners. It was I who first made ragtime transcriptions of familiar classic selections" (114–15). By producing "ragtime transcriptions of familiar classic selections," the ex-colored man makes no pretense of authenticity but instead utilizes all aspects of his musical background and nature to create something overtly derivative that is also an original fusion of two "racial" traditions. More than his performances of European music allowed him to do, by "ragging the classics" he performs an African American "transformation" of the "required sounds" of European American performance practice and repertoire.

This "novel" performance style also promises him more financial and social rewards than his classical performances, and Johnson takes great pains to represent his narrator's new relationship to white audiences: "By mastering ragtime I gained several things: first of all I gained the title of professor. . . . Then, too, I gained the means of earning a rather fair livelihood. . . . Through it I also gained a friend who was the means by which I escaped from this lower world. And, finally, I secured a wedge which has opened to me more doors and made me a welcome guest than my playing of Beethoven and Chopin could ever have done" (115). This account of ragtime's cultural capital—as it grows to become greater even than that of Beethoven and Chopin—underscores why such classically trained black musicians as Rosamond Johnson would gravitate toward popular music in the 1890s. Moreover, it emphasizes the degree to which white audiences—like the narrator's new millionaire "friend"—seemed to approve of and reward a musical practice that entwined black culture with the more familiar context of the "classics." But while open to the black sounds of this music, the narrator's audience ultimately fixes both performer and music as projections of their seemingly unquenchable desire. The millionaire, who rescues him from the "lower world" of New York black culture, hires him to play at private parties in his home and the homes of his friends, all of whom crave, like the millionaire himself, an escape from the ennui of white culture in the consumption of black culture. While his father responded to—and seemed to require—the narrator's musical suppression of his blackness, the more modern millionaire and his friends, ever in search of "a new sensation" or "a fresh emotion," respond specifically to his musical expressions of blackness (119). Although it is not stated, one imagines that he becomes a comfortable bridge for this audience between a black culture perhaps too remote and dangerous (as suggested by the slumming white widow's murder by her jealous black lover) and their own more genteel world. Indeed, it is worth noting that the "natural" black musicians in this novel never play for white audiences, who only ever hear "black music" as it is performed—through imitation, transcription, and incorporation into "white" forms—by the narrator himself.

At first, the narrator enjoys his ability to grab his white listeners' attention with ragtime, as he himself had been grabbed upon first hearing it: "It was a pleasure to me to watch the expression of astonishment and delight that grew on the faces of everybody." True to its reputation of "demanding physical response," the narrator's ragtime creates the "curious effect" of leading "the whole company involuntarily and unconsciously [to dance] an impromptu cake-walk" (119–20). But the narrator's musical agency—his power to propel his white audience to perform a dance that is itself a parody of white culture—remains limited by his position as a commodity bought and paid for by this white audience. As the millionaire boasts at the end of the party: "Well, I have given them something they've never had before" (120). The white listener's desire for novelty and sensation, furthermore, reveals itself less as openness to the coupling of black and white sounds than as addiction to "novelty," addiction that requires the performer and his music to represent and maintain their difference from the (white) familiar. In thus becoming an object of obsessive desire, the narrator finds himself trapped in a seemingly endless performance of the same, represented by the private performances he must give his employer. Playing for three or four hours at a time, "I soon learned that my task was not to be considered finished until he got up from his chair and said: 'That will do.' . . . At times I became so oppressed with fatigue and sleepiness that it took almost superhuman effort to keep my fingers going; in fact, I believe I sometimes did so while dozing. During such moments this man sitting there so mysteriously silent, almost hid in a cloud of heavy-scented smoke, filled me with a sort of unearthly terror. He seemed to be some grim, mute, but relentless tyrant, possessing over me a supernatural power which he used to drive me on mercilessly to exhaustion" (121). The successful ragtime pianist thus experiences a link between commodification and the color line: as "ragging" acquires commercial value, repeatedly offered up for the consumption of white audiences, the critical and historical difference of its "blackness"—its basis in an inimitable and thus "freer" oral culture—becomes inaudible, as does any effort to unsettle the line between white and black.

The ex-colored man's final plan to write classical music based on Negro themes seems at first like a way out of the bind of ragtime, while it ultimately brings back into sharp focus the inescapably paradoxical situation of the "trained" black musician. Like all of his preceding musical innovations, this one involves imitation and improvisation. The very idea of making black music "classical" arises when he performs his ragtime transcriptions for a German musician who uses his own "training" to further develop this hybrid form: "He seated himself at the piano, and, taking the theme of my ragtime, played it through first in straight chords; then varied and developed it through every known musical form. I sat amazed. I had been turning classic music into ragtime, a comparatively easy task; and this man had taken ragtime and made it classic. The thought came across me like a flash—It can be done, why can't I do it?" (142). Ironically, the narrator is led back to black musical "origins" by hearing a German imitating and developing his own developed imitations of the "natural" ragtime pianist. The place of German musicality in the evolution of the narrator's musical style is crucial and takes us momentarily outside the field of American musical practices and into what was then considered the apex of European musical culture. Furthermore, unlike the narrator's white American audiences, this German pianist clearly appreciates and is himself interested in the hybridity at the heart of "ragging the classics." But in seizing upon the German's idea as a new possibility for situating his own bimusicality in American culture, the narrator once again finds himself threatening to silence the very "blackness" that he now quite explicitly hopes to make audible.

This is the first moment when the narrator imagines the possibility of creating American *classical* music based on African American themes. While the narrator had to argue for the significance of ragtime as an expressive form, he treats the potential cultural significance of an African American symphony—and the potential status of its composer as a "great Negro"—as self-evident. It remains quite difficult to determine Johnson's point of view in this part of the novel. On the one hand, the idea of the Negro composer recovers, for the narrator and for the trained black musician, a marked degree of freedom from the exploitative social and economic conditions surrounding the ragtime performer.[25] On the other, the narrator's project reproduces the very assumptions about the superiority of "trained" musicians that his earlier account of the black ragtime pianist strove to problematize. As he travels "back into the very heart of the South, to live among the people, and drink my inspiration firsthand," Johnson's language characterizes his narrator's stance toward "the people" as self-serving and piratical (142). The ex-colored man's relationship to black musical traditions, indeed, seems to become more fraught the more he tries to "imitate" them, reaching an extreme in his assumption that the raw "material" of black music is there for his taking: "I gloated over the immense amount of material I had to work with, not only modern ragtime, but also the old slave songs—material which no one had yet touched" (142–43). While he granted the "natural" ragtime player the status of originator, he seems here to assume that only the trained musician's "touching" of this material counts, while discounting the very "people" whose inspired performances he "drink[s] . . . firsthand." Traveling about various communities, the narrator echoes the work of postbellum ethnographers, "jotting down in my note-book themes and melodies, and trying to catch the spirit of the Negro in his relatively primitive state" (173).

The novel, however, refuses the narrator any significant success in this project and soon charts his transformation from an active musical subject, for whom "the South" exists as the raw material of his own artistry, to a passive recipient of southern musicality, which undermines his sense of agency and renders him silent. On his last stop at a "big meeting" that promises "a mine of material," he witnesses "Singing Johnson," whose function is to bring the large congregation together in song. With "every ear in the church . . . fixed upon him," Singing Johnson sings out "leading lines" that the congregation respond to in the "call and response" form of African American song (178). In what becomes a prelude to the novel's most dramatic turning point, the narrator's anthropological detachment suddenly breaks down in the overwhelming presence of these sounds and their collective performance: "As I listened to the singing of these songs, the wonder of their production grew upon me. . . . So many of these songs contain more than mere melody; there is sounded in them that elusive undertone, the note in music which is not heard with the ears. I sat often with the tears rolling down my cheeks and my heart melted within me. Any musical person who has never heard a Negro congregation under the spell of religious fervor sing these old songs has missed one of the most thrilling emotions which the human heart may experience" (181). Rather than moving from this "thrilling" musical "experience" to his own musical agency (as did Cather's Thea Kronborg after singing with Mexicans), this scene marks an end of the narrator's ambition to produce a new (African) American music. Echoing Frederick Douglass's claim that no one could hear the slave songs without being moved by them to tears (and to oppose slavery) and anticipating Zora Neale Hurston's insistence that spirituals must be heard in their original contexts to be fully understood, Johnson's narrator here relinquishes his own musical authority—based as it is on the ability to imitate and to notate—to that of Singing Johnson and of the Negro congregation.[26] As in Douglass's narrative, we are aware here of the narrator's dual position as character and writer: while the character cedes musical authority to a source that remains inaccessible to the reader, the narrator reclaims authority as the one who can, through his autobiographical narrative if not his musical score, let us know the significance of that which we cannot hear.

This scene marks the end of the narrator's musical aspirations, while it immediately precedes his flight from the South and from his own identification with blackness. Upon witnessing a black man being lynched, which, like his experience of the congregation singing, renders him silent and overwhelmed, the narrator is driven by "shame, unbearable shame" to abandon his black identity along with his musical project and move to New York to live as a white businessman. What this narrative turn suggests about the ex-colored man's relationship to music, and Johnson's attitude about his narrator's musical project, remains difficult to answer. The narrator's "shame" at being identified with a race subject to the brutal violence of lynchings encompasses, I would like to think, his shame, also, at having occupied the position of one who could "mine" the "raw material" of black music for white American audiences who might countenance (and even desire to witness) the lynching of black people. After his experience at the "big meeting," whose southern, collective, religious context defines its musical value for him, it is difficult to imagine how he would translate this value into a symphony or oratorio to be performed by professional musicians on a stage before a paying, silent, presumably white audience, an audience perhaps eager to own and consume the sounds of blackness.

The narrator's abandonment of blackness is punctuated by his ensuing marriage to whiteness, a marriage that once again draws our attention to music's capacity to perform, and mask, racial identity. Upon his return to New York, the narrator, now passing as white, and a woman who is "white as a lily" (198) fall in love through their "mutual bond of music" (201)—and specifically through their mutual enjoyment of the music of Chopin, which displaces ragtime as the narrator's signature music, now casually performed at cocktail parties. While their plan to marry is almost permanently stalled by the narrator's revelation of his racial heritage, the partnership is saved, as it began, by Chopin. Here, if not able to erase his blackness, the narrator's performance of Chopin at least succeeds in dissolving his beloved's resistance to miscegenation, by convincing her that his blackness can remain inaudible, and thus nonsignifying. Underscoring the emptiness of the urban middle-class white society he is about to join, Johnson's narrator performs one last improvisatory act, altering the "required sounds" of Chopin's piece so that it ends on a major rather than a minor chord, thus announcing a "happy" ending (209). While this musical act might be taken to signify his ongoing playfulness with both music and racial identity (as at least one critic has suggested), it seems on the contrary an ironic signal of the end of his more ambitious and interesting musical experiments, in capitulation to a banal cliché of (white) musical convention.[27]

This novel's ending clearly registers, among other things, Johnson's disillusionment with the various projects of turn-of-the-century American music promising to bring African American music into mainstream American culture. Standing in the way of a truly cross-cultural musical and national expression, Johnson implies, are obstacles not only of racism but also of an American "culture industry" that reifies racial difference, as it depends on the repeatability, marketability, and novelty of its products, separates performer and audience into commodity and consumer, and erases the social history of musical styles and forms. The narrator's efforts to express "blackness" within the dominant forms of white musical expression seem ultimately complicit in the silencing of black culture. Johnson's novel finally gestures to the idea of an authentic black music as existing essentially outside the domain of the American culture industry, defined not by distinct sounds, rhythms, and melodies so much as the distinct social rituals and relations that produce it. Thus defined, black music becomes inaccessible to anyone outside its social economy and thus loses its power to transform the "required sounds" of mainstream white America, while it remains invulnerable to (or at least imaginatively distinct from) efforts to "mine" its resources for commercial or cultural reward.

Finally, we should not discount the ex-colored man's last creative project, which is neither the aborted symphony nor his whitened performance of Chopin but rather his writing of his autobiography. The status of writing, as a process of translating the "elusive" spirit into a tangible, marketable, and repeatable artifact, has by the end of Johnson's novel been thoroughly problematized by the narrator's various experiments in cultural synthesis. Indeed, rather than preserving the narrator's "dead ambition" to give voice to his African American heritage, the "yellowing manuscripts" on the novel's final page can themselves, as text, only silently gesture to a musical world that lives off the page. And yet, in acknowledging the cultural cost of his attempts to revise, inspirit, and transform America's musical traditions by way of African American ones, the narrator remains committed to the project of writing and of crossing the "color line" *through* writing that cannot claim to represent, or reproduce, but can nonetheless silently gesture to a black musicality independent from, and inaudible to, the industries of American music.

Johnson's decision in 1905 to leave songwriting and turn instead to politics and literature reflected his growing sense of the limits of his work in musical theater: "Being light enough for Broadway," he writes in his memoirs, "was beginning to be, it seemed, a somewhat heavy task."[28] As, perhaps, its novelty wore off, the vogue for black music and musical theater would considerably wane in the 1910s, revealing the degree to which his group depended on the desires of white audiences. In December 1913, after a period of pronounced success in London, Rosamond wrote a letter to his brother that describes his own efforts to remain optimistic in spite of diminishing opportunities: "I have had a very hard drive of it, and just at the time when it looked like easy sailing—long came the storm. But they haven't licked me yet, they've knocked me down, but they haven't knocked me out. . . . If I keep my health, I am bound to find some work to do, and I am never afraid to tackle it no matter how hard, or embarrassing it may seem I've got to get hold of some real money, and I am willing to work work work and then work some more for it."[29] Rosamond and others would find work again, of course, in the various new musical venues of 1920s New York, but with a different sense of their relationship to both American culture at large and to African American identity in particular. With the growing emphasis on racial authenticity in black cultural production, African American musicians of the 1920s were involved in more racially specific expressive forms and gestures, as, with the birth of "race records" and a growing black urban audience, was the music industry itself.

Indeed, the Johnsons would become partners again in their publication of *The Books of American Negro Spirituals* (1925, 1926), a project that, unlike the ex-colored man's and Harry Burleigh's efforts to work the spirituals into "classic European form," attempts to reproduce them "authentically" as they once were. But in spite of this turn to the preservation of an authentic black culture, Johnson's preface makes very clear that such a project is itself inherently problematic and contradictory. Proclaiming their attempt "to recreate around [the spiritual] as completely as we can its true atmosphere," Johnson acknowledges the impossibility of totally recreating the original social context of the spirituals in their textual reproduction, and emphasizes the failure of European notation adequately to represent the nuances and improvisational performances of this music: "I doubt that it is possible with our present system of notation to make a fixed transcription of these peculiarities that would be absolutely true; for in their very nature they are not susceptible to fixation."[30] By acknowledging their status as "imitators" incapable of thoroughly translating one musical language into another, Johnson thus acknowledges his own difference from those now absent musicians whose music he wishes to preserve, at the same time that he delivers a deeply felt tribute to that different, improvised, oral culture of another moment in black cultural history.[31]

In spite of his implicit critiques of the racial politics of turn-of-the-century American music, Johnson at moments looked back with definite nostalgia at his stint as songwriter. I would like to close by describing Johnson's notes to a musical play he entitled "Down the Nile," which he may have intended as a vehicle for reviving the songs written by the Johnsons and Cole at the turn of the century. The first and only completed scene describes the household of a famous African American composer, whose "Negro Symphony" has been performed by the National Symphony and who thus embodies what the ex-colored man might have become (Johnson calls him only "Great Colored American Composer"). Through the nostalgic musings of the composer's housekeeper, we learn that this man once wrote popular songs, songs that the housekeeper decidedly prefers to his more recent output: "I'm certainly sorry he's started writing this newfangled[32] music—no tune to it," she says; "This here Negro Symphony—the only thing Negro about it is the name." The housekeeper is soon joined by the composer's devoted student, who initially scorns her lowbrow taste, but quickly finds himself moved by shared memories to sit at the piano and play some of these old songs. The titles Johnson indicates in his manuscript—"Nile—Congo—Bamboo"—clearly refer, in shorthand, to the most famous hits of the Johnsons and Cole: "Castle on the Nile," "The Congo Love Song," and "Under the Bamboo Tree."[33]

More explicit than any references in *The Autobiography of an Ex-Colored Man*, this insertion of his own contributions to musical history attributes their value not to their "higher degree of artistry" but to their popularity with audiences (here black rather than white), unlimited by any claims to racial authenticity. The scene clearly sides with the housekeeper's preference for tuneful songs over avant-garde symphonies that neither entertain nor seem connected to, even as they claim to speak for, black experience.

The housekeeper's nostalgia harkens back to more than just the songs of her employer. It suggests Johnson's own problematic nostalgia for a moment of "trained" black musical production that, before the explosion of the more racialized expressions of the 1920s, held out the promise of a biracial American musicality.

5
Fictions of the American Music Critic

> Music is a living thing for me, as living as any vital organism. It lives when it enters the porches of my ears, and it is a living memory. To write about it is quite hopeless.
>
> —James Huneker, *Steeplejack*

In its focus on music's place in American literature at the turn of the twentieth century, this book has been concerned, among other things, with the relationship between music and writing. To write about music, for the fiction addressed here, is to consider the nature and effects of music as well as to confront the gap between musical and textual expression. These realist/naturalist projects seem haunted by a musicality that promises not only to represent but also to make audible, and thus to make tangibly *present*, otherwise hidden truths, realities, and pockets of the self. At the same time, the novels considered here draw attention to the social circumstances that exert pressure on and qualify music's "realist" claims, by containing its potential for unmediated expressivity within conventional social meanings and performance situations. Dreiser, for example, presents Carrie's musical sensitivity as at once a sign of her freedom from fixed social identity and her marketability as a new kind of urban performer. Cather's brilliant singer similarly remains trapped within a musical space that allows her to channel the "stream of life" and, at the same time, confines her within a white, urban, leisure-class cultural milieu that renders her musical sources—Native American, Mexican, rural—invisible and silent. James Weldon Johnson's novel at once celebrates African American musical difference and music's potential for breaking down the foundations of racial ideology, while also recognizing music's inevitable reduction, by a racist, capitalist culture, to a titillating commodity, marketed to an enervated white America. To write, for Johnson's alienated narrator, is to retain a degree of agency over black self-representation, even as it removes the writer from scenes of embodied musical expressivity and community.

Indeed, James Huneker might speak for all the writers considered here: "To write about [music] is quite hopeless."

Only those with a serious interest in American classical music at the turn of the twentieth century would be likely to read William J. Henderson's *Soul of a Tenor* (1912) and Huneker's *Painted Veils* (1920), two novels that dwell specifically on what it means to write about music. If they pale as literature beside the other novels considered in this study, these two works give us access to the imaginations of two of the most significant music critics of their era. Both set in the context of opera culture in turn-of-the-century New York City, these novels underscore a number of central problems that have emerged in this study. Like *Song of the Lark* and *Tower of Ivory*, they consider what it means to be a white American singer of European opera. Like *Sister Carrie* and *Autobiography of an Ex-Colored Man*, they raise questions about the commodification of music and of the authentic experience it promises to deliver. And like all of the works included here, they associate American music and musical experience with a dramatic unsettling and redrawing of the boundaries and grounds of the lived experience of national identity. More than the other novels, however, both *Painted Veils* and *Soul of a Tenor* directly thematize the problem and process of writing about music through their inclusion of music critics as central characters. Fiction writing offers Henderson and Huneker a space to explore their own embodied, and embattled, position as writers within a music scene that includes a tangled web of relationships among musicians, audiences, critics, and those who pay the bills. These relationships become the locus, in both novels, of gender trouble and particularly of a troubled masculinity, as the critic struggles to define his difference and distance from a feminized opera culture that powerfully attracts him. This attraction at once legitimates the critic's claim to understand music and renders the act of writing truthfully about it particularly "hopeless."

Music critics enjoyed tremendous authority in American musical life at the turn of the century, shaping the evolving taste of concertgoers, determining the career paths of professional musicians, and navigating a rapidly changing musical world for their readers. Joseph Horowitz, who writes that "music critics, one hundred years ago, were influential, not marginal, purveyors of taste and opinion," suggests that no European city "ever hosted a more distinguished group of music journalists than the one headed by Henry Krehbiel, James Huneker, and William J. Henderson, the outstanding New York critics of the Wagnerite era."[1] Henderson began writing music reviews in 1883, the year the Metropolitan Opera House joined the

Academy of Music to give New York the busiest opera season to date, leading the *New York Times* to invest, for the first time, in two staff music critics. Besides reviewing concerts first for the *Times* and then the *New York Sun*, Henderson also joined several of his critic colleagues in writing books aimed at novice audiences, with titles including *What is Good Music?* (1898), *How Music Developed* (1899), *The Orchestra and Orchestral Music* (1902), and *Richard Wagner* (1901). Henderson was an expert in the history of vocal music and his *Art of the Singer* (1906) was long considered a standard text for singers-in-training as well as interested operagoers.[2]

Huneker, meanwhile, established his authority as music editor at the *New York Sun* and was best known as a champion of modernism who tended, unlike his more conservative colleague, to look down his nose on neophyte American concertgoers and write instead for a more sophisticated audience. In addition to his daily reviews, Huneker wrote books and essays about a much wider aesthetic field, elaborating his provocative positions on modern music, literature, and art in such titles as *Mezzotints in Modern Music* (1899), *Iconoclasts: A Book of Dramatists* (1905), *Egoists: A Book of Supermen* (1909), and *Ivory, Apes, and Peacocks* (1915). He also wrote, as mentioned in chapter 2, what was long considered the definitive biography of Frédéric Chopin, whose music he championed.[3]

Both Henderson and Huneker voiced skepticism about the emerging forms of musical nationalism, tending to the more cosmopolitan position that good music transcends the particulars of its time and place, or, as Henderson put it, is "nothing but music."[4] Both also maintained the idea, dominant within European musical thought since the early nineteenth century, that musical value lies in compositions rather than in performances and that it is the performer's job *not* to draw attention to him or herself but to serve the musical score and, thus, the composer's musical genius.[5] Similarly, both critics downplayed the importance of their own subjective attitudes about music and insisted on calling themselves "reporters." Huneker claimed the critic should "tell me a news story" rather than try, inevitably in vain, to "describe a symphony."[6] Henderson imagined his job as that of a reporter, whose beat happened to be the concert hall, and who remained unbiased, objective, and completely divorced from the realm of his imagination or subjective responses: "The only question is, 'can you hear it or can't you?'" he wrote in the *New York Sun*; "Whether an orchestra is out of tune, whether it is out of balance, whether its tone is coarse and vulgar, whether the men are playing with precision and accuracy, whether the strings are poor or the brass blatant are not matters of opinion at all. These are matters of fact and due to be reported upon by persons trained to hear them."[7] Henderson's sense of professional authority, as one "trained" to hear accurately, led him to scorn fictional attempts to capture musical experience. In a *New York Times* column entitled "The Musical Novel," Henderson insisted "there never has been such a thing and probably never will be" as a "musical novel," mainly because most novelists "know absolutely nothing about music or its literature."[8] And yet, both Henderson and Huneker felt compelled to step out of their roles as music-reporters to write fictional narratives about music and musicians. These novels, in dealing as novels do with relationships between people, focus on performers, audiences, and critics, while composers—and specifically Wagner—remain only disembodied names, perhaps responsible for stirring up certain emotions but not participating in the social dramas that follow.

Huneker began writing short stories about musicians and music early in his career, as a way of exploring what he found to be the complex and often disturbing relationship between music and the imagination. His only novel, which he began in the 1890s but did not finish until 1919, describes musical New York at the turn of the century from the perspective of a disaffected (or as Huneker repeatedly referred to him, "deracinated") critic as he interacts with his circle of bohemian sophisticates and develops complicated feelings for a rising American opera star. While his biographer claims the novel "sounded one of the first notes of the jazz age he had foreseen but whose wildest music he was not destined to hear," *Painted Veils*, like Johnson's *Autobiography* (which was only widely read after its reissue in 1927), focuses on a moment already buried in the past by the 1920s, when an earlier variety of "wild music" heralded a kind of spiritual anarchy.[9]

More middlebrow than Huneker's protomodernist novel, Henderson's *The Soul of a Tenor* (1912) also describes turn-of-the-century New York opera culture but channels any musical wildness into a portrait of the artist as a married, upstanding white American citizen, albeit one whose musical depth distinguishes him from the more typical image of the successful American male. But for Henderson, as for Huneker, the rise of the American opera star comes at the price of the status of the American music critic, a version of which in both novels remains marginalized, sexually ambiguous, and under threat of becoming irrelevant. Both novels situate their critics in dramatic, and at times erotic, tension with the forces of the opera world, forces associated with femininity and sexuality, as well as, if more vaguely, with racial difference. Modern incarnations of Odysseus (an increasingly multivalent referent for literature of this period), these critics heroically maintain their objectivity and duty to write the truth in the face of beautiful and seductive voices but end up overshadowed by the new musical celebrities of American culture, able only to report on a vitality they cannot themselves afford to experience.

"Opera land and its people"

William J. Henderson, son of a theatrical producer and an actress/playwright, was a life-long New Yorker and a career journalist, writing for New York newspapers from the moment he graduated from Princeton in 1876. After a decade working in apprentice positions, and on several different beats, he was made music critic at the *New York Times* in 1887; he moved to the *New York Sun* in 1902, and remained there until his death in 1937.[10] His only novel, *Soul of a Tenor*, was praised by critics mainly for its titillating revelations of the insider's perspective on "opera land and its people."[11] Anticipating that his readers would be looking for such insider gossip, Henderson prefaced his novel with a note insisting "there are no portraits in this story. I have dared to give a momentary glimpse of one supreme interpreter, but none of the other characters in this book ever existed. . . . But opera land is an existing country; and a real artist might be born in it in some such way as is hereinafter set forth."[12] Beyond the one "supreme interpreter," by which he surely means Lilli Lehmann, the real-life grand-dame of opera who makes an appearance early in the story, Henderson's novel nonetheless seems from the start to be referencing *types* of operagoers, critics, and opera singers alike, if not specific individuals. And he quite aggressively characterizes the people of "opera land" to be, with only a few exceptions, pretentious, shallow minded, and invested much more in the culture of celebrity than in serious art. The central focus of the novel, as its title announces, is the transformation of a tenor, Leander Baroni, from glory-seeking celebrity to soulful artist, who emerges both through and against the operatic "country" that remains his home.

Framing this narrative, however, is a parallel story about the transformation of a music critic. Philip Studley is presented, at the beginning of the novel, as a young idealist determined—as was Henderson himself—to be absolutely objective in his reporting on New York musical life. This determination puts him decidedly at odds with his journalist peers, who, as he observes, make "far more account of the private habits of singers than of their art" (85). It also puts him at odds with the tenor-protagonist, whose marriage to Philip's good friend Helen Montgomery has not kept the critic from writing honest reviews of his performances. Philip and Helen are almost isolated in this novel by their shared commitment to the idea that music's value rests not in the brilliance of its performance but in the quality of its composition. In a letter to Philip announcing her imminent marriage to Leander, Helen writes that while "it is all literature, art, and architecture" with her friends, who care little for music, she considers the "music masters" to be "just as much a demonstration of the intellectual life of their times as the painters and the authors" (17). Philip, whose job it is to "attend from two to five performances of music in each day and to prepare a page of comment and notes for the Sunday issue of his paper" (92), clearly represents a young version of Henderson himself, particularly in his conservative attitudes about aesthetic experiment or what he calls "smartness." Upon seeing a new opera in which Leander sings, Philip, whose musical heroes are Brahms and Beethoven, states, "It's all paint and mannerism, like the ridiculous fantasms of the cubists and the futurists" (90). Philip's perspective resonates with Helen's own, as she begins to recognize that her husband's singing is itself "all paint and mannerism" and to see that he uses his technical vocal brilliance merely to acquire fame and glory for himself. Philip's subplot, however, leaves Leander and Helen behind when he finds himself forced to choose between his objectivity and his own musical and erotic pleasure, which comes in the form of his seduction by the reigning diva of New York, the half-gypsy Nagy Bosanka. That he is attracted to Nagy rather than Helen (for whom he has tremendous respect, but no desire) is both a sign of and a threat to his professional identity as a writer about music.

The tenor's story, however, takes center stage in this novel, with the critic's professional crisis relegated to the wings. Henderson's *Soul of a Tenor* may be the first American novel to feature a male opera singer, and it certainly remains one of only a handful to do so.[13] The siren is gendered female in the Western imagination, while male opera singers inevitably raise the specter of gender trouble and complicate the narrative structures of heterosexual romance. We have so far encountered only one male musician among the protagonists of our novels, which for the most part imagine musicality as the domain of female pianists and singers whose growing presence and agency threaten to overwhelm or at least overshadow the male characters in their midst. (The male composers whose works these women perform—Chopin, Wagner, Dvořák—remain, it is worth noting, disembodied and abstracted from the social network of the performance occasion.)[14] The masculinity of Leander Baroni is under stress from the start of the novel, which speaks to the implicit question of how a man raised in the United States can end up a famous opera singer. Born Leander Barrett in Pittsburgh, Leander was just an "ordinary college boy" when discovered in the "glee club" by "one of those uncommon men who know something about the singing voice" (98). We don't get the scene of this discovery, which in diva literature typically entails an eroticized encounter between male master and female student, but we do learn, in this brief reference to it, that men who know something about singing (men like Henderson, who wrote books about it) are rarities in the United States. After proper training, including the requisite years with a European "master," Leander has risen in the opera ranks from his successful debut in Catania to impress audiences in Milan, Paris, and New York. He finally can claim, as these musical success stories typically go, that he has "conquered the world" after appearing at London's Covent Garden.

But this conquest, we learn along with his young wife Helen, rings somewhat hollow; the divo has merely learned to master "technical effects," while demonstrating no genuine musical artistry of his own. If not herself musical, the confident and pragmatic Helen understands Leander's deficiency in terms that have long dictated how classical music is valued, terms that Henderson himself, in his criticism, firmly espoused: rather than serve "the master who wrote the work," Leander is mistakenly interested only in the machinery of his own voice (99). With the composer unequivocally occupying the role of "master," Leander's role as singer/performer is thus doubly feminized: as ideally subservient to a "master"; and as, in actuality, preoccupied with surface effects (like Cather's "americanischen Fräuleins" who have nothing "on the inside"[15]). On the other hand, Leander's refusal to submit to any master, by instead asserting his own voice as the primary value, becomes the sign of his claim to masculine autonomy. Leander's refusal to submit to the "master" indicates, furthermore, that he recognizes and can profit from the market value of his own talent: audiences (mainly female) are paying not to hear him deliver Wagner and Bizet but to hear him hit the high notes with strength and tonal brilliance. The situation of the American male opera singer, then, entails an almost impossible choice: between an authentic artistry represented by subservience to the composer or aggressive self-promotion that turns one's voice into a mere ornament.

What rescues Leander from this dilemma, giving him both a musical "soul" and a stable "American" masculinity, is his intimate and transformative encounter with the same seductive voice that tests Philip. The relationship between Leander and Nagy echoes a number of musical relationships encountered in this study between an American and a musical *other*. The novel figures Nagy Bosanka, clearly the musical superior of the initially "soul-less" American tenor, as soulful by *nature* rather than training, by virtue of her primitive gypsy blood as well as her Old World European origins. Reminiscent of Cather's American Indians or Johnson's ragtime pianist, Nagy's musicality functions as a zone of musical authenticity that can never be fully appropriated by the white, Anglo-Saxon, Protestant American but can, nonetheless, catalyze (while itself remaining outside) a modern American version of musical authenticity. Nagy also resembles portraits of modern female musicality encountered in the novels of this study. Her past seems unknowable and distant, generating, like the unspeakable pasts of Atherton's Styr and Frederic's Sister Soulsby and the unreadable inner life of Chopin's Mlle Reisz, contradictory gossip: "Some held that she was the daughter of a Moscow Jew by a Tartar mother. Others declared that she was the child of an Austrian nobleman and a Dalmatian peasant woman. None of them really knew" (29). Her "true" origins, *we* do learn, are with Hungarian gypsies and supposedly account for her restlessness and the "soundless depths and elusive spaces" of her "soul." This soul, she insists, echoing Bizet's gypsy Carmen (a role she eventually performs) is "clean and honest and strong because it has always been free, because it has looked good and evil squarely in the eyes" (257). Rather than the roles of Wagner, which safely packaged the "wild" passion of Kronborg and Styr in unequivocal whiteness, Nagy remains identified with the darker feminine seductresses of nineteenth-century French opera. As Meyerbeer's African Selika, Nagy is "the most lissome, flashing-eyed, sinuous, and seductive of savage queens" (194); and she "flings" herself into the role of Carmen "with all the sinuous grace and abandon given her by her gipsy [*sic*] nature" (278). And unlike the Wagnerian divas who forgo sexual lives in their total devotion to art (Wagner, incidentally, hated Meyerbeer), Nagy crosses the boundary between stage and life in her "savage" will to seduce and "conquer" the men in her path. Her promiscuous femininity and her ethnicity remain inextricably linked, on stage and off, both appealing to and threatening the American professional men in her midst.

At first Leander keeps his distance from his co-star, apart from their scenes on stage together: he "liked to sing with [Nagy] because she was tremendous; but off the stage he preferred the American members of the company who were all cordially hated by the European members" (31). Unlike Nagy, who throws herself into her roles, Leander initially approaches his profession more as commercial enterprise than art: "We are not there for psychology or imaginations or aesthetics. We are there to make the public shout and clap its hands, and hasten to put more dollars in the box office" (81). Nagy puts it somewhat differently: "In this sordid America no one is great. You are a nation of hucksters. You see nothing, you know nothing, you feel nothing. . . . You are all dead, dumb, soulless" (128, 129). It is only when Nagy decides Leander "had something worth stirring" that she invites him into the private space of her apartment to conduct an "experiment" to see if she will be the one to awaken him. As she sings for him not opera but a Persian folk song, with a "queer sliding melody of melting intervals and oily scales," he responds in a manner reminiscent of Edna Pontellier's and Theron Ware's responses to their private piano recitals: "Leander, understanding nothing yet, felt strange waves running through all his sense. It was as if he had suddenly been thrust into the depths of a fragrant tropical garden" (127). Nagy completes her experiment when the company is on tour, during which "day after day the influence of this unique nature worked upon Leander" (271) until eventually something inside him begins to change: "The sleeping soul was approaching its hour of *awakening*. . . . The germs of spiritual force, which had so long been dormant in Leander, began to *vitalize*. . . . The tenor began to have *new and strange moods*" (274, emphases mine). Unlike Edna Pontellier's "awakening," which also aroused "new and strange moods" that led only to her heightened despondency, Leander's spiritual transformation unlocks his artistic potential. Rather than continue singing only "with tonal perfection and exquisitely finished nuance," he now begins to "publish [the music's] meaning. He became really eloquent" (275–76).

Leander's transformation does not simply bring "meaning" into what was once mere technical mastery, but also turns his one-dimensional, American masculinity into a more complicated mixture of masculine and feminine qualities and a new national identity that draws from something more "spiritual" than the mere drive to make money. By giving in to the influence of a powerful woman, and submitting more generally to a "strange new power" that he knows is "above and beyond him" (285), he gives up masculine control at the same time that he acquires greater musical authority and power. In submitting to this "new power," he also finally becomes independent of Nagy, internalizing his experience as enlightenment: "She knew that her dominion over him was gone forever. She had tried to show him his soul and he had begun to see the light" (287). A performance of *Carmen* clinches Leander's "awakening" as not only a recovery of his masculinity but also a reclamation of his American identity, which has received almost no explicit mention in this novel since its description of his "glee club" days: "There was something strange and potent and appalling in the relation between this Hungarian, who came of a race of lawless men and women, and this American, who was an illegitimate son of a nation of money grubbers. The house was aroused to extravagant demonstrations. Across the footlights it looked like a brilliantly realistic piece of acting and the audience was astonished at the vigor of the hitherto cold Americano" (287). The tenor has been transformed from a "cold" and "money grubbing" Americano (thus not belonging in opera) into a new operatic tenor of "vigor" and "soul," and all due to the passing influence of the "lawless" gypsy—an "appalling" relationship not only for its aura of miscegenation but also, perhaps, for its daring to admit a soulless American into a performance of *Carmen*. But the audience, as well as Leander, is won over by the "realism" of the performance, their intolerance of racial and aesthetic mixing overshadowed by the spectacle of his transformation. Just as, in Bizet's opera, Don Jose must kill Carmen in order to preserve his masculine, northern Spanish self from the gypsy's infectious, emasculating desire, Leander acquires a vigor that renders Carmen/Nagy's seductions powerless.[16] Rather than kill her, he abandons the gypsy diva by abandoning the operas that give her identity expression—operas like *Carmen*—for none other than . . . Wagner!

Besides effectively eliminating Nagy from his sphere, this operatic reorientation ushers the self-sacrificing, intellectual, and poised Helen Montgomery back in. Completely devoted to her husband's enlightenment, Helen harbors no resentment: she welcomes him back, grateful to Nagy for providing something she herself could not. American culture is returned to (white) Americans, enriched by their brush with the "primitive" and rescued from racial confusion by Wagner. The final scene gives us a subdued and conquered Nagy, who tells Helen that she is "a greater woman than I," even as Leander recognizes Nagy as the source of his newfound artistry: "I owe to her all that I know of the real meaning of Art" (365). Leander can now star again in *Carmen* opposite Nagy, but this time it will mean nothing to him. Recognizing that it is "one of those seductive 'special' performances . . . with a star cast" that the Met depends on for revenue, Leander is no longer subject to its charms, nor those of its diva/heroine. While the Met audience remains full of ignorant society ladies more interested in stars and their intrigues than "the real meaning of Art," the American tenor can distinguish between the two and thus claim to own a "soul."[17]

But while Leander's crisis of masculinity is thus tidily resolved, Philip's subplot leads to a less satisfactory if, in fact, more believable end. Unlike Leander, neither the critic's "soul" nor his aesthetic values need fixing, and, in the end, Philip seems to gain nothing of value from his intimate encounter with the diva, except a renewed commitment to maintaining a boundary between himself and the musical objects of his pen. The problem that she and her voice represent for Philip rests in the tension between his own musical responsiveness and his professional duty to write the truth about music he hears performed. His real crisis occurs when Nagy draws him, as she had drawn Leander, outside of the opera house, which is his professional domain, and into a more private space of musical experience, performing for him a private concert whose repertoire also takes him outside his comfort zone: "'No opera,' she murmured; 'something altogether different, something quite for—you.'" She begins with Greek melodies and Turkish love songs, challenging Philip's professionalized mode of musical reception: "The young man was able to contemplate the singing with his mind, though his soul confessed the marvelous witchery of the tones" (147). But when Nagy "seem[s] instinctively to realize that her songs were not conquering him," she moves on to the more familiar Brahms lieder, which indeed are Philip's "one musical weak spot." As he feels himself "drawn by some supernatural power against which his weakening will battled in vain," Philip finally submits to both the music and the singer, "cast[ing] away all thought" (148–49). The power of her singing raises for him the limits of his power as a writer to account for or describe the music that really moves him: "How this wild, untrammeled, undisciplined creature, with her imperfect training . . . ever acquired such a noble and potent art is something that remained forever one of the mysteries of Philip's life" (148). He almost immediately, however, recognizes the impossibility of occupying the position of both lover and critic as he faces the task of reviewing Nagy's singing: "I cannot write honestly about you. . . . I shall adore you if you sing out of tune" (151). But at her next public performance, he remains bound to write an honest review of her performance of Marguerite—calling it "the essence of polite convention" (160)—which puts an end to this temporarily confusing relationship, or what the narrator calls their "impossible compact" (152). The outraged diva, as expected, spurns him. After only a moment's regret, the critic quickly regains his senses and gladly returns to his solitary (and decidedly asexual) clarity.

In the final pages of the novel, Philip leaves the position of lover, spurned lover, or potential lover for that of mediator between lovers, as he orchestrates the reunion of Helen and Leander and then returns to the darkened background of the opera house from which he can write the objective truth about music, while keeping his "weakness" for both music and certain musical women at bay. This odd man out, who ultimately has little influence over either the romantic or musical plotlines of the novel, leaves us with the impression that to write about music is a rather joyless and, perhaps, irrelevant task. In the end, the "awakenings" and "vitality" that signify an emerging American musicality are located within musical experience that is beyond the power of newspaper reviews to represent. The critic remains, however, one of a select few who know the real thing when they hear it.

"Everything is unsettled"

James Huneker has been called the most important American music critic of the early twentieth century, and there is no question that he was one of the most influential. Famous for his defense of the "modern" artists in music, literature, and drama, Huneker's heroes included Ibsen, Wagner, Liszt, Chopin, Richard Strauss, Nietzsche, and Debussy. Unlike the more conventional Henderson, who appreciated the "moderns" but preferred nineteenth-century German "masters" like Brahms, Huneker made conventionality his enemy. But like Henderson, one of the chief objects of his scorn was a moralizing sentimentalism that he felt was keeping American taste and cultural production from realizing their potentials.

Born and raised in Philadelphia, Huneker was a life-long Francophile, having spent a year in Paris privately studying piano (after being denied admission to the Conservatoire) and devoting many years to the study of French language, literature, and philosophy. Though he was at times mocked for his Continental attitudes, he was, as one biographer insists, an aggressive promoter of "native" American artists and of the need for national styles and forms of music, opera, literature, and drama. (He focused as well, but with less command, on the visual and plastic arts.) He worried that European culture and European immigrants exercised too great an influence on the American scene, while he remained skeptical of Dvořák's brand of "folk" nationalism, which he considered overly simplistic and reductive. In reviewing the 1893 Carnegie Hall premiere of Dvořák's "New World" Symphony, he writes, with his typical bite: "Dvořák's is an American symphony: is it? Themes from Negro melodies; composed by a Bohemian; conducted by a Hungarian and played by Germans in a hall built by a Scotchman. About one-third of the audience was Americans and so were the critics. All the rest of it was anything but American."[18] Perhaps most striking in this typically irreverent pronouncement, given his "Continental" affiliations, is how it represents his own American identity (as one of the unified block of American critics among the minority American contingent in the audience) as more solid than that of "Negro melodies" or European immigrants. What it means to be an American critic is, in fact, precisely at the heart of his one and only novel, published at the end of his life.

Huneker was always struggling for the right language in which to write about music. While he wrote primarily in the genre of criticism (albeit with an impressionistic, nonacademic flair), he experimented throughout his life with fiction, which he considered a crucial form of commentary on music. For Huneker, music could be a powerful influence on, as well as expression of, the human psyche, and he was fascinated in particular by what he saw as an integral link between music and psychopathology. His book of short stories *Melomania* (1903), most of which had been published previously in *Musical Courier*, describes musical people—performers, composers, critics and listeners—as they undergo various kinds of musically induced altered states, including hallucination, hatred, mania, alcoholism, and obsession. *Painted Veils*, which he later described as bringing his own "suppressed complexes" to the surface, characterizes turn-of-the-century New York in terms of social and psychological instabilities that find their most telling expression in music.[19] Begun in the 1890s but not completed until 1919, the novel is preoccupied with the question of what a critic is to do with his awareness of music's dark truths, when the American public is content with the "painted veils" that are music culture's self-promoting lies.

Painted Veils is much more interested than *Soul of a Tenor* in the fate of the critic, although its first chapter might lead a reader to think it another "diva" novel. The novel opens with the arrival in New York City of a young singer from Virginia, Esther Brandès, who is determined to make a name for herself. We initially see a bohemian and decidedly French-influenced New York music scene through her fresh eyes, as she moves into the Maison Felicé, a morally lax hotel and gathering place for "singers, painters, actors and musicians," and then as she auditions at the "Conservatoire Cosmopolitaine" for the director and the reigning French tenor.[20] He is clearly referring here, with a certain wink to those in the know, to the National Conservatory, which employed a number of French musicians as teachers. (Unlike Henderson's novel, Huneker's is definitely a kind of roman à clef; he tells a friend, in a letter, that "you will definitely recognize the portraits," and writes to another that "it is the New York of 20 years ago, realistic."[21])

By the end of the first chapter, Esther (or Easter, as she is familiarly called) has demonstrated all the qualities necessary for an American diva's success: confidence, sex appeal, independence, and, above all, a strong, healthy, interesting voice. Like Cather and Atherton, Huneker gives us a modern diva who flouts sexual conventions without suffering for it, and in this respect his novel might be considered, with the others, a feminist revision of diva literature's conventional plot.

But the narrative quickly shifts its point of view to a character who *does* suffer as a result of the diva's choices: the critic. Music critic Ulick Invern's sensibility is already influencing the novel's tone before his entrance at the very end of the first chapter. With nothing available at the hotel when Easter first arrives in New York, she is given the young critic's rooms while he is on vacation. A pianist and teacher as well as a critic, Ulick has filled his rooms with books, music, and a piano, all of which give Easter a feeling of intimacy with him before she even meets him. A "flashback" soon reveals, however, that Ulick and Easter have indeed already met. The recounting of this meeting positions it as a kind of mythical origin of both Easter's modern musicality and Ulick's crisis of faith in his capacity, as critic, to tell the truth about music.

Earlier in the summer, Ulick had traveled to a small New Hampshire town in order to take a break from his work and do some serious thinking about the state of his world. Loaded down with books on mysticism and religion, he seeks to test his developing belief that the "time seems ripe" for a "new religion": "Everything is unsettled. We are on the verge of something tremendous" (40). On his first day, his solitary musing is interrupted by a "noisy, discordant music" that draws him to an unusual religious meeting and promises to answer his quest for modern spirituality. Led by a black man named "Brother Rainbow," the group, called the "Holy Yowlers," preaches temperance while drunk on rum and music. Intrigued, Ulick offers to buy drinks for Brother Rainbow and his white companion, Roarin' Nell. When they are denied entry at the local pub, Easter suddenly appears and offers to provide them with her own private stash of Kentucky whiskey. After a few drinks they rejoin the meeting, which quickly intensifies into a scene of bacchic revelry: "Ulick had seen camp-meeting revivals, yet they were a mere hymn carnival compared with this orgy of sound and motion" (48). When Brother Rainbow yells "lights out!" at the height of frenzy, Ulick finds himself pinned to the floor by a woman with whom he then has some kind of sexual encounter (the specifics of which remain murky); when the light returns he discovers Easter fainting in his arms, as

Brother Rainbow pronounces, "She has had true religion. She is now one of de Holy Yowlers" (49). When Easter awakens to Ulick's concerned attention, she flees the scene in apparent shock.

As it seems to parody the interracial scenario that, as we've seen, was increasingly informing narratives of white American musicality, the novel shows little interest, at least at first, of the influence of blackness or of primitive ritual on Easter's emerging musicality. This scene instead serves to initiate Ulick's plotline, by arousing in him a powerful if inchoate desire for Easter and for what she begins to represent for him. Decidedly unlike Henderson's Philip Studley, Ulick sees his salvation, as critic and as human being, in the eroticization of his relationship to the diva and to music generally, even if, eventually, this eroticization becomes his undoing. The "revival" meeting's confusion of sexual arousal and religious ecstasy throws fuel on Ulick's conviction, voiced throughout the novel, that sex is at the heart of all art, or, as he puts it, "the real protagonist of humanity," epitomizing "all creation" (181). The question becomes for Ulick as for the novel, whether not only American culture at large but Ulick himself is ready to confront and embrace this truth. Easter, we learn soon enough, will do so with neither shame nor sentimentality.

The "revival" scene announces this novel's concern with the place both of music and of those whose job it is to think and write about music in the United States. Ulick is an American who would really prefer to be living in Paris, where he was born to an American (New Yorker) mother and Irish father and where he received his musical training. In spite of his friends' insistence that his "soul" is "cosmopolitan" and in spite of his own disgust with what he perceives as a commercialized, shallow, and anti-intellectual American culture, he has moved to New York on the advice of his beloved French mentor, who insists, "You are deracinated in Paris. . . . Return to your native heath" (105). (Huneker claimed that Ulick was only a version of himself in their shared sense of "deracination," a term that marks one's relationship to one's "native heath" as racial.) But what constitutes a "native" alternative to the richness of French culture is nowhere in sight in Huneker's novel; the "Holy Yowlers" is, in fact, Huneker's only representation of an American "folk" culture beyond the scope of highbrow New York, which itself has little that appeals to Ulick. He has recently made a shift from music to theater criticism because the "same old arias, the same bad singing, and then the stale phrases that we are compelled to write" have given him "aesthetic nausea" (122). Whether Ulick will ever again find his footing as a music critic in his "native heath" seems to hinge on his relationship to Easter, who, as a new kind of American diva, promises a way out of his "aesthetic nausea." That she also seems to promise some kind of erotic satisfaction for the wayward Ulick reveals the degree to which, for Huneker as for many of the authors in this study, music's promises are bound up with desire, and specifically with desire that is authentic, primitive, and unsentimental and, furthermore, is free from conventional marriage plots and from the market forces that churn out the "same old arias" and the same "stale phrases."

What does set this novel apart from the others is its much more modern interest in sexual desire and in the consequences of a liberated sexuality for both society and aesthetics. This explicit focus on sex, in fact, is the primary reason Huneker, who had published so many books during his career, was unable to get his novel published and ended up publishing it privately for only a circle of friends. In a letter to Senator Henry Cabot Lodge, Huneker wrote "I fear the book [*Painted Veils*]—a serious one I assure you, despite some frills and thrills not precisely Rabelaisian, but enough to scare timid publishers. Hence the private publication."[22] Declaring himself a "feminist," Ulick espouses "free love" and the idea that women as well as men should be free to express their sexual desires without fear of moral judgment. Yet, Ulick's "aesthetic nausea" clearly pertains, at least in part, to the sexually liberated women in his midst, whose open expressions of desire he finds as unoriginal and inauthentic as a night at the opera. Easter, whom Ulick befriends back in New York without any explicit acknowledgment of their previous orgiastic encounter, represents a possible resolution to this contradiction—between Ulick's desire and disgust for sexually liberated women—by seeming to embody a more authentic sexual being.

Besides Easter, Ulick becomes involved with two women who represent two other versions of liberated female sexuality, both of which end up disappointing him in ways that underscore his own sexual confusion but also help clarify Easter's difference. One, a kind of modern Madonna, unites an intense "long[ing] for virility" (113) and strong sexual appetite with a fervent desire to have children, a combination that ends up repelling Ulick, who is no family man. He then meets Dora, a delightful if sometimes petulant prostitute, at an "orgy" hosted by a New York society bachelor. This gentlemen's event, which suggests that orgies are de rigueur among New York bohemian society (the scene contributed to Huneker's difficulty in getting the novel published), was purportedly based on an actual party thrown by a New York millionaire for the sculptor Augustus Saint-Gaudens.[23] But with its harem of semi-nude prostitutes, this orgy pales, in Ulick's imagination, before the more authentic New Hampshire episode: it is merely "the mimique of a monkey-cage. No enchantment of the sense beyond optical titillation" (149). Ulick's thoughts turn back to Easter, still convinced that something significant occurred between them: "What tremendous minutes they had been when he held her close to him in the mystic blackness; held and possessed her" (155). Compared to the legible mimicry and "optical titillation" of New York's party scene, the "blackness" that enshrouded his imagined moment of union with Easter in unnarratable mystery becomes the very sign of its authenticity.

Ulick's two closest friends function in the novel primarily as critics of his sexual inclinations and theories, both speaking from positions of celibacy that might be read as versions of Philip Studley's final retreat in Henderson's novel. Milt, a seminary student, acknowledges the growing influence of sexuality in the modern age but firmly believes in enlightened self-restraint. He claims "to be in the world, yet not of it, to wade through the sins and heresies of this ignominious age, yet never wallow in them. . . . Never did he lapse into that stupration of the soul, that mass of confused emotion evoked by the curves of the female form he never indulged in" (178). Alfred Stone, a cynical music critic himself, is "a woman-hater" (58), who "loathe[s] enthusiasm" (22), particularly as it is displayed by American audiences for such modern artists as Wagner. Where Ulick sees signs of "something tremendous" in the modern state of social, spiritual, and aesthetic confusion, Alfred sees disastrous chaos and sexual anarchy. Calling sex "a sickly thing . . . not health and conservation, but destruction, disease, death" (185), he shows particular disgust for women's sexual "freedom," which he associates with Wagner's music: "The world is hag-ridden by sexuality. And the worst of it is that with their 'new freedom,' as they call it, women are becoming more polyandrous. They, too, needs must have a staff of males for their individuality! Music is to blame a lot, Wagner's music in particular. What else is Tristan and Isolde but a tonal orgasm?" (281). Alfred's remarkably uncensored critique of American Wagnerism lays bare the degree to which musical "awakenings" like Edna's (and Thea's and Styr's and, even, Carrie's) raised the specter, in certain minds, of an unbridled, "polyandrous" female sexuality that could only spell the ruin of civilization as we know it.

But it is through Wagner that Easter herself rises to operatic stardom, and it is Wagner's music, particularly *Tristan und Isolde*, that seems first to awaken her sexual and musical desires. Although Huneker's treatment of Wagner is never without irony, the author devotes several pages to describing Easter's powerful reactions to the German "master": "She became a Wagnerian in a moment. No music before this had narcotized her senses, lapped her soul into bliss, hypnotized her faculty of attention until her consciousness had swooned" (56–57). Her response to *Tristan und Isolde*, the opera Alfred disparaged as "a tonal orgasm," is even more transformative: "At moments, Easter thought she couldn't longer stand the suspense. She wished to cry, to roll on the floor, to tear her hair out, to press her aching eyeballs till they fell out. She was in the center of an emotional typhoon. Her previous life shrivelled [*sic*] up like a scroll in the clear flame of the mighty master of musical elixirs" (59). Huneker makes Wagner's connection to sex more explicit than any other writer considered in this study and suggests that the music's sexual core is both its greatness and its bane—promising Nietzschean freedom and threatening not only creative chaos but a retreat into sickly sentimentality. Listening to Wagner, Easter becomes subject to a "spell" that is reminiscent of the previous "orgy of sound and motion" they shared in New Hampshire: "Music, the most sensual of the arts, for it tells us of the hidden secrets of sex, immersed her body and soul in a magnetic bath; the sound-fluid entered the porches of her ears. She was a slave manacled within the chalked circle of a wizard. To step across the line would have been an ineluctable attempt" (62–63). The spell is quickly broken, however, when the music stops and the opportunity to meet the great Lilli Lehmann turns her thoughts to her career.

According to Alfred, the danger for both women and men lies in allowing oneself to be susceptible to music's emotional and erotic effects and becoming, as he puts it, too "enthusiastic." It is, in fact, Easter's distinction as a woman and an aspiring professional that she never lets her enthusiasm get away from her. As Alfred remarks, she "never will waste herself in a swamp of sensual sentimentality" (25), nor will she ever be "manacled" to any man: "Easter might be profoundly immoral, but never a slimy odalisque. Her temperament was too tonic. Passion—yes, to the edge of tatters. Foaming passion; but no man would ever call her slave" (26). Alfred warns Ulick, however, that he will never succeed as a writer because he is "too receptive" (200), referring both to his sexuality and his relationship to music. Although Ulick has given up music criticism, he is, from the start, characterized as unusually susceptible to music's call. We are told, when his "unwilling ears" are struck with the "discordant music" of the "Holy Yowlers" that "he suffered from his sensitive hearing" (42). His "aesthetic nausea," he claims, is brought on not simply by "bad singing" and "the same old arias" but also by what he calls his "receptive frame of mind; always listening to other men's ideas, or the lack of them . . . what a sheer waste of time for anyone who wishes to be individual, to create, no matter how slight the performance" (123). Musicality and masculinity, if the latter is defined in terms of being "individual" and "creative" as opposed to "receptive," once again appear in conflict. Ulick's refusal to follow the lead of Alfred Stone, or Henderson's Philip Studley, or Johnson's ex-colored man, for that matter, and remain emotionally detached from music and women in order to maintain a productive and professional identity put him at the center of this novel's psychological drama.

In the end, Ulick—taking the place of the diva in one of grand opera's master narratives—is the one who suffers punishment for his sexual sins. When Easter triumphantly returns to New York, following her requisite early career in Europe, to sing Isolde at the Met (in the opera that Alfred calls a "tonal orgasm"), Ulick's professional and existential crisis finally comes to its point of no return. In her new glory as a celebrity soprano, Easter—now Istar—performs her "sexual freedom" at every opportunity and seems bent on unsettling all of the tenuously balanced sexual relationships in Ulick's circle. She befriends and seduces both of the other women in Ulick's life, although we never witness, or are sure of, how far these homoerotic seductions go. More devastating to Ulick, Easter threatens Milt's celibacy, by appealing to his "passion for music"—for which (reminiscent of Theron Ware) he "had been rebuked more than once" at his seminary: "She sang gloriously. Milt absorbed the luscious tones as if they were living corpuscles" (298). Finally, Easter reveals to Ulick the true nature of their experience with the Holy Yowlers and utterly shatters his "mystic" fantasy: in the dark, she claims, "we all got mixed-up," and she paired off not with Ulick but with Brother Rainbow. Furthermore, she claims that she "assented-physiologically" to sex with the black man, or, in Ulick's new assessment of his now rival, the "black monster" (302).

While Easter thus becomes another American diva who has been on intimate terms with primitive peoples, Huneker is much less interested in the effect of Easter's interracial sexual escapade on her operatic self than in its effect on Ulick. In his revulsion at learning that Easter had sex with Brother Rainbow and *liked* it, Ulick reveals his own sentimentality and indeed indulges in a sentimental ending by drinking himself to death. That his friends carry on quite well without him—the novel gives us little in the way of mourning of its hero's death—indeed underscores Ulick's sentimentality, his failure, ultimately, to live the modern perspective he preached. This failure supports Alfred's judgment that one can't be "too receptive," to music, to women, to anything that arouses desire, and maintain one's agency and authority in this modern world. The final words are, in fact, Alfred's—devoted to Istar in his own cynical and asexual way, and living to write her obituary. Only the "woman-hater" (the homosexual opera queen?) is free, among the novel's men, to appreciate the diva's power without risk of self-annihilation.

Huneker once wrote, back in 1896, "Let me . . . utter the awful truth that music is the most immoral and dangerous of the arts. . . . And lo! I am besieged with letters, cries of 'Shame' and hints of my awful responsibility as a critic and writer."[24] Ulick, himself an aspiring novelist, complains to his friends that "novels nowadays mean either the naked truth and that spells disaster, or slimy sensual sentimentality" (279). With the exception of Alfred, only Easter seems capable of living with the "naked truth"—neither falling into "slimy sensual sentimentality" nor denying sex only to succumb to it in self-annihilation, like Milt. Ulick, who dares to live with and write about the dark truths of music and human sexuality, is the novel's tragic hero whose downfall is his need for one last "painted veil," namely the idea that Easter needs him—or, put otherwise, that the diva and the critic are bound in some mystic, though conventionally heterosexual, way.

The critic characters in these two novels could not be more different, and their differences in many respects reflect the different personae of their critic authors. Philip Studley retreats from the limelight, maintains his dignity and objectivity, and remains determined to write about, and hear, music and musical performance, with his mind rather than his "soul." He chooses to remain comforted by the conviction that music's meaning and value remain stable, knowable quantities, transcending time and place, rooted in the composer's printed scores and representable by the critic's pen. For Ulick, however, music cannot be disentangled from the emotions and desires of those who perform and hear it; it is deeply caught up in its time and place. Those who deny this are merely lying to themselves; those who accept it, however, must face difficult, unsettling, truths.

But both critics, and both novels, nonetheless emphasize the "impossibility" of an intimate relationship between writer and musician. And whatever Ulick and Philip write in their reviews, whatever "awful truths" or "honest" accounts they offer in writing, both seem to recognize that the critic in the end has little influence over the new American musicality emerging in their midst. In their sense of powerlessness, marginality, and invisibility, these critic-characters underscore a common thread tying all of the works in this study together. To write about music—and, indeed, to write music—remains, for these novelists, something altogether different from the visceral, temporal, unsettling, and embodied experience of hearing and producing it.

Epilogue

Across their many differences, the novels considered in this study share a fundamental ambivalence about the presence and power of new forms of American musical experience. For many of their principal characters, music occasions the liberation or "awakening" of authentic pockets of selfhood and enables listeners to experience freer versions of themselves than their everyday lives allow. These musically awakened selves, however, inevitably face the impossibility of integrating their awakened selves into American social realities. The final paragraphs of *Sister Carrie* offer us resonant terms for this ambivalence. After suggesting that Carrie's musical responsiveness and musical voice have been instrumental in her transformation from poor Chicago migrant to successful New York actress, Dreiser leaves us with the image of her "singing and dreaming . . . such happiness as [she] may never feel."[1] To *sing* happiness, Dreiser finally implies, is something altogether different from, and perhaps even antithetical to, actually feeling it.

One can see versions of Dreiser's final image in the endings of our other novels, so many of which involve scenes of emotional paralysis or suicide. Edna Pontellier's suicidal walk into a sea of "voices" represents her choice of musical over social realism, a choice that the novel itself seems to make in its stylistic and protomodernist gestures. Theron Ware similarly attempts suicide after realizing the limits of his own musical "awakening." But Harold Frederic delivers an ending that contains music's power by holding onto the possibility that Theron will re-enter American society as a more modern American man. Thea Kronborg and Margarethe Styr both choose operatic careers that require their abandonment of social life, their "real" lives ultimately confined to the operatic stage. Thea ends up successful, but alone and exhausted, while Atherton's Styr dramatizes the diva's social death by actually becoming the character she performs and self-immolating as Brünnhilde on stage. The ex-colored man abandons blackness and music both, committing a kind of racial suicide (in becoming "ex-colored") to avoid what he imagines would be the suicide of living as a black man in a country that promotes lynching. Our two critic-novelists are alone in writing happy endings for their American musicians but only at the expense of the social life of the music critic himself, who alone seems capable of grasping the truth of musical experience.

While the relationship between music and society (and between music and writing) remains problematic for all of these novels, they offer a variety of historically resonant perspectives on the nature and causes of the problem. Debates about musical nationalism cast their shadow across most (if not all) of these works, I have suggested, in their recurring attention to the relationship between white Americans and ethnic and racial others who promise a more primitive, natural, and essential musicality. This relationship is constructed through various musical occasions and dynamics, all of which reinforce the notion that white (Protestant) American musicality is inevitably mediated, displaced, translated, or alienated. From Edna's and Theron's inability fully to claim the aesthetic and erotic freedom owned by the Catholic subcultures that surround them, to Thea's appropriation of Native American/Mexican voices, melodies, and rhythms, white Protestant audiences and musicians in these texts (including the "ex-colored" man) remain dependent on unassimilated sources who inhabit and embody seemingly more authentic forms of musicality. A defining feature of these "folk" sources is the sociality of their own musical cultures, in which music is inextricably bound up with rituals of communal expression and affiliation (the Mexican parties in *Song of the Lark*, the soirees in *The Awakening*, the church service and club scenes in *The Autobiography of an Ex-Colored Man*). White Americans can listen to these musical events and appropriate their sounds and styles, but they remain outside of what Frederick Douglass, in describing the music of slave culture, called "the circle."[2] Once this music crosses over into modern American bodies, settings, and economies, it becomes limited by the very forces it promises to transcend. To appropriate the musicality of those inside the circle—to transcribe, imitate, or internalize it—entails removing and translating it into an entirely different musical language, culture, and economy, one in which music is performed on stages for paying audiences, bought and sold as sheet music, and used to arouse consumers' desire to spend their money.

Music highlights for these texts a series of seemingly impermeable boundaries that variously stand in for one another: between folk authenticity and capitalist modernity, between blackness and whiteness, between music and writing.

New forms of American musicality call attention, in and for these novels, to limits in the project of realist writing, as they seem directly to arouse and access dimensions of the "real" that writing can only describe or analyze. But even as they variously gesture toward the gap between literary and musical claims to realism, the novels gathered here all nonetheless register the *impact* on Americans of emerging musical phenomena—of Tin Pan Alley's song-making machinery, of American Wagnerism and "Chopinitis," of women performing in public and going out to concerts, of "Indianist" forms of American composition, and of new urban black musical forms and practices. They help us, in ways unique to realist narrative, understand the terms by which Americans heard, and imagined, these new musical forms, which are always also (already?) mediated by those terms, however much they may seem immediate in their expressivity. Fiction, I have tried to demonstrate, can serve the cultural historian as a record of the musical imagination, taking us beyond stories of musical forms, styles, composers, performers, and venues and into the less tangible arena of emotion and desire; of felt connections between self, other, and place; and of the integration (or lack thereof) of musical experience into everyday experience of spaces, occasions, and relationships.

These novels, finally, capture a liminal, as well as transformative, moment in American musical ideology, and in American literature's relationship to music. By the time James Huneker published *Painted Veils* in 1920, Louis Armstrong had migrated from New Orleans to Chicago and would soon begin recording "hot jazz" that would once again lead to new notions of American music and of music's place in American cultural identity. White Americans would of course continue, and arguably continue still, to find the most compelling expressions of themselves in the music of others, particularly of African Americans. African American musicians themselves would come to occupy a national stage made possible by the recording industry, mass migration, and a host of other postwar circumstances. Meanwhile, Wagner's operas in the wake of the first World War would lose their place of grace, censored from American concert halls and opera houses along with German immigrant musicians, and would cede the stage to a new generation of American composers eager to build their own national voice on, among other things, the dominant popular musical styles of the Jazz Age. Huneker's novel anticipates this new moment most pointedly in his Freudian diagnosis that music, in the end, is a function of sexuality. While he, like his critic-hero Ulick, will not stick around for the ride, he nonetheless suggests that American music, and American culture more generally, is moving toward cultural desublimation, heralded by his hedonistic, bisexual diva, whose musical awakening is born, figuratively, out of orgiastic, interracial sex.

If a more dramatic explosion of modern American musicality is just around the corner, these turn-of-the-century elaborations of musical experience still harbor the memory of an earlier moment of change, a moment when Tin Pan Alley, the Metropolitan Opera, American Wagnerism, and the ragtime vogue were only just beginning to constitute new urban American realities. This was also a moment when the *idea* of American musicality was just beginning to become reified as a marketable idea and commodity. The liminal historical consciousness of the novels in this study accounts, perhaps, for the pervasive skepticism that accompanies their gestures toward music's capacity to express, arouse, and awaken real selves from their conventional slumbers. If Chopin's music can arouse an authentic sense of self, it also can "pass" as a Protestant hymn; if ragtime seems to express the "natural" self of an "untrained" black musician, it can also be harnessed to European musical forms as a novel form of entertainment for bored and disaffected white people; if popular song can give one a sense of connection to the "nation," it can also propel one into a never-ending cycle of consumer desire. These writers seem aware that music's emerging status as a language of authenticity is inextricably bound up with an emerging culture industry that profits from a promise of authenticity that it will never, in fact, fully deliver.

Notes

Introduction

1. James Weldon Johnson, *The Autobiography of an Ex-Colored Man* (New York: Vintage, 1989), 98.

2. This scholarship is too vast to cite comprehensively here. Of significant influence on my own thinking about music, and on this study, has been the work of "new musicologists" on gender and sexuality, particularly Susan McClary, Philip Brett, and Ruth Solie; the work of scholars in African American and diaspora studies, particularly Paul Gilroy, Ronald Radano, and Stuart Hall; the mostly British field of sociological analyses of music in everyday life, including Tia DeNora and Simon Frith; and the more foundational writings on music and political economy by Theodor Adorno and Jacques Attali.

3. This literature is also vast, and I will mention here only select works that have had a direct impact on this study. On black music, and the issue of race and music, at the turn of the century, see Lynn Abbott and Doug Seroff's *Out of Sight: The Rise of African American Popular Music, 1889–1895* (Jackson: University Press of Mississippi, 2010), and Edward Berlin's *Ragtime: A Musical and Cultural History* (Berkeley: University of California Press, 1980). On women in music, see Judith Tick's "Passed Away Is the Piano Girl," in *Women Making Music: The Western Art Tradition, 1150–1950*, ed. Jane Bowers and Judith Tick (Champaign: University of Illinois Press, 1987). On musical nationalism, see Michael Beckerman's scholarship on Dvořák in America and Michael Pisani's work on the "Indianist" music of American composers.

4. Keith Newlin, ed., *The Oxford Handbook of American Literary Naturalism* (New York: Oxford University Press, 2011).

5. Philipp Schweighauser's *The Noises of American Literature, 1890–1985: Toward a History of Literary Acoustics* (Gainesville: University Press of Florida, 2006),

47. This quotation is referring specifically to the strike scene in Dreiser's *Sister Carrie* but could stand for his larger argument as well.

6. Though not focused on literature, several important recent scholars have taken up the question of the historicity of American acoustics. See, in particular, Mark J. Smith's *Listening to Nineteenth-Century America* (Chapel Hill: University of North Carolina Press, 2000), Emily Thompson's *The Soundscape of Modernity: Architectural Acoustics and the Culture of Listening in America, 1900–1930* (Cambridge, MA: MIT Press, 2004), and Jonathan Sterne's *The Audible Past: Cultural Origins of Sound Reproduction* (Durham, NC: Duke University Press, 2003).

7. Jacques Attali, *Noise: The Political Economy of Music*, trans. Brian Massumi (1977; repr., Minneapolis: University of Minnesota Press, 1985).

8. The term "musicscape" has already been coined by management studies seeking to understand "the impact of music within various real and simulated service environments." See Steve Oakes and Adrian C. North, "Reviewing Congruity Effects in the Service Environment Musicscape," *International Journal of Service Industry Management*, 19, no. 1 (2008): 63–82.

9. Edward Said, "Music as an Extreme Occasion," in *Musical Elaborations* (New York: Columbia University Press, 1991).

10. Johnson, *Autobiography*, 99.

11. Kate Chopin, *The Awakening and Selected Stories* (1899; repr., New York: Penguin, 1986), 72.

12. See Joseph Horowitz, *Wagner Nights: An American History* (Berkeley: University of California Press, 1994), 3–4.

13. While Lawrence Levine's *Highbrow/Lowbrow* importantly historicized the "highbrow/lowbrow" dichotomy, accounts of postbellum U. S. culture nonetheless still tend to treat it as fixed and unchanging.

14. Houston Baker's *Blues, Ideology, and Afro-American Literature: A Vernacular Theory* (Chicago: University of Chicago Press: 1984) initiated an ongoing scholarly discourse about the relationship between black vernacular music and modernism.

15. See Nicholas Cook, *Music: A Very Short Introduction* (New York: Oxford University Press, 2000), particularly the first chapter. Also Tim Taylor, *Global Pop: World Music, World Markets* (New York: Routledge, 1997).

16. Karl Hagstrom Miller's important *Segregating Sound: Inventing Folk and Pop Music in the Age of Jim Crow* (Durham, NC: Duke University Press, 2010) demonstrates the degree to which academic folklorists and the recording industry in the early twentieth century imposed a musical "color line" on what had been a much more fluid and complex relationship between music, ethnicity, and race in the South.

17. The best book on Stephen Foster's life and place in American culture is Ken Emerson's *Doo-dah! Stephen Foster and the Rise of American Popular Culture* (New York: Da Capo Press, 1998).

18. This quote comes from the title of Eric Lott's compelling account of the

origins of and motivations for blackface minstrelsy, *Love and Theft: Blackface Minstrelsy and the American Working Class* (New York: Oxford University Press, 1995).

19. I will use, interchangeably, the terms "classical music" and "art music" to refer to music that has been composed in conscious relationship to the traditions of European art music. These terms are, of course, problematic, in ways that debates about American musical nationalism bring to the fore.

20. Arthur Farwell, "The Struggle toward a National Music," *North American Review* 86/625 (December 1907): 565–70, quoted in Michael J. Budds, ed., *Music in America: 1860–1918* (Hillsdale, NY: Pendragon Press, 2008), 13.

21. Antonin Dvořák, "Music in America," *Harper's New Monthly Magazine* 90 (February 1895): 429–34.

22. Ronald Radano makes this suggestion in his "Soul Texts and the Blackness of Folk," *Modernism/Modernity* 2, no. 2 (1995): 87.

23. A fascinating example of the confused relationship of sympathetic white listeners to the singing of African Americans is recorded in the "Introduction" to William Francis Allen, Charles Pickard Ware, and Lucy McKim Garrison, eds., *Slave Songs of the United States* (New York: A. Simpson and Co., 1867). This text was one of the first serious efforts by white Americans not only to transcribe African American music using Western notation but also to describe the difference and appeal of what they heard as African American music.

24. Henry Krehbiel, from "The American Composer of the Future," *Church's Musical Visitor* 25, no. 4 (April 1896): 98, quoted in Budds, *Music in America*, 11. Krehbiel was music editor for the *New York Tribune*, and wrote many articles and books that aimed to educate Americans about music.

25. Henry Krehbiel, *Afro-American Folksongs: A Study in Racial and National Music* (New York: Schirmer, 1914), v–vii.

26. See Berlin, *Ragtime* (particularly Chapter Three, "The Ragtime Debate," 32-60), on early discourses about ragtime, and Abbott and Seroff, *Out of Sight* (443-455), on ragtime's emergence out of diverse forms of black entertainment. James Weldon Johnson describes his and his brother's work as songwriters in *Along This Way: The Autobiography of James Weldon Johnson* (1933; repr., New York: Da Capo Press, 2000), 146–224.

27. For a good overview of European modernist musical strategies, see Alex Ross's *The Rest is Noise: Listening to the Twentieth Century* (New York: Farrar, Straus and Giroux, 2007).

28. Quoted in Budds, *Music in America*, 15.

29. Fiction thus implicitly accomplishes what Christopher Small urges musicologists to do in recognizing that modern Western art music—the "classical" tradition—is as much imbricated in social ritual as the "non-Western" music typically studied by ethnomusicologists. See, in particular, his *Musicking: The Meanings of Performing and Listening* (Middletown, CT: Wesleyan University Press, 1998).

30. See John Miller Chernoff, *African Rhythm and African Sensibility* (Chicago: University of Chicago Press, 1979), particularly "Introduction: Scholarship and Participation."

Chapter 1

1. Bill Brown, "The Matter of Dreiser's Modernity," in Leonard Cassuto and Clare Virginia Eby, eds., *The Cambridge Companion to Theodore Dreiser* (Cambridge: Cambridge University Press, 2004), 84.

2. Rachel Bowlby, *Just Looking: Consumer Culture in Dreiser, Gissing and Zola* (New York: Methuen and Company, 1985), 65, 62.

3. Walter Benn Michaels, "*Sister Carrie*'s Popular Economy," *Critical Inquiry* 7 (1980), 376.

4. See Nancy Warner Barrineau, ed., *Theodore Dreiser's "Ev'ry Month"* (Athens: University of Georgia Press, 1996) for a discussion of the impact of Dreiser's position as editor of a Tin Pan Alley magazine on his subsequent fiction. See also Jerome Loving's recent biography, *The Last Titan: A Life of Theodore Dreiser* (Berkeley: University of California Press, 2005), 95–114.

5. For a comprehensive collection of Dreiser's articles on the arts at the turn of the century, see Yoshinobu Hakutani, ed., *Art, Music, and Literature, 1897–1902* (Chicago: University of Illinois Press, 2001).

6. See Sandy Petry, "The Language of Realism, the Language of False Consciousness: A Reading of *Sister Carrie*," *Novel* 10 (1977).

7. The earlier critics include Alfred Kazin, *The Stature of Theodore Dreiser: A Critical Survey of the Man and His Work*, ed. Alfred Kazin and Charles Shapiro (Bloomington: Indiana University Press, 1965); F. O. Matthiessen, *Theodore Dreiser* (New York: Sloan, 1951); Donald Pizer, *The Novels of Theodore Dreiser: A Critical Study* (Minneapolis: University of Minnesota Press, 1976). Petry reads Dreiser's sentimentalism as irony that underscores "false consciousness" and thus supports a realist critique of the social conditions of capitalism. Walter Benn Michaels has been the most prominent proponent of an alternate reading that understands Dreiser's sentimental voice as an unironic, "unequivocal endorsement" of commodity capitalism, one that posits unquenchable "desire" as the engine of human nature. See Michaels, "*Sister Carrie*'s Popular Economy" (376).

8. See Amy Kaplan, "Sentimental Revolt of *Sister Carrie*," in *The Social Construction of American Realism* (Chicago: University of Chicago Press, 1989), 140–60.

9. Brown, "The Matter of Dreiser's Modernity," 87.

10. Theodore Dreiser, *Sister Carrie* (Philadelphia: University of Pennsylvania Press, 1981), 4. Unless otherwise noted, all quotations from *Sister Carrie* are from this edition. Future references to this work will be marked parenthetically in the text.

11. Theodore Dreiser, *Newspaper Days* (Philadelphia: University of Pennsylvania Press, 1991), 22, 20, 3, 4.

12. Ellen Moers writes that Dreiser had "mingled shame and admiration" for his brother's success. See her *Two Dreisers* (New York: Viking, 1969), 69.

13. I got this important word—and concept—from R. Murray Schafer's *The Soundscape: Our Sonic Environment and the Tuning of the World* (Rochester, VT: Destiny Books, 1994). Schafer sees his research as an attempt to answer the important, but typically unasked, question: "What is the relationship between man and the sounds of his environment and what happens when those sounds change?" (3–4). For a good discussion of early Tin Pan Alley, see David Ewen, *Tin Pan Alley* (New York: Funk and Wagnall's, 1964).

14. Lewis A. Erenberg, *Steppin' Out: New York Nightlife and the Transformation of American Culture, 1890–1930* (Chicago: University of Chicago Press, 1981); Kathy Peiss, *Cheap Amusements* (Philadelphia: Temple University Press, 1986).

15. Erenberg, *Steppin' Out*, 82; Peiss, *Cheap Amusements*, 98.

16. For a fascinating discussion of American women's devotion to Wagner at the turn of the century, see Horowitz, *Wagner Nights*. On the opera audience as homoerotic space for women, see Terry Castle, *The Apparitional Lesbian: Female Sexuality and Modern Culture* (New York: Columbia University Press, 1993), 203. See also Theodor Adorno, *In Search of Wagner* (New York: Verso, 2005).

17. Dreiser might be said to offer a version of Susan McClary's argument that music "channelizes" desire. See her *Feminine Endings: Music, Gender, and Sexuality* (Minneapolis: University of Minnesota Press, 1991).

18. Theodore Dreiser, "The Prophet," *Ev'ry Month* III (February 1897): 4.

19. Theodore Dreiser, "Words and Music," *Ev'ry Month* III (February 1897).

20. Quoted in Barrineau, *Theodore Dreiser's "Ev'ry Month,"* xvi.

21. Theodore Dreiser, introduction to *The Songs of Paul Dresser* (New York: Boni and Liveright, 1927), ix.

22. Quoted in Nancy Warner Barrineau, "The Second Issue of *Ev'ry Month*: Early Roots of Dreiser's Fiction," *Dreiser Studies* (Spring 1991): 27.

23. Theodore Dreiser, "My Brother Paul," in *Sister Carrie, Jennie Gerhart, Twelve Men* (New York: Library Classics of America, 1987), 910. *Twelve Men* was originally published in 1918.

24. Theodore Dreiser, "Birth and Growth of a Popular Song," *Metropolitan Magazine*, November 1898, 497–502.

25. Theodore Dreiser, "Whence the Song," *Harper's Weekly*, December 1900, 1166a, 1165, 1166a.

26. Henry Krehbiel, "Musical Guide" (1904), quoted in *Afro-American Folk-songs*, 2.

27. Quoted in Barrineau, *Theodore Dreiser's "Ev'ry Month,"* 90.

28. Ibid., 89.

29. See Yoshinobu Hakutani, *Young Dreiser: A Critical Study* (Rutherford, NJ: Fairleigh Dickinson University Press, 1980), 80–81. The review is reprinted in Blair

F. Bigelow's *Selected Newspaper Articles, 1892–1894, of Theodore Dreiser* (dissertation, Brandeis University, 1972).

30. Isaac Goldberg, *Tin Pan Alley: A Chronicle of American Popular Music* (New York: Frederick Ungar, 1961), 112. Dresser, it is important to note, did not move with the times into writing ragtime songs, and in this sense represented a kind of resistance to modernity, although I would argue that both sentimentalism and ragtime responded to and reflected modern circumstances.

31. Mark W. Booth, *The Experience of Songs* (New Haven, CT: Yale University Press, 1981), 168.

32. See Fredric Jameson's "Reification and Utopia in Mass Culture," *Social Text* 1 (Winter 1979): 133. Jameson uses the term "feeling tone" to describe the appeal of mass culture "since naturalism," which, like "the movie music that accompanies" screen versions of best sellers, already "floats above the narrative" as its most consumable element.

33. Krehbiel, *Afro-American Folksongs*, 3.

34. A big influence on, and register of, new approaches to music's "acoustic" dimension was Hermann von Helmholtz's *On the Sensations of Tone as a Physiological Basis for the Theory of Music*, originally published in 1863 and translated into English in 1875.

35. Brown, "The Matter of Dreiser's Modernity," 90.

36. Catherine Jurca, "Dreiser, Class, and the Home," in *Cambridge Companion to Theodore Dreiser*, 104.

37. In contrast, Frank Norris's representations of urban musicality in *McTeague* and *The Pit* take place almost entirely within public social spaces of vaudeville or the opera house and function primarily to elaborate class distinctions.

38. Brown's quotation is as follows, his elipses standing in for the sentences I quote: "Rocking to and fro and gazing out across the lamp-lit park toward the lamp-lit houses on Warren Avenue and Ashland Boulevard . . . She longed, and longed, and longed" ("The Matter of Dreiser's Modernity," 91–92).

39. Theodore Dreiser, *Sister Carrie* (Oxford: Oxford University Press, 1991), 441–42. The references to music in this scene do not appear in the "original" version of the manuscript, before he revised it for Doubleday.

40. Ibid., 440, 441.

41. Quoted in Richard Lingeman, *Theodore Dreiser: At the Gates of the City, 1871–1907* (New York: G.P. Putnam's Sons, 1986), 269.

42. *Sister Carrie* (Oxford), 464.

Chapter 2

1. James Huneker, "The Eternal Feminine," in *Overtones* (New York: Scribners, 1904), 292.

2. At the very moment when women began to form their own orchestras and professional organizations, and to distinguish themselves as soloists and compos-

ers, a number of critics felt compelled to defend music's masculinity and to return women to their proper place as the receivers or "inspirers" rather than the producers of musical art. Chicago critic George Upton's *Women in Music* (Chicago: A. C. McClung and Co., 1880, and reprinted several times in the following decades) implicitly polices the boundary between musical men and women by asking, "Why is it that music only comes to [women] as a balm, a rest, or a solace . . . and that it does not find its highest sources in her?" He concludes that while music "is the highest expression of the emotions" and women are "emotional by nature," they cannot "reproduce" emotion: "She herself is emotional by temperament and nature, and cannot project herself outwardly, any more than she can give outward expression to other mysterious and deeply hidden traits of her nature" (23). An 1894 *Atlantic Monthly* article similarly asserts that "the true creative force" in music is an emotional "virility" that "no femininity can infuse," given that "much of what passes in women for true emotion is mere nervous excitability." See Edith Brower, "Is the Musical Idea Masculine?" *Atlantic Monthly* 73 (March 1894): 332–39.

3. *Overtones*, 300. See Huneker, *Chopin: The Man and His Music* (New York: C. Scribner's and Sons, 1900).

4. For a discussion of Chopin's reception (mainly in Europe), see Derek Carew's very interesting "Victorian Attitudes to Chopin," in *Cambridge Companion to Chopin*, ed. Jim Samson (Cambridge: Cambridge University Press, 1992), 222–45. For a rich collection of quotations from nineteenth-century reviews of performances of Chopin, see Sandra P. Rosenblum's "'A composer known here but to few': Reception and Performance Styles of Chopin's Music in America, 1839–1900," in *The Age of Chopin: Interdisciplinary Inquiries*, ed. Halina Goldberg (Bloomington: Indiana University Press, 2004), 314–53.

5. Jeffrey Kahlberg, *Chopin at the Boundaries: Sex, History, and Musical Genre* (Cambridge, MA: Harvard University Press, 1996); see particularly the first two chapters. Kahlberg notes that, while much of Chopin's repertoire was considered dreamy, introspective, lyrical, and sentimental and thus deemed appropriate for the amateur bourgeois woman, on the whole Chopin's music refuses the conventional musical/emotional boundaries of both parlor and stage, with its frequent hints of melancholy, sickliness, and morbidity.

6. Huneker, *Chopin*, 300.

7. Ibid., 284.

8. Nicholas Cook, in his *Music*, describes the pyramid structure in Western musical discourse since the early nineteenth century by which the composer is deemed the most valuable repository of musical meaning, followed by the performer, and only lastly, the audience. In his *Music of the Common Tongue*, Christopher Small argues that we should approach all musical events as rituals whose meaning and effects are constituted by all people involved in their production and reception. See also Tia DeNora's *Music in Everyday Life* (New York: Cambridge University Press, 2000), in which she argues that "music analysis, tradition-

ally conceived as an exercise that 'tells' us about the 'music itself', is insufficient as a means for understanding musical affect, for describing music's semiotic force in social life. For that task, we shall need new ways of attending to music, ones that are overtly interdisciplinary, that conjoin the hitherto separate tasks of music scholars and social scientists" (23). I would make it a trio by adding literary critics as well.

9. For a discussion of Frederic's shifting place in the canon, see Glenn D. Klopfenstein, "'The Flying Dutchman of American Literature': Harold Frederic and the American Canon, a Centenary Overview," *American Literary Realism* 30, no. 1: 34–46.

10. Harold Frederic, *The Damnation of Theron Ware* (1896; repr., New York: Albert and Charles Boni, 1924), 307. All subsequent page numbers will be given parenthetically in the main text and refer to this edition.

11. This research is mentioned in Scott Donaldson's introduction to *The Damnation of Theron Ware, or Illumination*, by Harold Frederic (1896; repr., New York: Penguin Books, 1986), xiv. Donaldson is one of the few critics to recognize Sister Soulsby's use of "the power of music" (xxvi).

12. Aaron Urbanczyk, "A 'Study of Church in America': Catholicism as Exotic Other in *The Damnation of Theron Ware*," *Religion and the Arts* 10, no. 1 (2006): 42. Urbanczyk argues that Frederic's "inescapably religious" novel registers late nineteenth-century Protestant American anxieties about a growing and increasingly powerful Catholic population.

13. While the evidence to support my suggestion that Sister Soulsby may be mixed race is scarce (and perhaps not enough to make a good argument), one cannot ignore the degree to which her character defies categorization and legibility. Carrie Tirado Bramen sees blackness arising surreptitiously at the end of the novel, when Theron finally abandons his Celia fantasy: Theron's ultimate illumination, she argues, takes place among the "vilest of the vile" in New York's "low bar-rooms and dance-houses," which Bramen claims are clear references to "black and tans"—among the most racially heterogeneous spaces in the country. See Bramen's "The Americanization of Theron Ware," *Novel: A Forum on Fiction*, 31, no. 1 (Fall 1997): 80.

14. See Carew, "Victorian Attitudes to Chopin."

15. Raymond Williams used this phrase in many different contexts; the quote comes from *Drama from Ibsen to Brecht* (1952; repr., Harmondsworth, UK: Penguin, 1981), 10.

16. Lisa Watt MacFarlane, "Resurrecting Man: Desire and the Damnation of Theron Ware," *Studies in American Fiction* 20, no. 2 (1992): 138.

17. Huneker's novel, *Painted Veils*, which I discuss in my final chapter, describes a Protestant minister's undoing by an American opera singer, a figure widely perceived as the most powerful incarnation of the new musical woman in early twentieth-century America.

18. Bramen, "The Americanization of Theron Ware," 81, 83, 67.

19. Ibid., 83.

20. Dreiser, "The Prophet," 4.

21. Chopin, *The Awakening*, 135–36. All subsequent page numbers will be given parenthetically in the main text and refer to the 1986 Penguin edition.

22. See Emily Toth, *Kate Chopin* (London: Century, 1990), 80.

23. Lynda S. Boren, "Taming the Sirens: Self-Possession and the Strategies of Art in Kate Chopin's *The Awakening*," in *Kate Chopin Reconsidered: Beyond the Bayou*, ed. Lynda S. Boren and Sara deSaussure Davis (Baton Rouge: Louisiana State University Press, 1992), 190, 186.

24. Melanie Dawson, "Edna and the Tradition of Listening: The Role of Romantic Music in *The Awakening*," *Southern Studies: An Interdisciplinary Journal of the South* 3 (1992): 87–98.

25. Elaine Showalter, "Tradition and the Female Talent: *The Awakening* as a Solitary Book," in *New Essays on "The Awakening,"* ed. Wendy Martin (Cambridge: Cambridge University Press, 1988), 33–57, 46.

26. Doris Davis, "The Enigma at the Keyboard: Chopin's Mademoiselle Reisz," *Mississippi Quarterly* 58, nos. 1–2 (Winter–Spring 2005): 89–104.

27. Dawson, "Edna and the Tradition of Listening." One important distinction between painting and music in the novel (and, indeed, between writing and music in Chopin's own experience) is that painting affords Edna an opportunity to make some money. While one assumes Mlle Reisz is earning a (meager) living as a pianist, the novel makes no reference to music as something that can be commoditized. (Edna's dream about Mr. Highcamp playing the piano in front of a music store is an exception that, I would argue, further associates the Highcamps with a musicality that, like Miss Highcamp's performance of Grieg, leaves Edna "cold.")

28. Nicole Camastra, "Venerable Sonority in Kate Chopin's *The Awakening*," *American Literary Realism*, 40, no. 2 (Winter 2008), 161.

29. Ibid., 155.

30. Both *Zampa,* an opera comique composed in 1831 by Louis Joseph Ferdinand Hérold, and *The Poet and the Peasant*, a light opera composed in 1848 by Franz von Suppe, represent conventional popular opera of the mid-nineteenth century, created and performed more for entertainment than for serious aesthetic consideration.

31. The music renders her blind as well as mute, as she becomes, entirely, a listening self. Emily Toth notes that, as a girl, Chopin wrote in her diary, after hearing the great violinist Ole Bull, "I for the first time longed to be blind, that I might drink it all in undisturbed and undistracted by surrounding objects." (Quoted in Toth, *Kate Chopin*, 86.)

32. Patricia Yaeger, "'A Language Which Nobody Understood': Emancipatory Strategies in *The Awakening*," *Novel: A Forum on Fiction*, 20, no. 3 (1987): 197. Yae-

ger briefly focuses on one of Mlle Reisz's more private performances for Edna in New Orleans. Here, the pianist gives Edna Robert's letters to read while she plays, a gesture that, for Yaeger, encourages Edna to replace both the music and "her own particular sonority" with Robert's voice. Yaeger supports this claim by citing a passage—"Robert's voice was not pretentious. It was musical and true. The voice, the notes, the whole refrain haunted her memory"—that comes from a different scene in the novel not involving Mlle Reisz (and, indeed, a scene that precedes by several chapters her performance that accompanies Edna's letter reading).

33. Lawrence Kramer, *Music as Cultural Practice, 1800–1900* (Berkeley: University of California Press, 1990), 147, 142.

34. Horowitz, *Wagner Nights*, 113, 229, 220n, 110. The Nietzsche quotation is from his essay "Wagner as a Danger."

35. Bryan Magee, *Aspects of Wagner* (1969, repr., New York: Oxford University Press, 1988), 71.

36. Adorno, *In Search of Wagner*, 100.

37. Michele A. Birnbaum, "'Alien Hands': Kate Chopin and the Colonization of Race," *American Literature* 66, no. 2 (1994): 303.

38. Wai Chee Dimock, "Rightful Subjectivity," *Yale Journal of Criticism* 4, no. 1 (1990): 25–47.

Chapter 3

Epigraph. Krehbiel made this comment in 1888, referring to the characters in Wagner's Ring Cycle in a review of its American premiere; quoted in Joseph Horowitz, *Classical Music in America: A History of its Rise and Fall* (New York W. W. Norton, 2005), 140.

1. Clara Louise Kellogg, *Memoirs of an American Prima Donna* (New York: G. P. Putnam's Sons, 1913), 9, 1.

2. Willa Cather, "Three American Singers," *McClure's* 42, no. 2 (December, 1913): 42. Emily Leider, Gertrude Atherton's biographer, claims her diva heroine is based on Zdenka Fassbender, Munich's resident soprano whom Atherton, who lived in Munich before writing the novel, saw often on stage as Isolde and Brünnhilde. I would suggest that Atherton also drew from the character, if not the life, of her childhood San Francisco friend Sybil Sanderson. For Atherton's intimate involvement in Sanderson's life, see Jack Winsor Hansen, *The Sibyl Sanderson Story: Requiem for a Diva* (Pompton Plains, NJ: Amadeus Press, 2005).

3. Gertrude Atherton, *Tower of Ivory* (New York: Macmillan Company, 1910), 19. All subsequent page numbers will be given parenthetically in the main text and refer to this edition.

4. Willa Cather, "The Passing Show," *Nebraska State Journal* (December 13, 1896): 13.

5. See Horowitz's *Wagner Nights*, particularly his chapter "Protofeminism." I discuss Horowitz's book in chapter 2.

6. Krehbiel praised American ears as "unbiased" and Lilli Lehmann referred

to "the peculiar sense of freedom that is at once felt by everyone in America." Both are quoted in Horowitz's *Wagner Nights*, 108, 118.

7. See, in particular, Susan J. Leonardi and Rebecca A. Pope's *The Diva's Mouth: Body, Voice, Prima Donna Politics* (New Brunswick, NJ: Rutgers University Press, 1996).

8. Leonardi and Pope, *The Diva's Mouth*, 85.

9. See, particularly, Elizabeth Wood, "Sapphonics," in *Queering the Pitch: The New Gay and Lesbian Musicology*, ed. Philip Brett, Elizabeth Wood, Gary Thomas (New York: Routledge, 1994), 27–66.

10. Kevin Starr, *Americans and the California Dream: 1850–1915* (New York: Oxford University Press, 1973), 360–61, 356.

11. Sharon O'Brien, *Willa Cather: The Emerging Voice* (Cambridge, MA: Harvard University Press, 1997), 167, 171.

12. Leonardi and Pope, *The Diva's Mouth*, 89.

13. Richard Giannone, *Music in Willa Cather's Fiction* (Lincoln: University of Nebraska Press, 1968), 1, 15, 85.

14. More recent scholarship on *Song of the Lark*, like that of Leonardi and Pope and others already mentioned, tends to focus on its gender politics, underscoring and celebrating Cather's feminism without, I would argue, adequately situating her constructions of the female artist in the historical context of turn-of-the-century American opera culture. An exception is Debra Cumberland's "A Struggle for Breath: Contemporary Vocal Theory in Cather's *The Song of the Lark*," *American Literary Realism* 28, no. 2 (1996): 59–70. Cumberland demonstrates the ways in which Thea's vocal training reflects new theories about women's voices in the early twentieth century. For a less historicized, but nonetheless provocative, discussion of how Cather's choice of operas for her diva reflect Thea's/Fremstad's ambiguous or liminal gender identity, see John H. Flannigan, "Thea Kronborg's Vocal Transvestism: Willa Cather and the 'Voz Contralto,'" *Modern Fiction Studies* 40, no. 4 (1994): 737–63.

15. Giannone, *Music in Willa Cather's Fiction*, 21.

16. Willa Cather, *The Song of the Lark* (1915; repr., Boston: Houghton Mifflin Co., 1988), xxxii. (All subsequent page numbers will be given parenthetically in the main text, and refer to this edition.) Cather's later disavowal of this early novel is interesting for a number of reasons, not least of which for its elision of the role played by Indians and Mexicans in Thea's musicality. Instead, she writes, "What I cared about, and still care about, was the girl's escape; the play of blind chance, the way in which commonplace occurrences fell together to liberate her from commonness. She seemed wholly at the mercy of accident; but to persons of her vitality and honesty, fortunate accidents will always happen" (xxxii). By reducing her success to "chance" and disconnecting her "vitality and honesty" from her American context, Cather misreads her own novel, and resorts to a much more conventional model of the autonomous artist.

17. In this 1896 review of a performance of Dvořák's symphony, Cather ad-

mits to hearing hints of the sound of "Negros" singing (with which she claims familiarity from a recent trip to the Blue Ridge Mountains), but she clearly finds these voices much less significant than those of the European peasantry and the midwestern landscape. The review, originally published in the *Courier*, December 25, 1897, 2–3, is reprinted in *The World and the Parish*, vol. 1, of *Willa Cather's Articles and Reviews, 1893–1902* (Lincoln: University of Nebraska Press, 1970), 413–14.

18. See my introduction for a discussion of the critical debates surrounding Dvořák's symphony and his suggestions for American music composition.

19. See, for example, Wayne Koestenbaum, *The Queen's Throat: Opera, Homosexuality and the Mystery of Desire* (New York: Poseidon, 1993); Castle, *The Apparitional Lesbian*; Christopher Nealon, "Affect Geneology: Feeling and Affiliation in Willa Cather," *American Literature* 69, no. 1 (March 1997): 5–37; and Jonathan Goldberg's chapter "Cather Diva" in his *Willa Cather & Others* (Durham, NC: Duke University Press, 2001).

20. Nealon, whose reading of *Song of the Lark* in many ways resonates with my own, associates the "secret" of Thea's musicality with both a means of escape from "the demands of market-driven female heterosexuality" ("Affect Geneology," 13) and a means of affiliation with the Native American culture during her visit to the Cliff Dwellings. But while I consider Thea's cross-racial affiliation in relation to contemporary debates about musical nationalism, Nealon identifies her "secret" nexus of sexuality, musicality, and race as primarily a "lesbian strategy for imagining an America in which feeling, not family, would be the basis of affiliation." Nealon thus steers our attention away from considering how Cather's "strategy" might represent, and benefit, more than a lesbian subject position.

21. I refer here to stories Cather published after *Song of the Lark*—"The Diamond Mine," "A Gold Slipper," and "Scandal"—that feature female opera singers who have markedly more pragmatic and entrepreneurial relationships to their profession than Thea. The tone of these stories is much darker and more cynical than that of *Song of the Lark*, whose ending nonetheless betrays her sense of the difficulty of maintaining a commitment to musical artistry in the United States. These diva stories were first published in magazines and then included in Cather's collection *Youth and the Bright Medusa* (New York: Alfred Knopf, 1920).

22. See Loretta Wasserman, "Cather's Semitism," *Cather Studies* 2: 1–22. Wasserman importantly argues that Cather's "Semitism," while informed by commonly held stereotypes, also significantly complicates them and thus distinguishes Cather from other non-Jewish fiction writers of her day.

23. Max Paddison, *Adorno's Aesthetics of Music* (New York: Cambridge University Press, 1993), 246.

Chapter 4

Epigraph. "Our Musical Condition," *Negro Music Journal* 1 (March 1903): 137–38; quoted in Berlin, *Ragtime*, 44. Hiram K. Moderwell, "Ragtime," *New Republic* 4 (October 16, 1915): 286.

1. Quoted in Berlin, *Ragtime*, 44.

2. See Jean E. Snyder, "Harry T. Burleigh and the Creative Expression of Bi-Musicality: A Study of an African-American Composer and the American Art Song" (Ph.D. dissertation, University of Pittsburgh, 1992).

3. See my "James Weldon Johnson and the Autobiography of an Ex-Colored Musician," *American Literature* 72, no. 2: 249–74.

4. Salim Washington's important article, for example, understands the novel's use of music as a "racial metaphor," by which the color line is reflected in a line between orality and literacy. Noting that the narrator ultimately embraces a "mulatto-centered nationalism" that reflects the dominant racial-musical hierarchies of his day, Washington regrets Johnson's failure to recognize adequately and celebrate the more radical aesthetics of ragtime and spirituals. Salim Washington, "Of Black Bards, Known and Unknown: Music as Racial Metaphor in James Weldon Johnson's *The Autobiography of an Ex-Colored Man*," *Callaloo* 25, no. 1 (Winter 2002): 233–56. Bruce Barnhart argues that the novel represents black music and European "classical" music as expressions of distinct and opposed ideas of time; ragtime and spirituals reveal, through their "improvisational flexibility and responsive suppleness," the bodies and relationships that "classical music," with its linear movement towards an idealized timelessness, works to suppress. Bruce Barnhart, "Chronopolitics and Race, Rag-time and Symphonic Time in *The Autobiography of an Ex-Colored Man, African American Review* 40, no. 3 (2006): 558.

5. This is a version, of course, of the postcolonial question, posed by Gayatri Spivak, of whether the "subaltern" can "speak." Katherine Biers, who reads both the novel and its idea of ragtime as subversive, importantly draws our attention to the ways in which ragtime is itself a form of writing (which she calls "phonographic") and thus moves us beyond the limiting binary, upheld by so much scholarship, that divides authentic black "voices" and inauthentic white "writing." Putting the novel (as do I) in the context of the "ragtime debate" and debates about musical nationalism, she considers how notions of "the national archive," in this case, the archive of transcribed "folk" material available for appropriation for a national musical expression, requires an erasure of the historical conditions of musical production. The novel itself, like the ragtime it represents, reveals what the archive silences, as "a record of missed moments, a ragged voice." Katherine Biers, "Syncope Fever: James Weldon Johnson and the Black Phonographic Voice," *Representations* 96 (Fall 2006): 111, 118.

6. Letter dated October 10, 1912, Box 40, Series III, Folder 11, James Weldon Johnson Collection, Beinecke Library, Yale University.

7. Joseph T. Skerrett Jr., "Irony and Symbolic Action in James Weldon Johnson's *The Autobiography of an Ex-Colored Man*," *American Quarterly* 32 (Winter 1980): 554. Skerrett quotes from *Along This Way*, 223.

8. Nigel Thomas, *From Folklore to Fiction: A Study of Folk Heroes and Rituals in the Black American Novel* (Westport, CT: Greenwood Press, 1988), 114.

9. The parallels between the two authors are likewise notable: Dreiser and

Johnson were born in the same year (1871), both moved to New York at the turn of the century to work with their musician brothers in popular music, and both left that work to, among other things, write their first novels.

10. Johnson, *The Autobiography of an Ex-Colored Man*, 74. Subsequent page numbers will be given parenthetically in the main text.

11. James Weldon Johnson, *Black Manhattan* (1930; repr., New York: Knopf, 1991), 119, 118, 116.

12. The opportunities that black musicians saw in ragtime and classical music resemble the possibilities that dialect fiction provided to writers like Charles Chesnutt and Paul Lawrence Dunbar around the same time. In both music and literature, black artists could claim a more authentic voice while recognizing the degree to which they were, in fact, involved in imitating white constructions of authenticity.

13. Dvořák, "Music in America," 430.

14. Rupert Hughes, *Contemporary American Composers* (Boston: L. C. Page and Co., 1900), 22.

15. Radano, "Soul Texts and the Blackness of Folk," 88; W. E. B. Du Bois, *The Souls of Black Folk* (New York: Penguin, 1989), 205.

16. Quoted in Anne Key Simpson's *Hard Trials: The Life and Music of Harry T. Burleigh* (Metuchen, NJ: Scarecrow Press, 1990), 15, 14. The former quotation comes from a letter from Burleigh published in the program notes of a 1918 performance of Dvořák's "New World" Symphony.

17. Simpson, *Hard Trials*, 19.

18. For more on these shows and the larger contexts of black musical production see Eileen Southern's *The Music of Black Americans, A History* (New York: W. W. Norton and Co., 1983), 293–302, and Johnson's *Black Manhattan*, 94–110. These shows, unlike white musical theater, combined European and African American musical traditions in their program by typically including opera scenes or arias as one of their "acts."

19. James Weldon Johnson, *Along This Way: The Autobiography of James Weldon Johnson* (1933; repr., New York: Da Capo Press, 2000), 147–50.

20. In *Along This Way*, Johnson describes his response to a letter in the *Ladies Home Journal* that indicated the writer assumed the Johnsons were white: "I laughed too; but my laughter was tempered by the thought that there was anybody in the country, notwithstanding the locality being Georgia, who knowing anything at all about them, did not know that Cole and Johnson Brothers were Negroes" (196).

21. See Michael Rogin, *Blackface, White Noise: Jewish Immigrants in the Hollywood Melting Pot* (Berkeley: University of California Press, 1996), 73–120.

22. See David Krasner's "Parody and Double Consciousness in the Language of Early Black Musical Theatre," *African American Review* 29, no. 2: 317–23.

23. *Along This Way*, 153.

24. R. C. Simmons, "Europe's Reception to Negro Talent," *The Colored American Magazine*, November 1905, 635, 639.

25. A letter from Rosamond, written just after the publication of *The Autobiography*, indicates the distance James Johnson himself felt from ragtime (perhaps increased by his new careers in writing and politics as well as his geographical dislocation). Responding to several songs James had sent him, Rosamond writes, "I don't think that you'll be able to write a *low* class rag song for some time to come as you have not been in touch with the sayings of the day—you may practice on this style by writing words to the tunes of some of the now famous ones. And in that way you'll get the run of the peculiar metre. Your 'Ark' song is a good poem of its kind but it's rather too regular in its construction. Of course there is no need of advice when it comes to lyrics like 'The Awakening.'" Johnson is more at home writing lyrics to songs like "The Awakening"—which is in the style of an "art" song and, incidentally, contains no explicitly racial references—than writing a "low class rag." See letter dated August 29, 1913, Box 40, Series III, Folder 12, James Weldon Johnson Collection, Beinecke Library, Yale University.

26. See Frederick Douglass, *Narrative of the Life of an American Slave, Written by Himself* (New York: Laurel, 1997), and Zora Neale Hurston, "Spirituals and Neo-spirituals," originally published in Nancy Cunard's *Negro: An Anthology* (New York, 1934) and reprinted in *The Sanctified Church, The Folklore Writings of Zora Neale Hurston* (Berkeley: Turtle Island, 1981), 79–84.

27. Kathleen Pfeiffer reads the narrator's improvised "major triad" at the end of the Nocturne as a sign of his continued refusal of racial binarisms, choosing instead a third (i.e., "triadic") position of racial ambiguity. But rather than emphasize the triad (the original Chopin chord is also a triad), Johnson clearly intends to emphasize that it was a *major* as opposed to minor harmony. The character (if not the author) thus seems to be reproducing, rather than evading, the conventions of "whiteness," and indeed plays right into a major/minor binarism. Kathleen Pfeiffer, "Individualism, Success, and American Identity in *The Autobiography of an Ex-Colored Man*," *African American Review* 30, no. 3 (1996): 403–19.

28. Johnson, *Along This Way*, 160. Johnson left at the moment when his brother and Bob Cole decided to take their most recent shows on tour, which meant enduring the racism much more prevalent outside New York (and particularly in the South).

29. Letter from Rosamond to James dated December 29, 1913, Box 40, Series III, Folder 12, James Weldon Johnson Collection, Beinecke Library, Yale University.

30. James Weldon Johnson, preface to *The Books of American Negro Spirituals*, ed. James Weldon Johnson and J. Rosamond Johnson (1925–26; repr., New York: Da Capo Press, 2002), 14, 30.

31. One could argue that this nostalgia, which consigns authentic black musicality to an irrecoverable past, denies the power and authority of contemporary black music of the 1920s, namely blues and jazz, a denial reinforced by the introduction's failure to accord any place to the emergent recording industry in the preservation and extension of black oral culture.

32. The term "new-fangled" dates this undated fragment in the post-tonal era of musical modernism and also at the moment when such "New Negro composers" as William Grant Still and Nathianel Dett gained a degree of fame (i.e., 1920s to 1940s) unknown to the earlier generation. For a discussion of these composers see Southern, *The Music of Black Americans*.

33. "Down the Nile," JWJ MSS 196, James Weldon Johnson Collection, Beinecke Library, Yale University.

Chapter 5

Epigraph. James Huneker, *Steeplejack* (New York: Scribner's, 1925), 201.

1. Horowitz, *Wagner Nights*, 4.

2. Long-time New York Philharmonic conductor Walter Damrosch writes that *Art of the Singer* "is of inestimable value to the vocal student and artist of today" in his biographical sketch, "William J. Henderson," *American Academy of Arts and Letters* (1938): 61.

3. James Huneker, *Chopin: The Man and His Music* (New York: Charles Scribner's Sons, 1900). The most recent hardcopy edition was published by Dover in 1966. For an overview of the era's critics, and their place in the larger music world, see Joseph Musselman, *Music in the Cultured Generation: A Social History of Music in America, 1870–1900* (Evanston, Ill.: Northwestern University Press, 1971).

4. W. J. Henderson, "The Function of Musical Criticism," *Musical Quarterly* 1 (1915): 73.

5. For an excellent distillation of the origins and history of this privileging of the composers over the performer (and listener), see the first two chapters of Nicholas Cook's *Music*.

6. Huneker, *Steeplejack*, 201.

7. Henderson, *New York Sun*, February 2, 1908. Upon his death in 1937, Henderson's friends and colleagues repeatedly singled him out for having been unbiased, fair, and objective in his reviews. See, for example, "W. J. Henderson, 81, Killed by Bullet," *New York Times*, June 6, 1937. The critic took his own life for reasons that never surfaced, although he was known to have been in poor health.

8. See W. J. Henderson, "The Musical Novel," *New York Times*, January 28, 1899, BR57.

9. Arnold T. Schwab, *James Gibbons Huneker: Critic of the Seven Arts* (Stanford, CA: Stanford University Press, 1963), 273.

10. The only extended source of information on Henderson's life is H. Paul Shurtz's unpublished dissertation, "William James Henderson: His Views on the New York Musical World, 1887–1937" (University of Colorado at Boulder, 1980).

11. "A Romance of Opera: Fiction from the Pen of a Musical Critic," *New York Times*, October 27, 1912.

12. W. J. Henderson, *The Soul of a Tenor: A Romance* (New York: Henry Holt

and Co., 1912), "Prefatory Note," iv. All subsequent quotations are from this edition and are marked parenthetically in the text.

13. Besides James Cain's *Serenade*, which would not be published until 1937, most prominent fiction centering on a male singers deals with castrati; see, for example, Balzac's "Sarrasine," Marc David's *Farinelli: Memoires d'un castrat*, Lawrence Goldman's *The Castrato*, and John Spencer Hill's *The Last Castrato*.

14. Johnson's exception to this rule goes only so far: both as performer and listener, his narrator experiences a loss of agency that causes him to flee his circumstances and take on more masculine pursuits and to distance himself from authentic musical sources, first as composer working with transcribed "Negro music" and then as a white businessman.

15. See my chapter 3.

16. For a compelling feminist reading of Bizet's *Carmen*, see Susan McClary's "Sexual Politics in Classical Music," the third chapter of her *Feminine Endings*.

17. Leander's new relationship to *Carmen*—in which rather than identify with his role he merely represents it—can be contrasted with the scene toward the end of *Sister Carrie*, in which Carrie is unable to grasp Ames's advice that she "represent" desire, rather than simply succumb to it.

18. Schwab, *James Gibbons Huneker*, 56. According to Schwab, Huneker also claimed, having taught at the National Conservatory when Dvořák was director, that the Bohemian composer "had mistaken Negro for Indian themes" (55).

19. Schwab, *James Gibbons Huneker*, 261.

20. James Huneker, *Painted Veils* (New York: Liveright, Inc., 1920), 16. All subsequent quotations are from this edition and are noted in the text parenthetically.

21. The first quotation is from a letter to Frida Ashforth, October 18, 1920; the second from a letter to Mrs. Josephine Ditrichstein, February 25, 1920. Both letters are included in *The Letters of James Gibbons Huneker*, ed. Josephine Huneker (New York: Scribner's Sons, 1922).

22. Huneker, *The Letters of James Gibbons Huneker*, 307, letter dated December 3, 1920.

23. Schwab, *James Gibbons Huneker*, 262.

24. Ibid., 125.

Epilogue

1. Dreiser, *Sister Carrie* (Oxford), 464.

2. Douglass, *Narrative of the Life of an American Slave*, 13.

Bibliography

Abbott, Lynn, and Doug Seroff. *Out of Sight: The Rise of African American Popular Music, 1889–1895*. Jackson: University Press of Mississippi, 2010.

Adorno, Theodor. *In Search of Wagner*. New York: Verso, 2005.

Allen, William Francis, Charles Pickard Ware, and Lucy McKim Garrison, eds. *Slave Songs of the United States*. New York: A. Simpson and Co., 1867.

Atherton, Gertrude. *Tower of Ivory*. New York: Macmillan Company, 1910.

Attali, Jacques. *Noise: The Political Economy of Music*. Translated by Brian Massumi. 1977. Reprint, Minneapolis: University of Minnesota Press, 1985.

Baker, Houston. *Blues, Ideology, and Afro-American Literature: A Vernacular Theory*. Chicago: University of Chicago Press, 1984.

Barnhart, Bruce. "Chronopolitics and Race, Rag-time and Symphonic Time in *The Autobiography of an Ex-Colored Man*." *African American Review* 40, no. 3 (2006): 551–69.

Barrineau, Nancy Warner, ed., *Theodore Dreiser's "Ev'ry Month."* Athens: University of Georgia Press, 1996.

———. "The Second Issue of *Ev'ry Month*: Early Roots of Dreiser's Fiction." *Dreiser Studies* 22 (1991): 23–32.

Beckerman, Michael. *New Worlds of Dvořák: Searching in America for the Composer's Inner Life*. New York: W. W. Norton and Co., 2003.

Berlin, Edward. *Ragtime: A Musical and Cultural History*. Berkeley: University of California Press, 1980.

Biers, Katherine. "Syncope Fever: James Weldon Johnson and the Black Phonographic Voice." *Representations* 96 (Fall 2006): 99–125.

Bigelow, Blair F. *Selected Newspaper Articles, 1892–1894, of Theodore Dreiser*. Dissertation, Brandeis University, 1972.

Birnbaum, Michele A. "'Alien Hands': Kate Chopin and the Colonization of Race." *American Literature* 66, no. 2 (1994): 301–23.

Booth, Mark W. *The Experience of Songs*. New Haven, CT: Yale University Press, 1981.

Boren, Lynda S. "Taming the Sirens: Self-Possession and the Strategies of Art in Kate Chopin's *The Awakening*." In *Kate Chopin Reconsidered: Beyond the Bayou*, edited by Lynda S. Boren and Sara deSaussure Davis, 180–98. Baton Rouge: Louisiana State University Press, 1992.

Bowlby, Rachel. *Just Looking: Consumer Culture in Dreiser, Gissing and Zola*. New York: Methuen and Company, 1985.

Bramen, Carrie Tirado. "The Americanization of Theron Ware." *Novel: A Forum on Fiction* 31, no. 1 (Fall 1997): 63–86.

Brett, Philip, Elizabeth Wood, Gary Thomas, eds. *Queering the Pitch: The New Gay and Lesbian Musicology*. New York: Routledge, 1994.

Brower, Edith. "Is the Musical Idea Masculine?" *Atlantic Monthly* 73 (March 1894): 332–39.

Brown, Bill. "The Matter of Dreiser's Modernity." In *The Cambridge Companion to Theodore Dreiser*, edited by Leonard Cassuto and Clare Virginia Eby, 83–99. Cambridge: Cambridge University Press, 2004.

Budds, Michael J., ed. *Music in America: 1860–1918*. Hillsdale, NY: Pendragon Press, 2008.

Camastra, Nicole. "Venerable Sonority in Kate Chopin's *The Awakening*." *American Literary Realism* 40, no. 2 (Winter 2008): 154–66.

Carew, Derek. "Victorian Attitudes to Chopin." In *Cambridge Companion to Chopin*, edited by Jim Samson, 222–45. Cambridge: Cambridge University Press, 1992.

Castle, Terry. *The Apparitional Lesbian: Female Sexuality and Modern Culture*. New York: Columbia University Press, 1993.

Cather, Willa. *The Song of the Lark*. 1915. Reprint, Boston: Houghton Mifflin Co., 1988.

———. "Three American Singers." *McClure's* 42, no. 2 (December 1913): 3–48.

———. *The World and the Parish*. Vol. 1 of *Willa Cather's Articles and Reviews, 1893–1902*. Lincoln: University of Nebraska Press, 1970.

———. *Youth and the Bright Medusa*. New York: Alfred Knopf, 1920.

Chernoff, John Miller. *African Rhythm and African Sensibility*. Chicago: University of Chicago Press, 1979.

Chopin, Kate. *The Awakening and Selected Stories*. 1899. Reprint, New York: Penguin, 1986.

Cook, Nicholas. *Music: A Very Short Introduction*. New York: Oxford University Press, 2000.

Cumberland, Debra. "A Struggle for Breath: Contemporary Vocal Theory in Cather's *The Song of the Lark*." *American Literary Realism* 28, no. 2 (1996): 59–70.

Damrosch, Walter. "William J. Henderson." *American Academy of Arts and Letters* (1938): 61.

Davis, Doris. "The Enigma at the Keyboard: Chopin's Mademoiselle Reisz." *Mississippi Quarterly* 58, nos. 1–2 (Winter–Spring 2005): 89–104.

Dawson, Melanie. "Edna and the Tradition of Listening: The Role of Romantic Music in *The Awakening*." *Southern Studies: An Interdisciplinary Journal of the South* 3 (1992): 87–98.

DeNora, Tia. *Music in Everyday Life*. New York: Cambridge University Press, 2000.

Dimock, Wai Chee. "Rightful Subjectivity." *Yale Journal of Criticism* 4, no. 1 (1990): 25–51.

Donaldson, Scott. Introduction to *The Damnation of Theron Ware, or Illuminations*, by Harold Frederic, vii–xxx. 1896. Reprint, New York: Penguin Books, 1986.

Douglass, Frederick. *Narrative of the Life of an American Slave, Written by Himself*. New York: Penguin Classics, 1986.

Dreiser, Theodore. "Birth and Growth of a Popular Song." *Metropolitan Magazine*, November 1898, 497–502.

———. Introduction to *The Songs of Paul Dresser*, v–x. New York: Boni and Liveright, 1927.

———. "My Brother Paul." In *Sister Carrie, Jennie Gerhart, Twelve Men*. New York: Library Classics of America, 1987.

———. *Newspaper Days*. Philadelphia: University of Pennsylvania Press, 1991.

———. "The Prophet." *Ev'ry Month* III (February 1897): 4.

———. *Sister Carrie*. Philadelphia: University of Pennsylvania Press, 1981.

———. *Sister Carrie*. Oxford: Oxford University Press, 1991.

———. "Whence the Song." *Harper's Weekly*, December 1900, 1165–66a.

———. "Words and Music." *Ev'ry Month* III (February 1897).

Du Bois, W. E. B. *The Souls of Black Folk*. New York: Penguin, 1989.

Dvořák, Antonin. "Music in America." *Harper's New Monthly Magazine* 90 (February 1895): 429–35.

Emerson, Ken. *Doo-dah! Stephen Foster and the Rise of American Popular Culture*. New York: Da Capo Press, 1998.

Erenberg, Lewis A. *Steppin' Out: New York Nightlife and the Transformation of American Culture, 1890–1930*. Chicago: University of Chicago Press, 1981.

Ewen, David. *Tin Pan Alley*. New York: Funk and Wagnall's, 1964.

Flannigan, John H. "Thea Kronborg's Vocal Transvestism: Willa Cather and the 'Voz Contralto.'" *Modern Fiction Studies* 40, no. 4 (1994): 737–63.

Frederic, Harold. *The Damnation of Theron Ware*. 1896. Reprint, New York: Albert and Charles Boni, 1924.

Giannone, Richard. *Music in Willa Cather's Fiction*. Lincoln: University of Nebraska Press, 1968.

Gilroy, Paul. *The Black Atlantic: Modernity and Double-Consciousness*. Cambridge, MA: Harvard University Press, 1993.

Goldberg, Isaac. *Tin Pan Alley: A Chronicle of American Popular Music*. New York: Frederick Ungar, 1961.

Goldberg, Jonathan. *Willa Cather & Others*. Durham, NC: Duke University Press, 2001.

Hall, Stuart. "What Is This 'Black' in Black Popular Culture?" *Social Justice* 20, no. 1 (1993): 104–11.

Hakutani, Yoshinobu, ed. *Art, Music, and Literature, 1897–1902*. Chicago: University of Illinois Press, 2001.

———. *Young Dreiser: A Critical Study*. Rutherford, NJ: Fairleigh Dickinson University Press, 1980.

Hansen, Jack Winsor. *The Sibyl Sanderson Story: Requiem for a Diva*. Pompton Plains, NJ: Amadeus Press, 2005.

Henderson, W. J. "The Function of Musical Criticism." *Musical Quarterly* 1 (1915): 69–82.

———. "The Musical Novel." *New York Times*, January 28, 1899, Saturday Review of Books and Art, p. BR57.

———. *The Soul of a Tenor: A Romance*. New York: Henry Holt and Co., 1912.

———. Untitled Review. *New York Sun*, February 2, 1908.

Horowitz, Joseph. *Classical Music in America: A History of its Rise and Fall*. New York: W. W. Norton, 2005.

———. *Wagner Nights: An American History*. Berkeley: University of California Press, 1994.

Hughes, Rupert. *Contemporary American Composers*. Boston: L. C. Page and Co., 1900.

Huneker, James. *Chopin: The Man and His Music*. New York: C. Scribner's Sons, 1900.

———. "The Eternal Feminine." *Overtones*. New York: C. Scribner's Sons, 1904.

———. *Painted Veils*. New York: Liveright, Inc., 1920.

———. *Steeplejack*. New York: C. Scribner's Sons, 1920.

Huneker, Josephine, ed. *The Letters of James Gibbons Huneker*. New York: C. Scribner's Sons, 1922.

Hurston, Zora Neale. "Spirituals and Neo-spirituals." In *The Sanctified Church, The Folklore Writings of Zora Neale Hurston*. Berkeley: Turtle Island, 1981.

Jameson, Fredric. "Reification and Utopia in Mass Culture." *Social Text* 1 (Winter 1979): 130–48.

Johnson, James Weldon. *Along This Way: The Autobiography of James Weldon Johnson*. 1933. Reprint, New York: Da Capo Press, 2000.

———. *The Autobiography of an Ex-Colored Man*. New York: Vintage, 1989.

———. *Black Manhattan*. 1930. Reprint, New York: Knopf, 1991.

———. "Down the Nile." JWJ MSS 196, James Weldon Johnson Collection, Beinecke Library, Yale University.

———. Preface to *The Books of American Negro Spirituals*, edited by James Weldon Johnson and J. Rosamond Johnson, 11–50. 1925–26. Reprint, New York: Da Capo Press, 2002.

Jurca, Catherine. "Dreiser, Class, and the Home." In *Cambridge Companion to Theodore Dreiser*, edited by Leonard Cassuto and Clare Virginia Eby, 100–111. New York: Cambridge University Press, 2004.

Kahlberg, Jeffrey. *Chopin at the Boundaries: Sex, History, and Musical Genre*. Cambridge, MA: Harvard University Press, 1996.

Kaplan, Amy. *The Social Construction of American Realism*. Chicago: University of Chicago Press, 1989.

Kazin, Alfred, and Charles Shapiro, eds. *The Stature of Theodore Dreiser: A Critical Survey of the Man and His Work*. Bloomington: Indiana University Press, 1965.

Kellogg, Clara Louise. *Memoirs of an American Prima Donna*. New York: G. P. Putnam's Sons, 1913.

Klopfenstein, Glenn D. "'The Flying Dutchman of American Literature': Harold Frederic and the American Canon, a Centenary Overview." *American Literary Realism* 30, no. 1: 34–46.

Koestenbaum, Wayne. *The Queen's Throat: Opera, Homosexuality and the Mystery of Desire*. New York: Poseidon, 1993.

Kramer, Lawrence. *Music as Cultural Practice, 1800–1900*. Berkeley: University of California Press, 1990.

Krasner, David. "Parody and Double Consciousness in the Language of Early Black Musical Theatre." *African American Review* 29, no. 2: 317–23.

Krehbiel, Henry. *Afro-American Folksongs: A Study in Racial and National Music*. New York: Schirmer, 1914.

Leonardi, Susan J., and Rebecca A. Pope. *The Diva's Mouth: Body, Voice, Prima Donna Politics*. New Brunswick, NJ: Rutgers University Press, 1996.

Levine, Lawrence. *Highbrow/Lowbrow: The Emergence of Cultural Hierarchy in America*. Cambridge, MA: Harvard University Press, 1988.

Lingeman, Richard. *Theodore Dreiser: At the Gates of the City, 1871–1907*. New York: G. P. Putnam's Sons, 1986.

Lott, Eric. *Love and Theft: Blackface Minstrelsy and the American Working Class*. New York: Oxford University Press, 1995.

Loving, Jerome. *The Last Titan: A Life of Theodore Dreiser*. Berkeley: University of California Press, 2005.

MacFarlane, Lisa Watt. "Resurrecting Man: Desire and the Damnation of Theron Ware." *Studies in American Fiction* 20, no. 2 (1992): 127–43.

Magee, Bryan. *Aspects of Wagner*. 1969. Reprint, New York: Oxford University Press, 1988.

Matthiessen, F. O. *Theodore Dreiser*. New York: Sloan, 1951.

McClary, Susan. *Feminine Endings: Music, Gender, and Sexuality*. Minneapolis: University of Minnesota Press, 1991.

Michaels, Walter Benn. "*Sister Carrie*'s Popular Economy." *Critical Inquiry* 7 (1980): 373–90.

Miller, Karl Hagstrom. *Segregating Sound: Inventing Folk and Pop Music in the Age of Jim Crow*. Durham, NC: Duke University Press, 2010.

Moderwell, Hiram K. "Ragtime." *New Republic* 4 (October 16, 1915): 285–86.

Moers, Ellen. *Two Dreisers*. New York: Viking, 1969.

Musselman, Joseph. *Music in the Cultured Generation: A Social History of Music in America, 1870–1900*. Evanston, IL: Northwestern University Press, 1971.

Nealon, Christopher. "Affect Geneology: Feeling and Affiliation in Willa Cather." *American Literature* 69, no. 1 (March 1997): 5–37.

Newlin, Keith, ed. *The Oxford Handbook of American Literary Naturalism*. New York: Oxford University Press, 2011.

O'Brien, Sharon. *Willa Cather: The Emerging Voice*. Cambridge, MA: Harvard University Press, 1997.

Oakes, Steve, and Adrian C. North. "Reviewing Congruity Effects in the Service Environment Musicscape." *International Journal of Service Industry Management* 19, no. 1 (2008): 63–82.

Paddison, Max. *Adorno's Aesthetics of Music*. New York: Cambridge University Press, 1993.

Peiss, Kathy. *Cheap Amusements*. Philadelphia: Temple University Press, 1986.

Petry, Sandy. "The Language of Realism, the Language of False Consciousness: A Reading of *Sister Carrie*." *Novel* 10 (1977): 101–13.

Pfeiffer, Kathleen. "Individualism, Success, and American Identity in *The Autobiography of an Ex-Colored Man*." *African American Review* 30, no. 3 (1996): 403–19.

Pisani, Michael V. *Imagining Native America in Music*. New Haven, CT: Yale University Press, 2006.

Pizer, Donald. *The Novels of Theodore Dreiser: A Critical Study*. Minneapolis: University of Minnesota Press, 1976.

Radano, Ronald. "Soul Texts and the Blackness of Folk." *Modernism/Modernity* 2, no. 2 (1995): 71–95.

Rogin, Michael. *Blackface, White Noise: Jewish Immigrants in the Hollywood Melting Pot*. Berkeley: University of California Press, 1996.

"A Romance of Opera: Fiction from the Pen of a Musical Critic." *New York Times*, October 27, 1912.

Rosenblum, Sandra P. "'A composer known here but to few': Reception and Performance Styles of Chopin's Music in America, 1839–1900." In *The Age of Chopin: Interdisciplinary Inquiries*, edited by Halina Goldberg, 314–54. Bloomington: Indiana University Press, 2004.

Ross, Alex. *The Rest is Noise: Listening to the Twentieth Century*. New York: Farrar, Straus and Giroux, 2007.

Ruotolo, Cristina. "James Weldon Johnson and The Autobiography of an Ex-Colored Musician." *American Literature* 72, no. 2: 249–74.

Said, Edward. *Musical Elaborations*. New York: Columbia University Press, 1991.

Schafer, R. Murray. *The Soundscape: Our Sonic Environment and the Tuning of the World*. Rochester, VT: Destiny Books, 1994.

Schwab, Arnold T. *James Gibbons Huneker: Critic of the Seven Arts*. Stanford, CA: Stanford University Press, 1963.

Schweighauser, Philipp. *The Noises of American Literature, 1890–1985: Toward a History of Literary Acoustics*. Gainesville: University Press of Florida, 2006.

Showalter, Elaine. "Tradition and the Female Talent: *The Awakening* as a Solitary Book." In *New Essays on "The Awakening,"* edited by Wendy Martin, 33–58. Cambridge: Cambridge University Press, 1988.

Shurtz, H. Paul. "William James Henderson: His Views on the New York Musical World, 1887–1937." Unpublished dissertation, University of Colorado at Boulder, 1980.

Simmons, R. C. "Europe's Reception to Negro Talent." *The Colored American Magazine*, November 1905, 635–42.

Simpson, Anne Key. *Hard Trials: The Life and Music of Harry T. Burleigh*. Metuchen, NJ: Scarecrow Press, 1990.

Skerrett, Joseph T., Jr. "Irony and Symbolic Action in James Weldon Johnson's *The Autobiography of an Ex-Colored Man*." *American Quarterly* 32 (Winter 1980): 540–58.

Small, Christopher. *Musicking: The Meanings of Performing and Listening*. Middletown, CT: Wesleyan University Press, 1998.

———. *Music of the Common Tongue: Survival and Celebration in African American Music*. Middletown, CT: Wesleyan University Press, 1998.

Smith, Mark J. *Listening to Nineteenth-Century America*. Chapel Hill: University of North Carolina Press, 2000.

Snyder, Jean E. "Harry T. Burleigh and the Creative Expression of Bi-Musicality: A Study of an African-American Composer and the American Art Song." Ph.D. dissertation, University of Pittsburgh, 1992.

Solie, Ruth. *Musicology and Difference: Gender and Sexuality in Music Scholarship*. Berkeley: University of California Press, 1995.

Southern, Eileen. *The Music of Black Americans, A History*. New York: W. W. Norton and Co., 1983.

Starr, Kevin. *Americans and the California Dream: 1850–1915*. New York: Oxford University Press, 1973.

Sterne, Jonathan. *The Audible Past: Cultural Origins of Sound Reproduction*. Durham, NC: Duke University Press, 2003.

Taylor, Tim. *Global Pop: World Music, World Markets*. New York: Routledge, 1997.

Thomas, Nigel. *From Folklore to Fiction: A Study of Folk Heroes and Rituals in the Black American Novel*. Westport, CT: Greenwood Press, 1988.

Thompson, Emily. *The Soundscape of Modernity: Architectural Acoustics and the Culture of Listening in America, 1900–1930*. Cambridge, MA: MIT Press, 2004.

Tick, Judith. "Passed Away Is the Piano Girl." In *Women Making Music: The Western Art Tradition, 1150–1950*, edited by Jane Bowers and Judith Tick, 325–48. Champaign: University of Illinois Press, 1987.

Toth, Emily. *Kate Chopin*. London: Century, 1990.

Upton, George. *Women in Music*. Chicago: A. C. McClung and Co., 1880.

Urbanczyk, Aaron. "A 'Study of Church in America': Catholicism as Exotic Other in *The Damnation of Theron Ware*." *Religion and the Arts* 10, no. 1 (2006): 39–58.

Washington, Salim. "Of Black Bards, Known and Unknown: Music as Racial Metaphor in James Weldon Johnson's *The Autobiography of an Ex-Colored Man*." *Callaloo* 25, no. 1 (Winter 2002): 233–56.

Wasserman, Loretta. "Cather's Semitism." *Cather Studies* 2: 1–22.

Williams, Raymond. *Drama from Ibsen to Brecht*. 1952. Reprint, Harmondsworth, UK: Penguin 1981.

"W. J. Henderson, 81, Killed by Bullet." *New York Times*, June 6, 1937.

Wood, Elizabeth. "Sapphonics." In *Queering the Pitch: The New Gay and Lesbian Musicology*, edited by Philip Brett, Elizabeth Wood, Gary Thomas, 27–66. New York: Routledge, 1994.

Yaeger, Patricia. "'A Language Which Nobody Understood': Emancipatory Strategies in *The Awakening*." *Novel: A Forum on Fiction* 20, no. 3 (1987): 197–219.

Index